JOHNSON, GRANT, and the
POLITICS of RECONSTRUCTION

JOHNSON, GRANT,
and the
POLITICS of
RECONSTRUCTION

Martin E. Mantell

 Columbia University Press
New York & London *1973*

Library of Congress Cataloging in Publication Data

Mantell, Martin E   1936–
    Johnson, Grant, and the politics of reconstruction

    Based on the author's thesis, Columbia University,
with title: The election of 1868; the response to
Congressional Reconstruction.
    Bibliography: p. 187
        1. United States—Politics and government—1865–
1869.   2. Reconstruction.   3. Johnson, Andrew, Pres.
U. S., 1808–1875.   4. Grant, Ulysses Simpson, Pres.
U. S., 1822–1885.   I. Title.
E668.M34   973.8   72-13452
ISBN 0-231-03507-1

To my Mother and the memory of my Father

ACKNOWLEDGMENTS

This study is largely based on my doctoral dissertation, The Election of 1868: The Response to Congressional Reconstruction, done at Columbia University. Professor Eric McKitrick has had an especially important influence on it, both as my dissertation sponsor and through his own groundbreaking work on the Johnson administration. Professors James Shenton, Harvey C. Mansfield, Harvey A. Levenstein, and Eric Foner, all of Columbia, also offered many helpful suggestions and comments. A special word of thanks is due to Professor Henry Graff, who first taught me the essentials of historical research and writing. I would also like to express my appreciation to the staffs of the manuscript divisions of the Library of Congress, Historical Society of Pennsylvania, State Historical Society of Wisconsin, Iowa State Department of History and Archives, Ohio Historical Society, Henry E. Huntington Library, and New York Public Library, and to the reference librarians in Butler Library at Columbia University for their advice and assistance.

CONTENTS

JOHNSON, GRANT, and the
POLITICS of RECONSTRUCTION

INTRODUCTION

The years of the presidency of Andrew Johnson are filled with a drama and significance rarely equaled in the nation's history. Beginning with Johnson's succession to the presidency in an atmosphere charged with the emotional reaction to the assassination of his predecessor, they were also to witness a large part of the nation placed under direct military rule, the United States Senate come within one vote of removing the President from office, and, finally, a presidential campaign marred by widespread fraud, violence, and intimidation of voters. All of these events were part of a single larger conflict between men struggling to control the shape of the new political order that would be established as the issues of the war were settled and the nation reunited.

But in studying the period, attention has very strongly focused on the first two years of Johnson's term, as historians have been most intrigued by the origins of the President's split with the Republican Party and the reasons why a program for reconstruction that had almost no support at the end of the war was adopted by Congress just two years later. In the revisionism of the past decade, therefore, there have been no fewer than four major works dealing primarily with these problems, while Charles Coleman's thirty-five-year-old study of the election of 1868, which deals mainly with the selection of the Democratic nominee, remains the only book whose major concern is the events of the second half of Johnson's term.[1]

The disparity between the attention paid to these two periods would also seem to be based on a widespread assumption that 1866 was "the critical year," as Howard K. Beale called it, after which, "the Radical Congress [had] complete power over President and South alike."[2] But was the situation so clear at the time? Recent works have shown that the Reconstruction Acts were not written by a radical Republican clique in Congress operating on the basis of a carefully conceived and long-nurtured plan of action. Rather, they were hastily written measures, reflecting a process of give and take between various Republican factions who were forced to compromise their differences by the need for unified political action.[3]

Because of this it was not at all certain what the political results of the passage of the Acts would be. Thus there were at first both northern Democrats and southern conservatives who urged quick acceptance of the congressional terms, arguing that the outcome would be defeat for the Republican Party as southern blacks would vote with their former masters and help sweep a reunited Democratic Party back into national power. There had to be a long and complicated struggle over the interpretation and implementation of the Reconstruction Acts before the congressional program could achieve a measure of success with the inauguration of Republican-controlled governments in most of the southern states in June and July of 1868. Even then the attack on the validity of the congressional requirements did not end, as the Democratic Party carried the issue of the validity of the Acts to the voters in the presidential campaign of 1868. It was only after the Republican victory in November of that year that there was general acquiescence in the basic decision of the 1866 elections, that the South would have to accept whatever terms for reconstruction Congress established.

But by itself the Republican majority in Congress could not have succeeded in thus imposing its will and forcing the creation of the type of southern government it desired, for it had no way to control the manner in which the laws were executed, except indirectly by threatening to remove the President. To provide day to day implementation of the Reconstruction Acts on the local level in conformity to Republican policy, the leaders of Congress had to rely on the cooperation and support of the army, and in particular its commanding general, Ulysses S. Grant. The major role that Grant played in the postwar years has been too little appreciated, the generally accepted opinion of him being reflected in Avery Craven's recent description of "a pathetic, bewildered, shuffling figure whom others used for ends he never understood." [4]

This picture is in strange contrast to that of the bold and aggressive wartime commander, and Benjamin Thomas and Harold Hyman have opened the door for its revision by showing that Grant played a much more active political role in the early years of reconstruction than previous historians have ascribed to him. But Thomas and Hyman are looking at Grant from Edwin M. Stanton's point of view. Convinced that the general protected himself by hiding behind the Secretary of War, they accuse Grant of keeping his policies secret and building a "safe haven of apparent neutrality," from which he could still have jumped in either direction as late as January, 1868.[5]

This belief that Grant was pushed into the radical camp by his dispute with Johnson over the reinstatement of Stanton is also evident in most studies of the period. It ignores, however, the extent to which Grant's support for congressional reconstruction had already been openly stated in official correspondence and the fact that his nomination by the Republican Party was virtually certain prior to his public conflict with the President.[6] The fact that at the same time as the army was given responsibility for implementation of the Reconstruction Acts, a measure was passed to insure that Grant would remain as its commander, is strong evidence of the degree of faith Republican leaders had in him from the very beginning.

But even against this alliance between Congress and the army the President was not reduced to a nullity. While, as Thomas and Hyman have shown, some argued that Congress had created a "second army" free from presidential control, a study of congressional debates and the laws actually passed shows that the majority of the party felt that they could not seriously reduce Johnson's powers as commander-in-chief, but could only threaten to impeach him if he used his authority to obstruct enforcement of the laws.[7] The result was that in 1867–1868 the President and the commanding general engaged in an intricate duel on a tightrope, as it were, with Johnson using all of the powers of the presidency to hinder the completion of the congressional program as much as possible without providing the Republicans with grounds for his own impeachment, while Grant was trying to enforce that same program in the way desired by Republican leaders while avoiding direct insubordination to his commander-in-chief. It should be noted that in the end it was the political novice, Grant, who kept his balance, while the experienced politician, Johnson, fell.

In this context the impeachment of the President also takes on new meaning. The previous view that the Republicans had essentially won absolute control of reconstruction in the elections of 1866 has led historians to look elsewhere than to events in the South for an explanation of the attempt to remove the President. Thus Avery Craven assumes that Congress could only have been motivated by the desire to humiliate the President, while Eric McKitrick suggests that impeachment was largely an emotional reaction on the part of the Republicans.[8] But against the background of the discussion above, it becomes possible to see the impeachment as an essentially political act in which the major concern of Republicans was the success of the reconstruction program they had established. This becomes even more evident when it is noted that impeachment occurred at a time when congressional reconstruction faced major threats from a number of different directions and was in the greatest danger of failing. This political explanation also throws new light on the final acquittal of the President, as during the course of the trial almost all of these threats to the completion of the congressional program were eliminated. From this point of view the trial, far from being a Republican defeat, saw the accomplishment of everything the majority of Republicans desired as within a short time after Johnson's acquittal Republican-controlled state governments were inaugurated in all but three of the ex-Confederate states.[9]

The culminating major event of Johnson's administration then came in the presidential election that fall, which was also the first major test of the postwar political system. The Republican Party, which had originated in opposition to slavery and grown strong in opposition to secession, now had to demonstrate that it could survive emancipation and peace. In 1865 some were unsure that it could, feeling that its reasons for existence had been eliminated and its various elements would now naturally fragment. Felice Bonadio, in a recent study of Ohio politics, has placed great emphasis on these predictions and portrayed an essentially weak and divided party that held on to power by the narrowest of margins. Describing in great detail the rivalry between the various Republican factions, he feels that each preferred defeat for the party to victory for the opposing wing.[10] But Bonadio fails to reconcile this view with the fact that the Republicans won every gubernatorial election in Ohio between 1856 and 1874. Intense intraparty struggles can be a sign of vitality as well as of decay, and the ability consistently to win close contests is usually considered the mark of a champion.

Another indication of the great underlying strength of the Republican Party was its ability to respond to the new policy requirements of an everchanging situation, both during the war and after. The evolution of the Republican platform on racial issues is the most striking example of this, as a party that had originally been committed only to keeping black slaves out of the territories eventually became responsible for the adoption of the Thirteenth, Fourteenth, and Fifteenth Amendments to the federal constitution and the passage of the Civil Rights Acts of 1866 and 1875. The fact that there was resistance to this change from within the party and that strong racial prejudices continued to exist among the people of the North, only makes the progress of the Republican Party in this field more remarkable.[11]

This is not to suggest that the party's actions were determined solely by idealism and altruism, for the change occurred only because original Republican ideology, practical political considerations, and the logic of events all happened to be exerting their influence in the same direction. But whatever the motivation, the essential consideration here is that the party did have a large number of able and energetic leaders, who despite differences between themselves were able to define new basic policy positions that met the needs of rapidly changing times while maintaining the essential unity of their own party organization.

Such major change in the party's policy within such a short time and without significant permanent loss of voter support was possible only because the success of the war against secession and slavery, far from eliminating the adhesives that had bound the party together, created a loyalty to the Republican Party among its rank and file that would be a major political consideration in the North for decades to come. Thus, the election of 1868 would only be the first of a long series of postwar presidential elections in which the great strength of wartime symbols and party commitments would be demonstrated.

If the Republican Party faced a problem in the postwar years it was not internal division or inability to find a reason for existence, but the fact that it had only minor support within the dominant white segment of the population in ten southern states. It was this that endangered Republican control of the national government, for despite the closeness of the party struggle in some northern states, the Republicans generally could carry that section as a whole by safe majorities. The congressional program for reconstruction was, at least in part, an attempt to broaden the party's base by enfranchising large numbers of black voters who, it was hoped, would help create strong southern Republican parties. The state and national elections in 1868 were the first test of the effectiveness of that effort, and they seemed to indicate that the Republicans had succeeded as the party carried the great majority of the contests. But the possibility of eventual failure was also made evident by the ability of the white community in a number of places effectively to deny the ballot to blacks, despite all legal and constitutional provisions to the contrary.

The elections of 1868 also indicated that what had been an extremely fluid political situation in the South after the war had solidified to a great extent, as the section for the first time in over a decade became fully integrated into the national two-party system. In 1865 it had been unclear if white southerners would again support the Democratic Party to the extent that they had before 1860, particularly as some had felt that the northern Democrats had betrayed them by the failure to prevent the use of military force to reunite the nation. For the first years after the war, therefore, the section had generally followed an independent political course. But the events of 1867–1868 evidently convinced the mass of southern whites that they had no alternative but to affiliate with the national Democratic Party, thereby reestablishing the powerful antebellum coalition that had governed the nation for so many years.

Thus, to the extent that the South was a danger to the Republicans, it represented hope of a restoration to power for the Democrats. For the latter the problem was not so much one of extending their base of support as of bringing together the various elements of their party that had been so disastrously split in 1860 and finding a way to win the support of just a small fraction of Republican voters who were, for whatever reason, dissatisfied with their own party. One cannot help but feel that the immediate postwar years must have been a frustrating period for the Democrats, who deeply believed that they represented the true majority opinion of the nation, but were unable to find in either coalition or "straight-out" candidates, or in any combination of issues a strategy that would bring victory. Denied the votes of the South by the exclusion of that section until it had been, at least temporarily, Republicanized, Democrats discovered that they could not win the support of a significant number of conservative northern Republicans without surrendering their own policies and organizational identity to an extent most of them considered unacceptable.

The wartime experience, in fact, had created emotional ties within the Democratic Party quite as strong as those among Republicans, as the Democratic rank and file had generally remained loyal to their party in the face of what they considered outrageous and unconstitutional persecution by Republican officials.[12] The obvious tactic of winning Republican votes by supporting dissident Republicans for office was, therefore, generally unavailable to the Democrats, as large parts of the party were unwilling to surrender leadership positions to their former enemies. Nor was the party prepared for any basic change in its essential war-related policies. Instead, it tended to aggressively defend the propriety of the actions of all of its leaders during the war and to intensify its appeals to strict constitutionalism and racial prejudice, thereby reinforcing its own internal unity but limiting its appeal to Republican voters. It was natural, therefore, that in 1868 the Democrats chose the course that involved the least threat of a party split during the campaign, rather than the one that offered the best chance for converting opposition voters, and then went down to defeat in the national election.

These then were the critical elements in the events of 1867–1868: the struggle between Johnson and Grant for control of the army in the South, the response of the Republican Party to the political requirements of the postwar situation, the definition of the place of the South in the national political system, and the effort of the Democrats to regain national power. But before considering these things in greater detail it is necessary to go back to April, 1865, and briefly sketch the events that resulted in the passage of the First Reconstruction Act.

CHAPTER ONE

THE PROBLEM OF RECONSTRUCTION

In April of 1865, as the Civil War came to a close, it might have seemed that the North had completely achieved its war aims and there was therefore no need for a long or complicated process of reconstruction. Even before Appomattox it had been clear that the effort to establish an independent southern nation had failed, and after the surrender of the Army of Northern Virginia even the most ardent Confederate had to admit that the struggle was over. With southern resistance to national authority thus virtually ended at least one northern leader, Major General William T. Sherman, thought that peace could be made quickly and easily. On April 18th, he signed a convention with Confederate General Joseph E. Johnston that represented the first effort to deal with the problem of reconstruction within the postwar context. The terms of the Sherman-Johnston Convention were simple enough: the remaining Confederate armies would lay down their weapons, the authority of the national government would be reestablished, and everything would then be restored essentially to the status quo ante bellum.[1] This agreement thus represented an effort to settle the war on the simplest basis possible by having the South renounce its claim to a right of secession, which had been the most obvious and immediate cause for the start of hostilities.

But the administration at Washington immediately and emphatically refused to ratify these terms, which were in fact a totally inadequate effort to deal with the situation as it existed at the end of the war. Instead, the new President, Andrew Johnson, established a much more far-reaching program for reconstruction. Where the Sherman-Johnston Convention would have left the Confederate state governments in existence, the President's plan abolished them, giving power instead to existing Unionist governments in four states; Arkansas, Louisiana, Tennessee, and Virginia, and to men appointed as provisional governors elsewhere. In the latter seven states elections were then held to create entirely new state governments, which the President subsequently required to rescind their secession ordinances, abolish slavery, repudiate the Confederate war debt, and ratify the proposed Thirteenth Amendment to the federal constitution. At the same time, in an obvious effort to deny power to the old leaders of the "slavocracy," Johnson issued an amnesty proclamation from which he excluded all the political and military leaders of the Confederacy as well as all Confederate supporters worth over twenty thousand dollars. Thus presidential reconstruction in addition to demanding the renunciation of the right of secession also refused to concede any degree of legitimacy to Confederate state governments and sought a settlement of what may be viewed as the underlying cause of the war, the South's "peculiar institution." By the fall, these conditions had been almost totally accepted by the South, although in some cases strong executive pressure had had to be applied in order to secure compliance.[2]

Even this, however, proved to be insufficient for the majority of northern voters, and Johnson's program in turn went down to defeat. Some historians have suggested that this was because the roots of the sectional conflict were not only in slavery and secession, but more basically in the growing antagonism between two different economic systems. Radical reconstruction, in this view, would then be required in order to complete the establishment of northern economic supremacy which had begun during the war. Recent works, however, have raised much doubt about the accuracy and sufficiency of economic explanations for reconstruction and suggest instead that the reasons for the rejection of the Johnson program must be sought not in terms of the original causes of the conflict but in energies and commitments developed during the war itself.[3]

For the North in particular the war had been one of movement and change, as the need to organize military and economic power on an unprecedented scale had provided the new Republican administration with both motivation and justification for breaking with the past and setting the nation on a new course. Abraham Lincoln had put this spirit into words in his Second Annual Message of December, 1862, when he had told Congress: "The dogmas of the quiet past are inadequate to the stormy present. . . . As our case is new, so we must think anew and act anew." From the start the President had acted on this basis, increasing the size of the army on his own authority, spending funds without congressional appropriation, arresting and exiling opposition leaders, emancipating slaves in the Confederacy, and creating new southern state governments, all without regard to strict constitutional theory or legal scruple, but solely in response to the need to do everything necessary to win the war.[4]

This same spirit of total commitment to the war effort had also served as a vital unifying force for Republicans, holding that party together despite numerous policy and personality clashes and permitting a rapid evolution of administration programs in certain key areas without a loss of majority voter support. The operation of these factors can be seen in the changing Republican reaction to the issue of slavery. Certainly prior to the war the vast majority of Republicans had had no intention of interfering with that institution where it already existed. But within the wartime situation the extreme anti-slavery wing of the party had no longer been restricted in its activities by charges that talk of abolition would bring disunion, while to large numbers of other Republicans an attack on slavery had seemed to be a logical and necessary step in a vigorous prosecution of the war. Once the administration had been converted to this point of view and emancipation had become official policy, even conservative Republicans had been forced to defend it because of the need to keep the pro-war party united in the face of its enemies, both North and South. At the same time the fact that white, slaveholding southerners had been identified with rebellion, while emancipation had been adopted as a measure that would help preserve the Union, had resulted in a growing sense among Republicans of a national responsibility to aid and protect the freedmen in the period of transition from slavery to freedom.

This same process of rapid change in a Republican policy in order to meet the needs of the war effort, with totally new commitments emerging at the end, can be seen on the question of the use of Negro troops. Initial widespread opposition to the use of black soldiers had been overcome by the ever increasing demands of the army for manpower. Employed at first for use only as laborers, Negroes had finally been used as combat troops also, as the war had become bloodier and more costly. The value of their services in the field had then been recognized by Republicans, again creating a sense of national obligation to black men who had fought to save the Union, in contrast to white southerners who had fought to destroy it. Thus, by the end of the war the Republican Party, which had originally been committed only to limiting the expansion of slavery, had moved a very great distance. Despite the undeniable fact that its members harbored deep-seated racial prejudices they now had an alternate method of judging people, that of loyalty or disloyalty, in which the mass of Negroes ranked higher than large groups of whites. With the intensity of the emotional reaction to the war, growing out of the great cost and sacrifice involved, this had led at least some Republicans by 1865 to feel the need for a general reassessment of the position of the Negro in the nation.[5]

But while Republicans had developed a total commitment to the war effort and accepted any actions or policies that seemed required for victory, a totally different spirit had also existed in the North. This had been that of the great majority of Democrats, who had been essentially conservative and dedicated to the maintenance of the federal Union as conceived by Andrew Jackson. Thus while it is a mistake to view the Democrats as basically anti-war or pro-Confederate, they had been consistently opposed to the type of war that the Republicans had insisted on fighting. They had attacked all of Lincoln's extraconstitutional measures as being as destructive of the nation as secession itself, and instead had dedicated themselves to a strictly limited war designed to preserve "the Union as it was and the Constitution as it is." Their reaction to the slavery issue had been consistent with this spirit, as they had persisted in their opposition to emancipation to the end and had made strong and open racist appeals to the northern electorate.[6]

In this situation, party politics had taken on a character reminiscent of the early years of the Republic. It had not simply been a question of specific policy differences or competition for office, but each side had tended to question the essential legitimacy of the role being played by the other. To the Democrats, with their insistence that the only Union worth saving was the constitutional Union, Republican support for any and all measures needed to win the war had seemed revolutionary and treasonable. From the Republican point of view, in contrast, the persistence of the Democrats in raising constitutional issues and refusing to become totally committed to the war effort had proven that the opposition party was less than completely loyal.

This political situation would have major importance in the early years of reconstruction, when the mass of Republicans would continue to identify themselves as the sole party of loyalty while the Democrats would apply the label "Radical" to all Republicans without distinction. At the same time, the Republicans during reconstruction would still be the great party of movement and change, showing the ability to adjust and compromise to meet new situations and to maintain the unity required to overcome all obstacles. Where this had been possible before in order to win the war, it was now done under the imperative of "protecting the results of the war." This latter phrase could encompass a number of different issues, but in general they can be summed up in the single idea that the final effects of the war should be in some measure favorable to groups identified with loyalty and unfavorable to those who had been in any sense disloyal.

It is only against this background that the reaction against Johnson's program can be understood, for the President's policies seemed to be taking the nation in exactly the opposite direction. In the summer of 1865, elections had been held to create new state governments in the South under the Johnson plan, with prewar voting requirements in effect and the ballot as a result limited to whites. The great mass of the voters, therefore, were men who had been supporters of the Confederacy and, quite naturally, they showed a strong inclination to vote for those who had been their leaders during the war. By the same token, men who had been wartime Unionists found themselves largely excluded from power, and southern loyalists complained to Republicans in Congress that they were being subjected to legal harassment and even being physically assaulted and forced to leave their homes. For the freedmen the situation seemed to be even worse, as the newly created governments began to pass severely discriminatory Black Codes which seemed to indicate a determination on the part of white southerners to keep them in a permanent state of peonage. The final unacceptable element in the situation, from the Republican point of view, was that the emancipation of the slaves would actually increase the congressional representation of the South, making its influence in the national government greater and setting the stage for a possible recapturing of national power by a renewed coalition of southerners and northern Democratic "doughfaces." [7]

To Republicans the possibility that the glorious victory that had been won after four years of bloody and costly conflict would be quickly followed by a restoration to power of the men who had opposed them during the war must indeed have had nightmarish qualities. Therefore, despite the fact that as Congress met in December of 1865 Republican Congressmen held widely differing views as to what should be done, they were in general agreement that further progress of reconstruction had to be halted until Congress had had a chance to study the situation. By almost unanimous party votes then they denied seats to the representatives from the newly created southern governments and established the Joint Committee of Fifteen on Reconstruction to investigate the problem and make recommendations for legislation.

In trying to frame a program, however, Republicans faced immediate difficulty because the man in the White House was no longer Lincoln, who had been extremely sensitive to the needs of the Republican Party during the war, but Andrew Johnson, who suddenly proved to be totally unresponsive to Republican desires. This requires some comment because Johnson had been something of a radical during the war, who as military governor of Tennessee had not hesitated to take any steps necessary to maintain the Unionist cause in his state. His first postwar amnesty proclamation had reflected somewhat this same spirit, representing as it did an effort to remake the political power structure of the South. But, as a recent study of the subject has suggested, the key requirement for the success of presidential reconstruction was the voluntary cooperation of the southern electorate. As a result Andrew Johnson quickly became the prisoner of southern voters, who were not prepared to disavow their Confederate past. Thus, the results of the 1865 elections left the President with the choice of either issuing special pardons to all of the men elected who had been excluded from the general amnesty or refusing to accept the election results, in effect declaring that his entire program had been premature. Despite the fact that he was greatly upset by the results Johnson adopted the former course, thereby giving up his effort to eliminate the old political leaders of the South. At the same time the situation was not without its benefits for him, as the liberality of his policies made him extremely popular in the South, a fact that would be of some importance if his program were pressed to completion and the section completely restored prior to the presidential election of 1868.[8]

It is not sufficient, however, to explain Johnson's reversal solely as a shrewd political maneuver, as there was no certainty that the gains would balance the losses and there were other roads open that also seemed to lead to reelection in his own right. Johnson's southern birth and the effects of flattering appeals from the southern aristocracy are other factors that have been offered as influencing him, but perhaps the most useful way of approaching Johnson's policy is to recognize that it was essentially a return to the states-rights, strict-constructionist views that he had held before the war. It may then be suggested that his apparent radicalism during the war had been only a temporary response to a situation in which he had found himself cut off from his own political base, so that his only hope for a future career had lain in total support for the national administration and the war effort. After the war, however, with the power of the presidency at his command and the entire South looking to him for leadership, he suddenly held great political power in his own right and could revert to the political philosophy he found most congenial, one of conservatism and constitutionalism. By early 1866, he had gone so far in this direction that he was openly agreeing with the Democratic view that at least the extreme wing of the Republican Party was revolutionary and as responsible for causing the war as the original secessionists.[9]

As the congressional session began, however, the extent of the gulf between the President and Congress was not yet clear. A large number of Republicans, therefore, still hoped to find common ground with him, assuming that all that he had done had been experimental and was still subject to change. The Republican congressional majority began to define what it was hoped would be a mutually acceptable program in a bill to extend the life of the Freedmen's Bureau and give military courts in the South the power to protect the legal rights of Negroes. This measure Johnson vetoed, despite the fact that the overwhelming majority of Republicans in Congress had voted for it and he himself had raised no objections to it in discussions with its sponsors. His objections to it were largely on constitutional grounds, but he also questioned the right of Congress to pass such legislation while the southern states were unrepresented.

After an attempt to override the veto failed, Republicans responded with a second bill, the Civil Rights Bill, which conferred federal citizenship on all persons born in the United States, established the right of everyone to full and equal benefit of the law without regard to race or color, and made it a federal crime to deprive anyone of his civil rights. A number of conservative and moderate Republicans strongly urged Johnson to accept this bill, warning that it was supported by the rest of the party and that rejection would make the rupture between Congress and the President final and complete. However, he rejected this advice, sending the bill back with a message that indicated his absolute opposition to any legislation of this type, again on constitutional grounds. The result, as had been predicted, was that Republicans in Congress became unified in their opposition to the President and the measure was repassed over his objection, the first time in the nation's history that a veto of a major piece of legislation was overridden.[10]

With an irreparable breach thus established between the President and Congress, congressional Republicans proceeded to develop their own program of minimum demands for the readmission of the southern states. These took the form of a proposed Fourteenth Amendment to the constitution, recommended by the Joint Committee on Reconstruction after long debate. It essentially would write the legal protections of the Civil Rights Act into the constitution, reduce southern representation if Negroes were not given the vote, disqualify for federal or state office anyone who had held such office before the war and then supported the Confederacy, and guarantee the payment of the national debt while prohibiting the payment of either the Confederate debt or compensation for emancipated slaves. Congress took no action on an enabling bill, also recommended by the Joint Committee, which would have provided for readmission of the states upon acceptance of the amendment. But Tennessee, the only southern state that had a Republican-controlled government, was immediately readmitted upon ratifying it.

The amendment then provided a perfect platform upon which the Republican Party could unite in the approaching congressional elections. It met a number of Republican requirements for any settlement of the war issues by providing a degree of protection for loyal blacks in the South, while making possible a reduction of southern political power in the nation and excluding from an active political role those whom it was felt had been most disloyal. At the same time it made no extreme demands that might alienate moderate Republicans, while more radical Republicans could insist that it was merely a first measure and not a final settlement. Republican state platforms in the fall reflected this latter division, as Massachusetts Republicans insisted that Negro suffrage be made an additional condition, while New York Republicans accepted the Fourteenth Amendment as the final terms and most state platforms simply ignored the question.[11]

Andrew Johnson, meanwhile, remained fixed in his determination that no new conditions be demanded, and indicated that he would oppose the Republican Party in the election. He would not do this by returning to the Democratic Party, however, but rather hoped to create a great middle party based on the support of moderate Republicans, Democrats, and southerners. This latter plan had great advantages for the President, who would be the single dominant figure in any such new party formation. In addition, it would make it possible to exclude the extreme "Peace" Democrats, who were still distasteful to him, while attracting the maximum support from the Republican Party. In June, 1866, to further this aim, a call was issued for a National Union convention of all supporters of the President's policy, to meet in Philadelphia in August. At the same time the cabinet was purged, with all members who were unwilling to support this National Union movement resigning, except Secretary of War Edwin M. Stanton. To replace them the President drew entirely upon the conservative wing of the Republican Party, thereby avoiding identification of his administration as Democratic, despite his agreement and cooperation with the latter party on policy questions.[12]

This situation was not at all unsatisfactory to the Democrats, who were themselves not yet prepared to totally commit their party to Andrew Johnson. Various elements in the party had welcomed his succession to the presidency, recognizing that his ties to the Republican Party were weak and hoping that he would lead a movement of War Democrats out of the Republican coalition and back to their original party allegiance. But while Johnson's policies had certainly been more acceptable than those of his Republican opponents, Democrats still had many doubts about the completeness and permanence of his conversion to "correct" constitutional principles. They had been particularly upset by the trial of the assassination conspirators in a military court and the President's delay in restoring the right of *habeas corpus* throughout the nation. Even after reassurance on these points Democrats continued to complain that the President was giving only halfhearted support to his own policies and permitting the patronage to be used in behalf of his enemies. Nor were most Democrats willing to consider the possibility of a political realignment that would result in the disappearance of the party to which their loyalties were so strongly committed. The Democratic response to the call for the Philadelphia convention therefore was one of widespread hesitation and suspicion, and it was only after they were assured that they could retain their own party organization and would be given the full support of the administration in the campaign that the bulk of the party agreed to participate.[13]

The National Union Convention then met with a great show of apparent strength and unity. It had the support of the national administration and the dominant political group in the South, while Democrats and conservative Republicans had joined to choose the northern delegates. The keynote for the convention was sounded when the Massachusetts and South Carolina delegates entered the hall in pairs, from which it received the nickname, the "arm-in-arm" convention. Its main work was the adoption of a platform stating that the South fully accepted the results of the war and should be immediately readmitted without further conditions.

In fact, however, the National Union coalition contained elements of great weakness that were to prove fatal. The unity shown at Philadelphia was achieved only by careful stage managing and the willingness of Peace Democrats like Clement Vallandigham and Fernando Wood to surrender their claims to seats in the convention. But the difficulty of establishing working cooperation between the various groups involved became evident as the coalition was actually implemented at the state level and the process of choosing local tickets began.[14]

The situation in New York provides perhaps the best illustration of the weaknesses inherent in the movement. In that state its chances for success appeared to be particularly good as it brought together an already strong Democratic Party and such major Republican supporters of the President's policy as William Henry Seward, Thurlow Weed, Henry J. Raymond, and John A. Dix. But a struggle immediately developed over the nomination of a candidate for governor, growing out of the unwillingness of either element to concede the leading role in the coalition to the other. The Johnson men felt that the Democrats should take a back seat in order to bring over as many Republican voters as possible and therefore supported the nomination of one of their own number, the former Union general, Dix. The Democrats, however, recognized that they would have to provide most of the voting support for the ticket and therefore saw no reason why they should give control to someone else, especially when the men involved were their oldest political enemies, Seward and Weed. As they were the strongest element within the coalition, the Democrats were able to nominate a candidate from their own ranks, Mayor John T. Hoffman of New York City. This pattern was followed in other places also, as in state after state local nominations were controlled by the Democratic Party.[15]

But with this Democratic domination of the National Union movement clearly established, its appeal to conservative Republican voters was very greatly reduced, particularly as their own party's Fourteenth Amendment platform was fully acceptable to them. In addition, northern feeling against the South was strengthened following a riot in New Orleans in July, in which a large number of Negroes were killed as the result of what General Philip Sheridan described as "an absolute massacre by the police." Johnson further weakened his own cause by a series of intemperate speeches in August and September, during a tour of the North popularly known as the "swing around the circle." The consequences of all of this showed in the fall elections in the North as National Union tickets went down to defeat almost everywhere.[16]

For this result Johnson and the Democrats blamed each other. The latter believed that their new allies had proven to be of very little value and that the President in particular had shown great ineffectiveness as a political leader by his failure to use the patronage properly to support his true friends. At the same time, conservative Republicans were convinced that they had been denied victory only because the Democrats had insisted on taking a leading role in the coalition, thereby tainting the movement with the image of Copperheadism in the minds of northern voters. As a consequence Johnson would continue to run an essentially personal administration, politically isolated from both parties, while the Democrats would increasingly turn away from ideas of coalition and be strengthened in their resolve to maintain the independence and purity of their own party identification.[17]

The results left the Republicans in complete control of the governments of every northern state and three of the border states, West Virginia, Missouri, and Tennessee, where stringent registration laws still kept ex-Confederates from the polls. The Democrats had power only in Delaware, which they had carried throughout the war, and Kentucky and Maryland, where the lifting or relaxation of voting restrictions had restored the ballot to large numbers who had previously been disfranchised for their wartime activities.[18] In the House of Representatives the Democrats held about a third of the seats from the mid-Atlantic states and about a fifth of those from Ohio, Indiana, Illinois, and Wisconsin, but none from any of the thirteen remaining northern and Pacific states. While the net gain by the Republicans in House seats was only four, it must be remembered that they already had an oversized majority and would now hold a 129–35 advantage. In addition, the increase in the radicalism of the Fortieth Congress would be even greater than indicated by the number of seats changing hands, as many of the more moderate Republicans had not been re-elected and Congress now felt that it had a mandate to control Reconstruction and overthrow Johnson's policies.[19]

Despite this, neither the Democrats nor the southerners felt compelled to accept the Republican program by ratifying the proposed Fourteenth Amendment. On the contrary both groups generally resisted all suggestions of compromise, insisting, as they had from the first, that the President remain adamant in his position. Neither accepted the election results as a mandate to Congress, pointing out that while the Republicans had won a large majority of the seats, they had carried the total popular vote for Congress by only 400,000 votes. If to this were added the number of voters in the South who supported Johnson's policies, there was a popular majority of at least a million in favor of those policies in the nation as a whole. In addition they stood on constitutional grounds, claiming that the amendment had not been properly proposed, as the South was not represented in Congress, and that no matter what public opinion in the North might desire the southern states could not be forced to ratify an amendment to which they were opposed. The war had been fought solely to prevent the southern states from leaving the Union; they were now prepared to return to the government and resume their places under the constitution, and this was all that could be demanded of them.

From the southern point of view even Johnson's actions had been unconstitutional, as he had had no right to destroy the existing state governments and create new ones. His conditions had been unwarranted and contrary to the terms of surrender, but they had strongly desired peace and reunion and had therefore agreed to them. But the promise that they would then be restored had been broken, and they were not now ready to agree to the disqualification for office of their leaders and the reduction of their congressional representation when they had no guarantee that these were the final terms.[20]

The southerners were encouraged to adopt a policy of "masterly inactivity" by assurances from northern Democrats and Johnson that Congress could not do much more than had already been done. There might be an attempt to declare the amendment ratified by a vote of three quarters of the states represented in Congress, but once readmitted they could attack the validity of such a ratification. As for any attempt by the radical Republicans to establish new governments and black suffrage in the South, they would have difficulty getting a two thirds vote in Congress for such an act, and in any case the President and the Supreme Court would prevent its enforcement. At the same time the passage of such an extreme measure would quickly bring a reaction against the Republican Party and its defeat in the northern states. Despite some warnings of the dangers involved the overwhelming majority of southern legislators accepted this reassuring view of the situation, and the amendment was rejected by almost unanimous votes in all of the states. This, with similar action in Kentucky and Delaware, ensured that the amendment would fail unless Congress took more drastic action.[21]

In December and January, southern hopes were further increased by a series of Supreme Court decisions that attacked two of the major tools available to Congress, military courts and test oaths. On December 17, 1866, in *ex parte Milligan*, a unanimous Court held that the President had no power to authorize trial of civilians by military courts in areas where the civil courts were open, and a majority of the Court held that there was a similar limitation on the power of Congress. Then, on January 14, 1867, in *Cummings* v. *Missouri* and *ex parte Garland*, it struck down requirements of test oaths, in the first case for a priest to teach in Missouri, and in the second for a lawyer to practice before the Supreme Court.[22]

During this same period Republicans in Congress were unable to agree on a policy, dividing between moderates who remained committed to the terms of the Fourteenth Amendment and radicals who wanted to create entirely new southern governments controlled by the freedmen and loyal whites. Then in February the administration took the initiative with a compromise proposal that had been developed in conferences between Johnson and moderate southern leaders. It was based on a revised Fourteenth Amendment, with the disqualification clause replaced by a section guaranteeing the equality of all the states, plus southern acceptance of impartial suffrage with a property holding or literacy requirement for new voters only. Southern legislatures and newspapers, however, were not prepared to accept the proposal without more consideration and some indication of congressional feeling.[23] In the meantime, with the session drawing to a close, the Republicans reached agreement on what was to be the First Reconstruction Act.

The process by which the act was written shows again the ability of the Republicans to overcome factional differences that had produced an apparent legislative deadlock in order to produce a compromise measure to deal with what all Republicans viewed as an immediate emergency. The need for some kind of congressional action had become clear in the early months of the session as the nearly unanimous southern rejection of the Fourteenth Amendment had been accompanied by increasing reports of persecution of Unionists and Negroes in the South. On February 13th, therefore, the House approved a bill proposed by Thaddeus Stevens which provided for the division of the South into five districts, under military commanders who were made responsible for the preservation of law and order. It was intended to be an interim measure, which would give congressional sanction to the army's role in the South as the protector of the Unionists and freedmen until a permanent settlement could be established. In order to prevent obstruction of the congressional policy by the President, power to appoint the district commanders was given to Ulysses S. Grant, as commanding general of the army.

In the Senate, however, the essential nature of the bill was changed by amendments proposed by John Sherman of Ohio which provided for the readmission of the southern states if they ratified the Fourteenth Amendment and adopted new constitutions acceptable to Congress. The latter would have to provide for universal suffrage, and Negroes were to vote in the elections for delegates to the conventions and on ratification of the constitutions. In addition, the President was given the power to appoint the district commanders, discussion in both Houses showing the general belief that Congress could not reduce his powers as commander-in-chief, but could only hold him accountable, under threat of impeachment, for proper execution of the laws.[24]

The amended version was unacceptable to radical Republicans in the House, who wanted to immediately create new state governments from which ex-Confederates would be excluded, and they combined with the Democrats to prevent acceptance of the Senate version of the bill. Moderate and radical Republicans then united to amend the Senate bill by adding provisions disfranchising those men disqualified for office by the Fourteenth Amendment and stating that the existing southern state governments were provisional only, and subject to the power of the federal government to "abolish, modify, control, or supersede [them]." The bill was sent to Johnson in this form with less than ten days remaining in the session, so that he could have defeated it with a pocket veto. But provision had been made for an immediate special session of the Fortieth Congress, which was expected to be even more radical, and he therefore returned it with a veto message in time for it to be repassed over his objection.[25]

During this same period two other major acts affecting reconstruction were passed. Johnson was forced to accept a rider, known as the Command of the Army Act, which was attached to the army appropriation bill. It provided that Grant could not be removed as commanding general of the army or ordered from Washington against his will, and all orders to the army concerning military operations had to be issued through him. An additional section forbade the organization of militias in any of the ten southern states until authorized by Congress. The other law, the Tenure of Office Act, had been proposed in order to limit Johnson's use of the patronage. It made the consent of the State necessary for the removal of any officer whose appointment required Senate approval. When Congress was not in session the President could suspend such officers for cause, but he had to submit his reasons to the Senate for approval when it next convened. Originally, cabinet officers had not been included, but before final passage a provision was added protecting them from removal during the term of the President who had appointed them. This was generally seen as an effort to protect Secretary of War Stanton, the only supporter of the congressional policy still in the cabinet, but his status under it was questionable as he had been appointed during Lincoln's first term.[26]

As the First Reconstruction Act had not specified the details of how the conventions were to be called, the Fortieth Congress, in a short session, passed the Second Reconstruction Act, again over Johnson's veto. It placed the initiative for calling the conventions in the hands of the military commanders, who were to complete a registration of all eligible voters by September 1, 1867. Elections were then to be held at which voters would both elect delegates to a convention and decide whether it should be called. To be carried, the convention call had to be approved by a majority of those voting in an election in which a majority of the registered voters had participated. The act also specified an oath to be taken by all voters which somewhat increased the extent of disfranchisement. The First Reconstruction Act had simply referred back to the section of the Fourteenth Amendment which disqualified those who, as federal or state officeholders, had taken an oath to support the constitution and then aided the Confederacy. Voters were now required to swear not only that they had never broken an oath, but that they had never been a member of any state legislature or held any executive or judicial state office and then engaged in rebellion against the nation or given aid or comfort to its enemies.[27]

With this act the essentials of the Republican plan for reconstruction were completed and the Senate was prepared to adjourn until the next regular session in December. House members, however, warned that Johnson still had the power to obstruct reconstruction and they demanded that provision be made for a summer meeting. It was finally decided that the session would resume on July 3d, if a quorum of both Houses were present at that time. If either House did not have a quorum, both Houses would automatically adjourn *sine die*, which would mean that they could not meet again until December, unless called by Johnson.[28] On this understanding Congress recessed, leaving control of the South in the hands of the President and the army.

CHAPTER TWO

GRANT, JOHNSON, AND RECONSTRUCTION

The passage of the Reconstruction Acts created a situation unique in American history in that a major legislative program, directly affecting over one third of the nation, was to be carried out despite the opposition of the President. This could only be done if the army officers responsible for the enforcement of the Acts were sympathetic to the congressional policy and prepared to resist presidential obstruction. That Republican leaders themselves were sure that this was the case is shown by their decision to place reconstruction entirely in military hands, rather than adopting an alternate plan to create new provisional governments under the control of southern unionists.[1] Nor is this situation surprising, as the army was more aware than any other group of the price that had been paid for victory and thus more responsive than any other to the felt need to "protect the results of the war."

In addition, problems of reconstruction were not entirely new to the army commanders, who as the conquerors and occupiers of the South had played a direct role in southern government since the end of the war. During that time they had dealt with exactly those problems of security for southern Unionists and equality for the freedmen which had been of concern to congressional Republicans. Military courts had taken jurisdiction in cases involving freedmen, while commanders had nullified provisions of the Black Codes. In testimony before the Joint Committee on Reconstruction military men had reported instances of violence against Unionists and Negroes, and warned of the results of an early removal of federal troops. In addition, as Thomas and Hyman have shown, army officers had come to rely on Congress for support and legal aid against the threat of civil suits brought against them for official acts committed during the war.[2]

While the First Reconstruction Act gave no special role to Grant, his views were actually doubly important because of his influence on the other generals and his popularity with northern voters. As early as 1864 he had been mentioned as a presidential possibility, and at that time he had expressed a view, which he had maintained ever since, that as a military officer he could not publicly express his opinions on political questions. In private, however, he had supported Johnson's policies in 1865, seeing them as a continuation of Lincoln's, and if anything had acted as a moderating influence on the President in questions relating to the treatment of Confederate leaders. When General Carl Schurz had stated that there was a lack of loyalty in the South, Johnson had called on Grant for a report and had used the latter's statement that "the mass of the thinking men of the South accept the present situation of affairs in good faith," to show that congressional action was not needed.[3]

But during 1866 Grant had moved away from this position, undoubtedly influenced by reports coming from the South. On January 12, 1866, in General Order No. 3, he had ordered commanders in the South to protect soldiers, government agents, and loyal persons from prosecution for acts done under orders or acts against rebel forces and to prevent the prosecution of freedmen for offenses for which whites were not punished in the same manner and degree. A month later he had indicated his concern with the development of a disloyal spirit in the South by directing that copies of newspapers that were persistently hostile to the government should be sent to army headquarters so that he could order them suppressed. On July 6th he had taken an additional step in General Order No. 44, which instructed southern commanders to arrest persons charged with violence in cases where the civil authorities had not acted, and to hold such persons until a proper court was ready to try them.[4]

In all of this Grant had been moving in the opposite direction from Johnson, who had issued peace proclamations on April 2, and August 20, 1866, which had restored civil authority in the South and seemed to nullify General Orders 3 and 44.[5] At the same time the general's public silence on political issues had created confusion as to his position in the developing split between Johnson and Congress. Therefore, while some Republicans had felt that he was in basic sympathy with their policy and had regarded him as their party's probable nominee in 1868, Johnson had also hoped to use Grant's prestige to support the administration. Thus the President had arranged for Grant to be at his side to greet a delegation from the National Union convention and had asked the general to accompany him on the "swing around the circle." [6]

These appearances had brought increased speculation as to Grant's political allegiance, administration supporters claiming that they indicated his approval of the President's policy, while the Republican press maintained that he had been forced into going on the trip and was greatly annoyed by the persistent efforts to misrepresent him. Fortunately we have a letter from Grant to his wife that does indicate the general's private opinion at this time. In it he characterizes Johnson's speeches as a national disgrace, while cautioning her to keep his views confidential as he has to respect the President's office and remain in his confidence. It is clear, then, that Grant had strongly disapproved of Johnson's actions, but had felt equally strongly that he could not make his views known.[7]

Grant's desire to avoid public opposition to the President, however, did not mean that he played a passive role in the government. In October he had resisted suggestions from Johnson that troops be used in Baltimore to support the Democratic state government against the Republican city government, intervening personally instead to prevent a threatened outbreak of violence. His private feelings about the President had hardened by this time, and he had written Sheridan that few people who had been loyal during the war now had any influence on Johnson. Grant even had feared that the President might attempt to declare Congress itself unconstitutional, and he had considered the situation so serious that he had ordered the weapons in southern arsenals shipped North.[8]

Nor had Johnson been unaware of the growing divergence between his views and those of Grant. In late October he had ordered the general on a mission to Mexico, intending to make General William T. Sherman, who was believed to hold views very similar to the President's, commanding general of the army and probably secretary of war also. That Grant had felt that vital issues were involved became evident when he had refused to obey the direct order, on the grounds that he could not be forced to accept a diplomatic mission. That Johnson had strongly desired to replace Grant became equally clear when he had persisted in his efforts to force Grant to go, despite the latter's rejection of the proposal, twice in writing and once before a full cabinet. The President had finally been convinced that Grant would not go under any circumstances only by the arguments of Sherman himself, and the latter had then been sent on the mission instead.[9]

Then in the winter of 1866–67 Grant had moved into a somewhat more direct political role. He had urged General Edward O. C. Ord, commanding in Arkansas, to use his influence in favor of ratification of the Fourteenth Amendment, explaining that while he normally opposed army interference in political questions this was not a party, but a national matter. Grant had been sure that if the amendment were ratified the state would be readmitted, while delay would only result in additional demands being made. The same advice had been given directly to southern leaders, while he had sought from Republicans in Congress pledges that ratification would result in both the readmission of the southern states and the removal of the majority of disqualifications. When this effort had failed, Grant had played an active part in drafting the First Reconstruction Act, hoping that it would provide a final basis for a settlement, and he had dismissed Johnson's veto of it as "ridiculous." However he had been evidently still unwilling to engage in a direct power struggle with the President, as he seems to have been responsible for the amendment that had given Johnson rather than himself the power to appoint the district commanders.[10]

In addition both Grant and Stanton, according to newspaper reports, had urged Congress not to adjourn until the regular session in December, desiring continued congressional support if a conflict should develop over implementation of the Acts. However, when Johnson had appointed the district commanders recommended by Grant, it had been seen as an indication that he would not attempt to obstruct the congressional policy. The men appointed, John Schofield, Daniel Sickles, George Thomas, Edward O. C. Ord, and Philip Sheridan, had been considered in the main supporters of the congressional policy and Republican papers had expressed full confidence in them.[11] As has been seen, Congress had then felt that it could safely adjourn, making only provisional arrangements to reconvene in July if necessary.

At first everything proceeded smoothly, with the President making no effort to control the actions of the commanders. Grant adopted the view that Congress had intended to give the latter full responsibility for the execution of the Acts, and that he, therefore, could not give them orders on civil matters. When problems of interpretation did arise, however, and the administration questioned certain actions of the commanders, he made obvious efforts to avoid a direct issue on the subject of their powers. The first area of possible serious dispute was the interpretation of the disfranchisement provisions. Their effect would vary greatly according to the definition of which prewar offices were included within their scope and what constituted support of the Confederacy. These questions were referred to the attorney general for an opinion and there was an obvious intention to abide by his decision. When Sheridan removed three officials in New Orleans and Pope threatened to remove the governor of Georgia, some claimed that they were exceeding their powers. Grant, thereupon, suggested that in the future they suspend officials and try them by military court, as their power to do this was unquestionable.[12]

But, sooner or later, it had to be decided whether the President or the military were in control of reconstruction, and the issue came to a head in Louisiana. Sheridan had begun registration there before any of the other commanders had acted, and he had initially proposed to limit it to thirty days in New Orleans and sixty days in the state. But as registration began, W. H. C. King, the editor of the New Orleans *Times* and an administration supporter, warned Johnson that early returns in the city showed a large black majority and the registration period would have to be extended if his friends were to win the election. Johnson ordered this to be done, but the question of his authority to do so was avoided when his order was transmitted in permissive terms and Sheridan replied that an extension had already been granted. A few weeks later, however, he was again told to extend the registration period, this time in a direct order signed by Stanton. In early June, at the request of Governor James Wells of Louisiana, Sheridan was further directed to suspend an order he had issued removing the Levee Commission of that state and appointing a new one. Both orders were obeyed without question, but Sheridan vented his feelings by removing Governor Wells.[13]

At this same time the long awaited opinions of Attorney General Henry Stanbery were issued. He interpreted the disfranchisement provisions narrowly, exempting many prewar office holders whom the district commanders had excluded from registration, making oath-taking as well as office-holding a requirement for disfranchisement in all cases, and defining support of the Confederacy as the voluntary commission of an overt act intended directly to further the rebellion. In addition, he declared that the registration boards could not exclude anyone who was prepared to take the required oath of eligibility. A second opinion, on the powers of the district commanders, denied that they had the power to remove officials or alter state laws. He interpreted the Reconstruction Acts as making the provisional governments coequal with the military governments, with the latter limited to those basic police functions necessary for the protection of persons and property. The power set forth in the First Reconstruction Act to "abolish, modify, control, or supersede" the civil governments was, he believed, reserved to Congress itself, rather than delegated to the commanders.[14]

Before taking action on the basis of the opinions, Johnson called a cabinet meeting to discuss the question of his authority over the commanders and the form and content of the official communication that would be sent to them. It can only be assumed that he hoped to reinforce the opinions, and perhaps protect himself as well, by obtaining the endorsement of a unanimous cabinet for them. But in this he failed, as Stanton steadfastly insisted that the registration boards had the power to refuse applicants and that the southern governments were completely subject to military authority. While not claiming absolute independence for the commanders, the secretary of war maintained that the President had only general supervisory powers over them, to prevent "willful neglect or wanton abuse of authority." [15]

The final result, after three days of cabinet meetings, was the transmission to the district commanders of a summary of Stanbery's opinion on registration, "for their information in order that there may be uniformity in the execution of the said acts." This phrase Grant interpreted for the commanders as meaning that the opinion was advisory, and he told them to enforce their own interpretations of the Acts. He then made his own position clear by taking strong exception to Ord's decision to follow Stanbery's opinion in the registration in the Fourth District. Sickles and Sheridan also opposed the attorney general's views, the former stating that without the power of removal he could not protect the people of his district, while the latter warned that the opinion on registration would open "a broad macadamized road for perjury and fraud." [16]

Despite this, there is every reason to believe that a direct order enforcing the opinions would have been obeyed by the commanders, and Johnson was aware of this fact. Sickles had written privately to the President, stating his belief that as commander-in-chief he had full power to issue either general or specific orders to the commanders, while both Pope and Sheridan had stated in official correspondence that they would obey a direct order.[17] The failure of Johnson to insist on such an order is, therefore, interesting. As with his decision to enforce the Reconstruction Acts, even though he thought them unconstitutional, it must be taken as an indication of his unwillingness to commit any act which might be interpreted as a breach of his oath to execute the laws. The threats of impeachment made in Congress when power to appoint the district commanders had been left in his hands had been reinforced by the authorization of an investigation of his conduct. With Republican papers charging that he was deliberately obstructing enforcement of the Acts and Stanton and Grant rejecting his interpretation of his powers, he may well have felt that it was too risky to attempt to enforce his views.

In any event the timing of the opinions proved to be a major mistake, as they ensured the reconvening of Congress on July 3d. At that session, to the surprise of no one, Congress speedily reversed Stanbery's opinions. In the Third Reconstruction Act, also passed over Johnson's veto, the power of the district commanders

over the state governments was made explicit and complete. It was
further stated that the commanders should not be bound by the
opinion of any civil officer of the United States, but Grant was
given supervisory power over appointments and removals made by
them. The disfranchisement provisions of the previous acts were
somewhat clarified and expanded beyond the limits set by Stanbery, with the registration boards given authority to decide on the
eligibility of any applicant. In addition, all future appointees to office in the provisional governments were required to take the
"iron-clad" oath that they had never supported the Confederacy.[18]

With the powers of the district commanders thus reinforced by
Congress, Johnson gave up the effort to control them, even though
the Act in no way reduced his authority as commander-in-chief
over them.[19] Instead, once Congress had adjourned, he began to
consider use of his power of removal which, against the advice of
Grant, had been left unrestricted in the new law. Sheridan, Sickles,
and Pope were his most likely targets, while Schofield and Ord
were considered the more conservative of the district commanders.
Sheridan was particularly objectionable to Johnson because of the
language of his attack on Stanbery's registration opinion and the
circumstances under which he had removed Governor Wells of
Louisiana. Pope, for his part, had made his position clear in a long
letter to Grant complaining about the activities of "pardoned rebels" and warning that reconstruction might not be possible while
"these unrepentant and reactionary political leaders are suffered to
remain in this country." Sickles, in contrast, had urged universal
amnesty, but had also used his power to open the jury lists to all
taxpayers, outlaw racial discrimination on public transportation,
and prohibit the distillation of whiskey.[20]

But Johnson, unexpectedly, made his initial move against Secretary of War Stanton. On August 5th the nation was startled when
he requested Stanton's resignation, on the grounds of "public considerations of a high character." When Stanton replied that "public
considerations of a high character" required him to remain in office
until Congress convened, he was suspended and Grant made Secretary of War *ad interim*. Grant's acceptance of the office created
confusion as to his views on reconstruction, a situation not dis-

pleasing to Johnson. Shortly before making the appointment the President had told an interviewer that he had regarded Grant as a supporter of his policy and would "be surprised to find out at this time that he [Grant] has been opposed to what I have been attempting to do." [21]

Historians have tended to take Johnson at his word, but there can be no question about Grant's support of the Republican policy, and there is every reason to believe that Johnson was well aware of this. While Grant had not made any public statements, his basic policy had been made clear in official correspondence. His advice to the district commanders to enforce their own interpretations of the Acts, his telegram to Ord opposing Stanbery's registration opinion, and a message to Sheridan stating that he did not disapprove of the removal of Wells were all part of the public record. When Johnson, on August 1st, suggested that he might remove both Stanton and Sheridan, Grant had responded with a letter strongly opposing either action. Stanton, he stated, was protected by the Tenure of Office Act, and he pointedly asked why Johnson had not acted while the Senate was in session if he desired a new secretary of war. As for Sheridan, he had done great service for the country and the loyal people would not easily accept his removal. Later, when asked by Johnson if there were any conflict between them, Grant replied that there was nothing personal, but they did disagree on the Fourteenth Amendment and the Reconstruction Acts. In discussion with Secretary of the Navy Gideon Welles, Grant took the position that the South was conquered territory and it was the duty of the Executive to enforce the congressional policy there. Welles warned Johnson of the trend of Grant's thinking, but the President did not need this advice, for he had himself, four months previously, stated that Grant was as radical as anyone.[22]

In appointing Grant, therefore, Johnson was not getting a secretary of war who agreed with his policies, but he had undoubtedly acted with two other purposes in mind. With Grant holding the office the reaction to Stanton's removal would be softened as the Republicans could not charge Johnson with attempting to obstruct enforcement of the laws without at the same time implying that

Grant was cooperating with him. With Grant in the cabinet, also, it might become possible to gain an influence over him, and in any case the impression would be created that he approved of administration measures. This last is very likely the reason why Johnson waited until after Grant was in the cabinet before making his next move, the removal of Sheridan from command of the Third District.

But any hope of convincing the public that Grant endorsed the President's course was very quickly removed as the newspapers obtained copies of a strongly worded letter of protest from the new secretary of war. The conflict continued over the question of future control of the Third District. George Thomas was first named as Sheridan's successor, and in the order appointing him Grant instructed him not to change any of Sheridan's orders without Grant's approval. This was done under the erroneous impression that the Third Reconstruction Act gave Grant general supervisory powers over the district commanders, when in fact his control extended only to questions of appointment and removal. Johnson realized this, and when Thomas declined the appointment he directed that the orders to the new commander, Winfield Scott Hancock, authorize him to use, at his own discretion, all of the powers given him by the laws. Grant, continuing his mistaken interpretation of the Act, protested in writing, stating that he had been given special responsibility by Congress for the execution of the Acts and would not permit his power to be usurped. Johnson, in a private interview with the general, righteously proclaimed that the law made the commanders independent of all control, and he would not permit Grant to obstruct the will of Congress. Grant was forced to admit the validity of Johnson's statement of the limitations on his power and he requested and received permission to withdraw his letter. He then issued the order in the form desired by Johnson, but, acting within the area of authority he did have, ordered that no commander should reappoint to office a man who had been previously removed.[23]

Johnson continued to take the initiative by ordering that General Edward R. S. Canby replace Sickles in the Second District, after the latter had refused to obey the federal courts in North

Carolina. The President followed this, on September 7th, with a sweeping amnesty proclamation that some hoped would have the legal effect of restoring the vote to most of those disfranchised by the congressional legislation.[24] Thus again, as in June, Johnson seemed to be embarking on a course of bold and vigorous action designed to give conservative forces in the South as much aid as possible. But, again, it all came to little in practice.

Superficially he had won a victory over Grant by forcing the general to give up his claim to supervisory powers over the district commanders. But he had done this by declaring the commanders independent of all control, which was the interpretation of the Acts that the general had favored from the beginning. In practice this gave Grant, who was privately advising the commanders and keeping them informed of political events in Washington, greater influence over reconstruction than anyone else. Nor did the change in commanders make much immediate difference, as Canby proved to be just as receptive to Grant's advice as the other commanders, and even Hancock, the only one of them who would ever oppose Grant, immediately stated that he would not change Sheridan's arrangements for the elections in Louisiana without Grant's approval.[25]

The amnesty proclamation also proved to be meaningless, as Johnson stated that he did not believe that he could order the commanders to register all those pardoned. If he attempted to do so, he stated, he would be impeached, so that amnestied southerners who were denied the vote must seek their redress in the courts.[26] Despite this flurry of activity in August and September, therefore, Johnson's actual influence on events in the South was minimal. The consequences of his failure could be seen as the Republicans won all of the elections held in the South in the fall of 1867. The developments in southern politics that had contributed to that result next need study.

CHAPTER THREE

RECONSTRUCTION IN THE SOUTH

Until the passage of the Reconstruction Acts southern politics had been relatively simple. In general there seems to have been little interest in political questions, as most people had been much more concerned with the need to rebuild the section after the physical destruction of the war. Under the Confederacy there had been no organized two-party system, and this continued to be true for most of the South during the immediate postwar years. With the collapse of the war effort men who had been strongly identified as original supporters of secession had tended to drop out of public life, so that leadership in the Johnson governments had been taken by men who had held more moderate antebellum views, many of whom were ex-Whigs. These latter had retained a large measure of their old hostility to the Democratic Party and had had no desire to join it, preferring to apply the label "Conservative" to themselves. But, as has been seen, they had accepted the President's leadership, supporting his National Union coalition and then defeating the Fourteenth Amendment by almost unanimous votes.[1]

It might have been expected that the southerners who had thus rejected the proposed Amendment almost out of hand, would now react even more quickly and decisively against the First Reconstruction Act, which demanded both ratification of the Amendment and the adoption of Negro suffrage. Such was not the case, however, for all of the expectations that had led the South to refuse to ratify the Amendment had proven false and the southern position required serious reexamination. Expectations of a deadlock in Congress or a split in the Republican Party had again proven false, and the strategy of "masterly inactivity" had only resulted in the formulation of a much tougher congressional policy. Hope that the implementation of the law could be prevented might prove to be equally illusory, as there was no assurance of a continuing conservative majority on the Supreme Court, while Johnson's decision to enforce the Act even though he considered it unconstitutional meant that reconstruction might be complete before the courts could act.

The first indication of a recognition of the need for an altered southern position came in late February, 1867, when Joseph E. Brown, the ex-Confederate governor of Georgia, returned from a trip to Washington and advised the South that it had to accept the terms of the First Reconstruction Act, or Congress would pass a much harsher measure. Then, in March, the Virginia state senate, which had rejected the Fourteenth Amendment unanimously, voted 25–4 to hold the required constitutional convention under the terms of the Act. Another major indication of a shift in southern thinking occurred on March 18th, when a black meeting in Columbia, South Carolina, which received national attention, heard ex-Confederate general Wade Hampton and Negro leader Beverly Nash call for political equality and cooperation between the races in the South.[2]

The strength of the movement toward acceptance of the congressional terms was increased by the passage of the Second Reconstruction Act. With the military commanders now taking the initiative in registration of voters and in the calling of conventions, a policy of "masterly inactivity" would simply mean exclusion from the political process. By the beginning of April, therefore, a major reversal seems to have occurred in southern thinking, as the majority of state governors and a growing list of ex-Confederate leaders were now urging an end to resistance and full participation in the process of creating new state governments as required by Congress. According to some observers there was even a tendency for ex-secessionists to be more likely to favor cooperation than men classified as "original Unionists," those who had opposed immediate secession in 1860–61 but then gone with their states. Nor is this surprising or illogical as the original secessionists, as has been seen, had not played a major role in the Johnson governments and therefore had less objection to their being replaced by a new political order. In addition while "original Unionists" might feel that they had done their best to save the Union and therefore should not be subject to any type of punishment, those who had supported secession from the first were more likely to argue, as Joseph E. Brown did, that the South had taken a risk, been beaten, and now had to agree to the victor's terms.[3]

But the movement in favor of participation was not limited to this latter group, and while it is impossible to define its exact strength or describe with any precision its political roots, the southern press, northern observers, and the newly appointed district commanders all agreed that this spirit of cooperation was the dominant mood of at least the vocal portion of the southern population at this time. Indicative of the new situation was the relatively cordial relations that were established between southerners and the district commanders. The orders issued by the latter when they took command, all of which left the existing state governments intact, were seen as an indication that they would enforce the Acts with moderation and liberality. Even as the commanders began to use their powers in ways that were subject to question, there was little criticism. The New Orleans press acquiesced in Sheridan's removal of three officials there, while Sickles in the Second District was applauded for issuing a stay order, even though courts in both North and South Carolina had declared stay laws unconstitutional.[4]

This totally unexpected southern response rested on two basic assumptions.[5] The first was that the South no longer had a choice. While it could not with honor have voluntarily accepted the Fourteenth Amendment, it could under duress accept the terms of the Reconstruction Acts. Constitutional arguments, valid as they might be, were no longer relevant, for the Republicans had revolutionized the government and made Congress, which they absolutely controlled, the supreme force. The essential thing was to be readmitted to the national government, at which time it might be possible to restore the constitution. Any attempt to delay reconstruction by defeating the call for a convention would be suicidal, as Congress would simply disfranchise enough additional voters to create radical majorities in the South, and it would then probably adopt confiscation measures as well.

They did not see how Democratic victories, even if they did

occur, would benefit the South, as the Fortieth Congress would remain in office until March, 1869, by which time reconstruction would be complete. In any case there was a strong feeling against relying on the Democratic Party, which it was felt had failed the South both during and after the war. There was also dissatisfaction with Johnson's course, many believing that his belligerent statements had merely irritated the congressional Republicans, resulting in harsher measures against the South, while he had done nothing to help them. The solution for many was that the South should not cooperate with either of the national parties, but should remain neutral until restoration was complete. On this basis a number of southern papers endorsed Grant for the presidency, seeing him as a non-party candidate, running on a platform of national unity based on acceptance of the Reconstruction Acts and the removal of all disqualifications.[6]

The other major assumption of southern thinking in the spring and early summer of 1867 was that conservative southern whites could continue to control southern politics, despite Negro suffrage. It was believed that the black population of the South had decreased and would continue to do so, so that a united white race would outnumber the Negroes in almost every state.[7] In addition, it was assumed that southern whites, particularly the planter class, who had dealt with the Negroes for so many years, would be able to exert a much greater influence over them than alien northern radicals. Beginning with Hampton's speech at Columbia, conservative whites sought black support by declarations that they were prepared to accept Negro political equality. Through the spring and summer of 1867, conservative white leaders addressed black meetings throughout the South, attempting to convince their audiences that they had the same interests as southern whites and should accept their leadership in politics.[8]

These efforts proved futile, however, as the Republican Party organized throughout the South in the spring of 1867 and gained almost unanimous Negro support. Prior to the war, of course, the Republican Party had been virtually nonexistent in the southern states. But during the first years of reconstruction local Republican or Union organizations had developed, particularly in areas that

had been strongly Unionist throughout the war or had been occupied at an early date by federal troops. As a result all of the border
and southern states had been represented at a southern loyalist
convention in Philadelphia, in September, 1866, which had called
for congressional action to protect Unionists in the South. The delegates from the ten unreconstructed states had, in addition, supported Negro suffrage, which they had seen as the only way to
counteract the strength of white ex-Confederates in their own states.
In contrast, therefore, to those southerners who favored accepting
the Reconstruction Acts as the better of two evils, white southern
Unionists welcomed the congressional program and only complained that it did not go far enough.[9] During the spring and summer of 1867 these "men of straitest sect," as they were sometimes
called, were joined in the Republican Party by the large mass of
newly enfranchised black voters, resulting in the creation of strong,
state-wide Republican parties throughout the South.

Since the end of the war there had been local movements among
Negroes in a number of southern cities demanding a greater measure of economic opportunity and civil equality. The Republican
Party was obviously a highly suitable vehicle for attaining these
goals and in almost every state, therefore, Negro leaders played a
major role from the first in the Republican organizing conventions.
In addition, the Union League of America, aided by the Freedmen's Bureau, engaged in a highly successful campaign to organize
southern Negroes in the interest of the Republican Party. Southern
conservatives were unable to match either the energy of these efforts or the effectiveness of Republican appeals for Negro support,
and in state after state Negro mass meetings endorsed the Republican Party. Conservative hopes that they would receive support
from a silent, conservative portion of the Negro population ended
when Negroes in Tennessee voted solidly Republican in elections
held on August 1st.[10]

While it seems reasonable to conclude that the bulk of Republican votes were provided by white Unionists in the upcountry and
Negroes in the Black Belt, Republican leaders came from a wide
variety of additional sources. Many, like Powell Clayton, Henry
Clay Warmoth, and Harrison Reed, the future governors of Arkan-

sas, Louisiana, and Florida respectively, were northerners who had entered the South either with the Union Army or as federal office-holders. For them participation in the Republican Party was both consistent with their previous history and the only road open to a political career in the South. In addition, the Republican Party attracted individual southern whites with widely varying backgrounds but the same belief that the best course for themselves and their states was cooperation with the national Republican Party. Thus, a wealthy planter like James Alcorn of Mississippi, an ex-Whig and opponent of secession who had served in the Confederate Army, hoped to secure adoption of economic policies that he favored by alliance with the Republicans and saw nothing to fear in granting political equality to a black population that could be controlled by men like himself. At the same time Joseph Brown of Georgia, a staunch Democrat and secessionist, was now convinced that the Republican Party represented the new power in the nation and it would be futile to fight it.[11]

The southern Republican parties established by this coalition of forces almost all adopted platforms that were broadly similar to each other. In general they favored the creation of systems of free public education and the establishment of the complete civil and political equality of all men. This last plank various state parties specifically interpreted to include the right to sit on juries and to hold public office. In some states economic planks were also adopted which favored a system of taxation based solely on property and measures to encourage the division of large landholdings into small farms. In certain states, in addition, the conventions indicated a developing radical strength that led at least some northern Republican papers to express concern that the southern party was becoming too proscriptive in spirit. Thus the platforms in South Carolina and Louisiana opposed an early restoration of the rights of ex-Confederate leaders, while in Virginia and Florida struggles between moderate and radical factions ended with the latter winning control. In North Carolina some moderate Republicans bolted the party after the state convention rejected resolutions stating that confiscation was not necessary and asking for a partial removal of disabilities.[12]

This sudden emergence of southern Republican parties capable of carrying their respective states had a major influence in reversing the current of opinion in favor of cooperation that had swept the South in the spring. From the first there had been a few men calling for resistance to the end and insofar as a pattern existed there seems to have been a tendency for them to be "original Unionists" from white, upcountry areas. As has been stated, these men felt it extremely unjust that they were now subject to the same disfranchisement provisions as were the original "fire-eaters." They were also men who represented areas within their states that had gained somewhat in political influence under the Johnson governments and they now stood to lose that increased power if the Negro populations of the Black Belt areas were given political equality.[13]

The first public appeal for rejection of readmission under the congressional terms came from Governor Charles J. Jenkins of Georgia. In an open letter, published in early April, he advised southerners that it would be better to remain under military rule and wait for a change in the mood of the country than voluntarily agree to the oppressive congressional conditions. He also joined with officials in Mississippi to bring suit before the Supreme Court to prevent enforcement of the Acts. Jenkins' actions came to little, however, as the Court refused to act on the grounds that it could not interfere with the President in the exercise of his executive powers, while the Governor was forced to cease making public statements opposing acceptance by threats of removal by General Pope.[14]

But by then a new opposition leader had developed in Benjamin F. Perry of South Carolina, who in a widely reprinted series of newspaper letters argued that Negro suffrage was the worst thing that could happen to the South and therefore it had to be resisted at all costs. He countered warnings of congressional confiscation by stating that the real danger was in the state governments that would be created under the Acts. Military rule was far to be preferred to governments controlled by "ignorant, stupid, demi-savage paupers" who would tax the whites and confiscate the land for their own benefit. There was still a chance for the whites to control the elections, before the blacks were fully organized, and all who were qualified should, therefore, register and then vote against the holding of a convention. They must preserve their honor and withhold their consent from the congressional Acts, so that after the inevitable Democratic victory in the northern states, whatever had been forced on them could be overthrown.[15]

As the summer progressed there was an evident major shift in southern opinion in favor of these views, the growth of the Republican Party giving added impetus to this movement. The activities of the Republican Congressional Committee, which was providing financial and other aid to the southern organizations and sending speakers like Senator Henry Wilson and Representative William D. Kelley on tours of the South, were considered particularly objectionable as an intrusion of outside forces into southern politics. The New York *Times* correspondent in Georgia reported that the speeches of Wilson and Kelley were causing a reaction against cooperation there, while a major riot occurred when Kelley spoke in Mobile, Alabama. Conservative whites charged that they were now to be required to elect radical governments and Congressmen before being restored, which represented the imposition of an additional condition. In addition, northern election returns caused renewed hope that a political reaction was occurring there, and it was feared that radicalized southern states might offset these Republican losses. In Georgia, Benjamin H. Hill began a major campaign against cooperation, attacking it in a series of speeches and newspaper articles, beginning on July 16th. Wade Hampton, also, now called for the defeat of the convention, reversing his previous position in a letter written just after the Tennessee elections.[16]

There was, in addition, an evident apathy among the white population, the editors of the New Orleans *Picayune* undoubtedly speaking for many when they said that they were powerless to influence political events and so would remain silent. This feeling was apparent from the beginning of registration, with white turnout low almost everywhere. In some places, particularly New Orleans, the registration boards were charged with arbitrarily refusing white voters. But in general the conservative press admitted the fairness of the boards and blamed the low registration on white lack of interest and unwillingness to vote with Negroes. Northern Democratic papers said the same thing, blaming the southerners for their failure to register and organize effectively and warning them that if they lost their own states they could expect no help from elsewhere.[17] Extensive campaigns to bring out white voters and the correction of the widely held misconception that all ex-Confederates were disfranchised did result in increased registration in some places. But the final figures still showed low white turnout in four states, Louisiana, Texas, Florida, and Arkansas, where only 67–72% of the adult white males registered. In the other six states, where turnout varied between 79% in Alabama and 87% in North Carolina, it is probable that most whites who did not register failed to do so because they were disfranchised.[18]

The other side of the coin was black turnout which, based on projections of census figures, ran from 89% in Florida and Georgia to 102% in Texas.[19] This combination of low white registration with Negro turnout figures that lend some credence to conservative charges of fraud created black majorities in Alabama and Florida, where the majority of the population was white, strengthened black control of Louisiana, Mississippi, and South Carolina, where a majority of the males of voting age were black, and reduced white majorities in the other five states to the point where white Republican votes might be sufficient to give that party victory. In addition, in Virginia and Georgia the apportionment of delegates was such that districts in which the Negroes were in a majority elected a majority of the convention delegates, even though there was a white voting majority in the state as a whole.[20]

Despite the fact that conservative control of any of the southern states was now unlikely, there were still some who favored cooperation rather than resistance. Conservative conventions which still sought Negro support were held in Alabama, Florida, and Mississippi in September, but they were lightly attended. In North Carolina and Virginia the Richmond *Whig* and the Raleigh *Sentinel* became the spokesmen for those who still favored voting for a convention and for delegates, even if the only choice were between different factions in the Republican Party. They attacked Johnson and the Democrats for continuing to agitate the issue of reconstruction when they could do the South no good in the face of Republican domination of the national government. Even though conservative whites could not retain control of the southern states, they still felt that the South had no choice but acceptance of the best terms that Congress would give. They did not think that a political reaction would occur in the North and did not see how, if it did happen, it would prevent the Republicans from carrying out the congressional program.[21]

The situation was drastically changed by both the size and the nature of Democratic victories in the fall elections in the North. Not only were the Democratic gains more sweeping than anyone had expected, but they seemed to depend on just that issue, Negro suffrage, which was most vital to the South. To conservative southerners the results indicated that northern voters had taken a strong stand against Negro suffrage and it might, therefore, be possible either to prevent the enforcement of the congressional Acts or overthrow them after Democratic victories in 1868. The most important question now was not how to make the best of the existing situation, but rather how to act so as to strengthen the northern reaction and at the same time delay the completion of reconstruction.[22]

In this situation the overwhelming majority of the whites boycotted the elections in six states, the five that had black voting majorities plus Georgia. While this tactic may have originated simply from a feeling of helplessness and a desire at least not to participate voluntarily, with the Democratic victories it became part of a more positive design. Abstention offered the best hope, slim as it might be, of defeating the convention call, because of the requirement in the Acts that a majority of those registered had to vote in order for the elections to be valid. There was also an evident desire to deny the legitimacy of both the elections and the governments created by them. The conservatives were sure that northern voters would not permit the recognition of governments based almost solely on black support. They were happy to see Negroes elected to office, believing that the blacker the governments created, the stronger the northern reaction against them would be. Only in Virginia, North Carolina, and Arkansas, the states with the largest white majorities, did a significant number of conservatives participate in the election. They hoped either to defeat the convention call or to elect delegates who would refuse to accept the congressional terms. They failed in both aims, however, as the result in every state was the calling of a convention and the election of predominantly Republican delegates.[23]

Unfortunately, at least from the historian's point of view, while the registration had been done by race, the voting, except in Virginia, had not. Returns from the latter state, however, show that less than 1% of the registered Negroes had voted against the convention, and estimates provided by commanders in other districts indicate that the same was true elsewhere. On the other hand the available information indicates that only in four states—North Carolina, Georgia, Alabama, and Arkansas—did more than 20% of the registered whites favor the convention call.[24] A study of county by county returns available for Alabama and Arkansas shows that those counties where the vote for the convention was greater than the total black registration were concentrated in areas that had been most anti-Confederate during the war, northwestern Arkansas and northern and southeastern Alabama.

It is possible to define the white pro-convention vote even more precisely in Virginia. There, white support for the convention was higher than the 12% registered statewide in 31 of the 102 counties and independent cities, concentrated in three distinct groups in widely separated parts of the state. Seventeen of them were in an almost solid bloc which included most of the southwestern tip of the state. A second group, consisting of the city of Alexandria and five nearby counties, was in the extreme north, while the remaining eight were scattered along Chesapeake Bay and the mouths of the rivers which feed it, running from Northumberland County on the Potomac, south to the City of Norfolk.[25]

There is little to tie these Virginia counties together on the basis of either their antebellum political loyalties or the racial makeup of their population. The southwestern counties were largely white, but included three counties with large black populations, while the northern and eastern counties were racially mixed, five of them having black majorities in their registration. On the basis of their voting in presidential elections from 1836 to 1848 the southwestern counties were again more homogenous, those classifiable being Democratic by a 9–3 margin as compared to an even split in the others. But over-all this factor also does not seem to have been decisive.

A much more significant relationship between the 31 counties would seem to be what had occurred in them during the war. The southwestern area had been a center for anti-Confederate activity, while Alexandria had been the seat of the Unionist government of Virginia. In addition, the northern area had been occupied by federal troops throughout almost the entire war, during which period, presumably, Unionist activities had been encouraged. The same was also partially true for the eastern counties, at least some of which had also been under federal control for a long time before the war ended.[26] These results would seem to clearly establish the relationship between wartime Unionism and large-scale voter support for Republican policies after the war.

At the same time the results for the South as a whole showed that those favoring reconstruction were a small minority of the white population and the section was badly split along racial lines. For conservative whites the results meant that they had lost control of their own states and now would have to place their entire reliance on their Democratic allies in the North.

CHAPTER FOUR

NORTHERN POLITICS AND THE ELECTIONS OF 1867

With the elections of 1866 reaffirming their firm control of the North and the congressional reconstruction program promising to give them a significant base of support in the South, Republicans in 1867 had good reason to feel well satisfied with their political situation. The differences that continued to exist within the party were essentially between those who thought that the legislation already passed was sufficient, and more radical elements who felt that the party's policies should continue to move forward as rapidly in the future as they had in the past. In reference to reconstruction these disagreements involved three separate issues, confiscation of the property of ex-Confederates, the removal of political disabilities, and the impeachment of the President. In the spring and summer of 1867 the future direction that the party would take on these questions was still undecided, as Republicans awaited the outcome of events in the South.

Thaddeus Stevens remained the principal spokesman for the radical group in the House of Representatives, his main concern being a confiscation bill under which the property of ex-Confederates would have been used to provide homesteads for ex-slaves and to pay for northern war damages and pensions. In this he had little immediate support from his own party, Congress taking no action on his proposal and not a single state convention in 1867 endorsing such a measure. But many times in the past the course of events had resulted in Republican moderates accepting measures that they had opposed as too radical just a short time before, and it was recognized that this might happen again. Congress held the threat of confiscation over the South by scheduling consideration of Stevens' bill for December, 1867, and even the moderate New York *Times* warned that if the congressional terms were rejected, all elements of the party would unite in support of harsher conditions.[1]

The operation of this process of radicalization could be seen on the question of impeachment. In January, 1867, its major advocate, Representative James M. Ashley of Ohio, obtained House approval for a Judiciary Committee investigation of Johnson's conduct. But the Republican press showed no great interest in the project, and in June the Committee informally voted, five to four, that the evidence did not warrant impeachment. With the publication of Stanbery's interpretations of the Reconstruction Acts, however, support for impeachment began to grow. Then, when Stanton, Sheridan, and Sickles were removed late in the summer a large number of Republican newspapers and leaders, including Grant's close friend, Elihu Washburne, became convinced that the removal of the President was necessary. The best measure of this change is the fact that, while through the end of August no Republican convention had supported impeachment, three out of four held in September did so.[2]

There was also some division within the Republican Party on the question of what would happen if the congressional terms were accepted by the South. Many Republican leaders promised that these were the final terms and that readmission would be certain if they were accepted in good faith. Some, most notably Henry Wilson and Horace Greeley, also favored the removal of all individual political disabilities, once reconstruction was completed. But Thaddeus Stevens attacked Wilson for promising restoration and amnesty, saying that he had no authority to commit the party to these actions. In this Stevens was supported by a policy statement issued by the Republican Congressional Committee, which stated that, even if the requirements of the Acts were fulfilled, a final decision on restoration would still have to be made by Congress. That body would look for proof that the South was loyal "by decisive and trustworthy majorities," and had accepted equal suffrage, public education, and policies favorable to land division.[3]

By early summer, however, it would seem that the majority of Republican congressmen had decided that it was not necessary to spell out any new conditions. At the beginning of the special session in July, therefore, a rule was adopted, over radical objections, which limited action to measures needed to interpret the previous laws, a decision that was approved by many of the most influential

Republican papers.[4] The question of whether additional conditions should be required then came increasingly moot as it became clear that the terms of the Reconstruction Acts would be accepted only if the southern Republican parties were successful in carrying their states. Thus, March, 1867, was to prove to be the highwater mark of Republican radicalism on the southern question, as the party's action thereafter would be essentially in defense of the program passed in that month, while all efforts to significantly expand it would be rejected.

But the Republican Party could not be concerned solely with questions of reconstruction and the South. From the beginning, slavery had been inextricably linked with the larger question of the position of the Negro within American society. In the 1830s abolitionists had recognized the relation between the two and their program had called not only for emancipation, but also for the eradication of prejudices of race that they had felt were an outgrowth of the slave system. The more militant anti-slavery elements of the freesoil movement had seen the same connection, and anti-slavery men had raised the issue of legal and political equality for black men in the North.[5] As has been seen, the movement in this direction had been strengthened during the conflict itself, although there can be no doubt that when the war ended the majority of people in the North had still held strong racial prejudices.

While it had been possible to remove the most extreme manifestations of northern racism, anti-black laws in Illinois and Indiana, voting discriminations had remained almost everywhere, Negroes having equal suffrage only in five New England states and a qualified suffrage in New York. Supporters of Negro suffrage had raised the issue in 1865, obtaining referendums on the question in Connecticut, Minnesota, and Wisconsin. But while these proposals had received much greater support than similar attempts prior to the war, they had still gone down to defeat in all three states, with large numbers of Republicans obviously voting against them. In 1866, then, facing an election that they had to win, Republicans had generally played it safe by avoiding the suffrage issue as much as possible. The Democrats, on the other hand, had tried to make it a major question in the campaign, attempting to take advantage of northern racial feeling by branding the Republicans as the party of social equality.[6]

This Democratic strategy, however, had the opposite effect to that intended, as its failure encouraged Republicans to believe that racist appeals were becoming less and less effective and that the progressive movement on racial issues which had been evident during the war was continuing. In response to this, and contrary to charges that the Republicans acted hypocritically by imposing equal suffrage on the South while permitting white-only suffrage to continue in the North, the great majority of Republican officeholders in 1867 were prepared to commit their party to Negro suffrage everywhere in the belief that the public was now ready to accept it.

Thus, while only six Republican state conventions had endorsed Negro suffrage in 1866, all but California and Pennsylvania did so in 1867. In Tennessee the franchise was given to black men by legislative action, while Republican-controlled legislatures or constitutional conventions in Ohio, Michigan, Kansas, New York, Missouri, and Minnesota all voted to place referendums for Negro suffrage on the ballot. In addition Congress provided for Negro suffrage in the District of Columbia and the federal territories, and it was made a precondition for the admission of Nebraska as a state. The distance that the party had traveled became clear in the Ohio campaign, when the moderate leader John Sherman made a plea for equal justice for those who "are only different from us in that their ancestors came from a different part of God's world than ours did," while he at the same time attacked the existing suffrage restriction as "based upon a narrow prejudice of caste, not founded upon reason or natural laws, but the offspring of . . . intolerance and bigotry." The major difference between moderates and radicals now was whether voting discriminations could be ended nationally by congressional action or only by referendum in each state.[7]

While Republicans were thus deciding that their reconstruction program was sufficient as it stood and that further progress toward political equality was possible in the North, some Democrats were arriving at strikingly similar conclusions. To at least one wing of the latter party the series of defeats that they had suffered indicated the necessity for a complete re-evaluation of their political strategy. Throughout the Thirty-Ninth Congress the Democrats had maintained a remarkable unanimity in an essentially negative policy of voting against all Republican measures relating to reconstruction or Negro rights. They had vigorously opposed the passage of the Reconstruction Acts, denouncing them as the unconstitutional imposition of Negro suffrage and military dictatorships on the South. Even before the final passage of the First Reconstruction Act, however, certain leading Democratic papers had suggested that the South should carefully consider the possibility of accepting the congressional terms. Thomas A. Hendricks of Indiana, a major Democratic leader in the Senate, had agreed, saying that the situation was not the same as when the Fourteenth Amendment had been proposed, and the Rhode Island Democratic convention had called on everyone to adapt to the new circumstances, "by all means consistent with honor."

Through the spring this group of Democrats who favored cooperation with conservative Republicans and had generally been in the moderate wing of the party during the war continued to favor an accommodation on reconstruction. Led by the New York Democracy and its organ the New York *World*, it also had strength in other areas of the East and the Midwest, where its views were supported by the Boston *Post* and the Chicago *Times*. Their assessment of the situation was very similar to that of those southern conservatives who were also moving towards acceptance of the congressional terms at this time. Thus, the New York *World* argued that the basic question was whether the southern whites or the northern Republicans were stronger in the long run, and as the latter would probably win eventually it was better for the southerners to accept while it was still possible for them to control the black vote. The Chicago *Times* considered the Second Reconstruction Act fair and was certain that under it southern conservatives could win their state elections. In general the situation seemed hopeful, as with the support of southern votes the Democratic Party could be restored to power, after which much that the South had accepted under duress could be reversed. The Republicans had unquestionably expected the South to refuse the congressional terms and were now shocked and surprised at the development of the movement in favor of cooperation.[8]

As part of this strategy this wing of the Democratic Party also gave some consideration to making Ulysses S. Grant its presidential candidate, again paralleling the thinking of southern conservatives at the same time. There seems in particular to have been a movement in the general's favor among New York Democrats in July. But it must be recognized that this was possible not because of any question as to Grant's position on the necessity for enforcement of the Reconstruction Acts, but only because these groups were for the moment prepared to accept his views. Actually the possibility of Grant being nominated by the Democrats was always remote, as a close examination of most statements about him by Democratic newspapers reveals that they were not so much interested in nominating him themselves as in insisting that he would neither be offered nor accept the Republican nomination.[9]

This reassessment of the Democratic position extended to the race issue. Those favoring a changed policy on reconstruction argued that racial appeals could no longer be used to advantage as the northern public was ready to accept equal suffrage. In November, 1866, the Chicago *Times* had startled the nation by declaring that Negro suffrage was inevitable, and the Democratic Party should therefore support an impartial qualified suffrage by state action, both North and South, to keep the Republicans from imposing universal suffrage by national action. This editorial had created a storm of controversy, being denounced as treason to the party's principles by most of the party press, but it had been endorsed by both the Boston *Post* and the New York *World*. This belief that the racial issue should be dropped in the North was entirely consistent with the southern strategy later adopted by these same papers, which depended on the ability of southern conservatives to control the black vote. As some Republicans were quick to see, it would place both northern Democrats and southern conservatives in a difficult position to have the former appealing to racial hatreds while the latter were seeking black support. In addition, some Democrats argued that it would help the party even in states like

Iowa in the North by making it easier to convert large numbers of German voters who favored equal suffrage but strongly opposed Republican prohibition measures.[10]

But despite the advantages it offered and the support it received from influential Democratic leaders this strategy of dropping the issues of race and reconstruction and turning to a national unity presidential candidate like Grant proved to be unacceptable to the party as a whole. The most determined opposition to any basic change in policy came from leaders in Ohio, and they proved to be representative of the thinking of the great majority of Democrats, especially in the Midwest. Racial feeling had always been stronger in that section than elsewhere in the North, and there seems little reason to doubt that most party members there were sincerely convinced of the need to maintain a "white man's government." The suffrage issue was also one on which the Republicans could be considered vulnerable, as prior elections had shown that many of their supporters were not in favor of political equality, so that the Ohio Democratic convention early in 1867 had come out strongly against it. When the Republican-controlled legislature had then placed an equal suffrage referendum on the ballot, race had become a major issue in the fall campaign with the Democrats appealing to racist fears of social equality, integrated schools, and miscegenation. While the racial issue was most important in Ohio, where it would influence a critical gubernatorial race, anti-Negro suffrage planks were also adopted by Democratic state conventions in Iowa, Minnesota, California, Kansas, and Pennsylvania. The only indication of a more moderate sentiment within the party was the failure of conventions in the New England states, New York, and Wisconsin to say anything at all on the subject.[11]

The same Ohio Democratic leaders also rejected from the first the strategy of accepting the Reconstruction Acts as a *fait accompli*, reflecting the non-compromising position that had been generally characteristic of midwestern Peace Democrats since the end of the War. In addition, by late spring even the more moderate wing of the party was becoming greatly upset, again along with the southern conservatives, by the success of Republican organizing efforts in the South. The New York *World* warned that if all the Negro voters joined the Republican Party, the result would be the creation of a white party in the South and a war of the races. The Republican efforts were taken as evidence that the southern states would be readmitted only if they elected radical governments. This, it was charged, was a breach of faith with the South, as were the provisions of the Third Reconstruction Act making the existing governments completely subject to the military commanders and giving the registration boards absolute power to exclude applicants.[12]

As the possibility of conservative victories in the South then decreased, the idea of accepting the results of the congressional policy lost most of its attractiveness and northern Democrats returned to a united attack on the Reconstruction Acts, state party conventions everywhere denouncing them as unconstitutional. Democratic campaign speakers invoked the racial prejudices of their audiences on this issue also, picturing the pitiful condition of southern whites who had been placed under black domination and calling on the white men of the North to rally to save their brothers. The Democrats were now optimistic about their chances in the northern elections, and they warned their listeners that the Republicans were trying to retain control of the country by creating black governments in the South.[13]

But while the leaders of the Ohio Democracy were thus successfully opposing any change in the party's policies on reconstruction and race, they were also taking the lead in making political use of an emerging set of economic issues, involving questions of the currency, the national debt, and the banking system. The problems involved had their roots in the immense cost of the war, which had left the nation with over $2 billion in bonded debt and over $400,000 in "greenbacks," government-issued legal tender notes, irredeemable in specie, which had been worth only 67% of their face value in gold when the war ended. It had been widely assumed that once the war was over the value of the greenbacks would increase and it would be possible for the government to make them redeemable within a short time. To accomplish this, Secretary of the Treasury Hugh McCulloch, in 1865, advocated reducing the amount of greenbacks in circulation, hoping that a contraction of between $100,000 and $200,000 would eliminate the gold premium and make possible a rapid return to a specie basis without otherwise affecting the economy adversely.

This policy was at first fully acceptable to Congress, the House endorsing it in principle by an almost unanimous vote in December, 1865, and McCulloch being authorized to begin contraction by an act passed early the next year. But strong opposition appeared in 1866 also, as the economy began to decline from the heights of wartime prosperity and some placed complete blame for falling prices on the reduction of the currency. This sentiment was particularly strong among midwestern businessmen and bankers, who had historically always felt that their section required more currency and who strongly associated their wartime prosperity with the greenbacks and the postwar recession with contraction. Their feelings were reflected in particular in the votes of Republican Congressmen from the Midwest, who in 1867 voted almost unanimously in favor of a resolution passed by the House opposing further retirement of greenbacks in that year. The Democrats, on the other hand, were the traditional hard money party, and they had opposed the original issuance of the greenbacks, which they had considered simply another unconstitutional war measure. In 1867 then, they voted very heavily in favor of continued contraction, midwestern Democrats splitting four to four on the issue.[14]

The business downturn, in addition, heightened interest in other economic issues. With taxes still at relatively high levels and a large part of the federal budget going just for servicing the debt, questions relating to the bonds also emerged as important political issues. The position of the bondholders was vulnerable on a number of accounts. Many of the bonds had been bought with severely depreciated currency, so that the payment of either the principal or the interest in gold or a currency whose value was now much greater meant very large windfall profits for the purchasers. In addition, while almost everything else in the country was subject to some kind of tax, a federal law exempted the bond principal from both federal and state taxes. The bondholders could thus be accused of both war profiteering and receiving special favors from the government, and on this basis a few midwestern Democrats in

1865 and 1866 had even suggested that repudiation might be justified. Early in 1867 Andrew Johnson himself took up this idea, charging that the prewar aristocracy of slavery had been replaced by an aristocracy of money, and warning the latter that no war debt in history had ever been paid in full.[15]

But attacks on the bondholders could always backfire, as the debt had been created as part of the struggle to save the union and threats that it would not be fully paid could be answered with extremely effective appeals to Unionism and the national honor. Even more importantly, such suggestions ran directly contrary to the overriding emphasis in nineteenth-century American thought on the sanctity of contract and private property, so that proposals that in any way involved violation of the government's legal obligation to the bondholders received almost no support. Instead attention focused on the one area where the exact meaning of the law was unclear, the method of repayment of the principal on the so-called 5-20 bonds.

By 1867 these bonds, which took their name from the fact that they could be redeemed five years after issuance and had to be paid in twenty years, constituted the largest part of the federal debt. They had first been authorized in 1862 by a law that clearly stated that the interest was to be paid in gold but made no provision as to the principal. Despite this, Secretary of the Treasury Salmon P. Chase and his successors had stated their belief that repayment in gold was required, and the sales agent for most of the bonds, Jay P. Cooke, had so promised in his advertisements. On the other hand, Thaddeus Stevens, wartime chairman of the House Committee on Ways and Means, had insisted that as payment in greenbacks was not prohibited by the law the paper currency was as much legal tender for this purpose as for any other.[16] The question had not been of great practical importance so long as it had been assumed that the Treasury would be able to make the greenbacks redeemable in specie before the bonds were repaid. But as opposition to McCulloch's contraction program developed, it became clear that specie resumption was many years off, and during the intervening time gold would continue to be worth significantly more than the paper currency. With $140 in greenbacks being required, on the average, in 1866–67 to buy $100 in gold, the amount of money potentially involved was quite large, for both the taxpayers and the bondholders.

Popular sentiment in favor of repayment of the bonds in greenbacks therefore began to grow. Again it seems to have been strongest in the Midwest, where a smaller amount of bonds was held than in the East, but this time the Republicans did not prove to be very responsive to the issue. Instead the most vigorous early exponent of repaying the bondholders in the legal tender notes was the Democratic editor of the Cincinnati *Enquirer,* Washington McLean, who in the spring of 1867 strongly urged his party to adopt this plan as the coming popular issue. It might seem that a program which would require vast new sums in greenbacks would have little appeal to a party that was still strongly committed to contraction of the currency, as shown both by votes in Congress and editorials in other midwestern Democratic papers at this time.[17] But from another point of view there was no inconsistency with Democratic ideology, which since the days of Jackson had emphasized the destruction of special privilege in order to guarantee equal treatment for all in the economic market place. From this perspective the question was not whether there should be a paper currency, which had already been decided, but only if a special group should be permitted to remain on a gold basis while everyone else was using greenbacks.

Democratic acceptance of the proposal to repay the bonds in greenbacks was made even easier under the specific plan most fully developed by George H. Pendleton of Ohio, which promised to eliminate the danger of currency inflation while directly attacking the most familiar Democratic demon, the national banks. The Pendleton Plan was based on the fact that under the banking system created during the war member banks were permitted to issue their own notes to the amount of 90% of the value of government bonds purchased and deposited with the Treasury. This itself, it was charged, was another instance of special privilege, as the banks received interest on both their capital invested in the bonds and their own notes secured by the bonds which they lent to their customers. What Pendleton and others suggested was that just these bonds, worth something over $300 million, be redeemed with newly issued greenbacks. Currency expansion would then be minimal, as the new greenbacks would, in effect, replace the roughly equal amount of bank notes that would be withdrawn from circulation, but the taxpayers would be saved almost $20 million in gold now being paid annually in bond interest. Pendleton claimed that with this saving and by halting the conversion of non-interest-bearing debt into interest-paying bonds, it would be possible to pay the debt in less than fifteen years without any additional taxes or an increase in the currency. This time period might be even further reduced by cutting government expenditures or issuing additional greenbacks, the latter to be done as required by the economy.[18]

The Pendleton Plan thus had appeal to both hard-money, anti-bank Democrats and inflationist business interests, while the fact that it could be argued that it was perfectly consistent with the law provided a defense against charges that it involved repudiation. The bond issue was used with particular emphasis by the Ohio Democrats in their fall campaign, all of the major party leaders and over forty county conventions endorsing the principle of repayment of the bonds in greenbacks. In addition, it gained support from Democrats in some other western states, being accepted by the Kansas convention and used in Iowa by Henry Clay Dean.[19]

But major elements within the party also rejected the plan. Many remained committed to repayment of the bonds in gold for reasons of either principle or personal interest, while others were unsure of the political effects of adopting this issue on which the party itself was split. Opposition was especially strong in the East, where most public figures were in favor of currency stability and payment of the bonds in gold. The New York Democratic Party, which had strong ties to the banking community, in particular took the lead in resisting any type of greenback proposal. The New York *World* and party leaders Horatio Seymour and John T. Hoffman endorsed payment in gold, while the Democratic state platform called the national debt a "sacred obligation."[20]

Even in the Midwest, many hesitated to follow Ohio's lead. The Wisconsin state convention rejected a resolution endorsing payment in greenbacks, while the Chicago *Times* carefully avoided a direct endorsement of the Pendleton Plan, even while stating that it was worthy of consideration and was not a measure of repudiation. This same reluctance to make a firm commitment to the new policy was evident in Ohio itself, where the Democratic candidate for governor, Allen J. Thurman, did not take a position until the campaign was more than half over and he had been directly challenged to state whether he agreed with Pendleton or not. The Cleveland *Plain Dealer*, representing a northern wing of the state party somewhat separate from the men who had originally advocated the issue, was also obviously happier attacking Negro suffrage than demanding that the bonds be paid in greenbacks, and on the day before the election its editorials concentrated on the former to the exclusion of the latter.[21]

The issue caused much less division among Republicans, who belonged in large part to the anti-Jacksonian tradition which had favored a national banking system and seen nothing wrong in government policies which aided special economic groups so long as they were in the national interest also. In addition the Republicans were much more likely to see those who had purchased the bonds as patriots rather than profiteers and to gloss over the legalities of the issue in order to emphasize morality and the need to maintain the national honor. The Republicans, after all, were the ones who had originally issued the bonds and promised payment in gold, and also presumably the ones who had bought most of the bonds in response to the great patriotic sales campaigns of Jay Cooke. Although no accurate figures are available on the number of individual bondholders, one estimate late in the war had been that three million people had purchased the bonds. Even if exaggerated, this figure indicates that the voting power of the bondholders was not to be ignored, especially if, as seems likely, they were concentrated within one party.[22]

With all of these factors acting on them, Republican leaders in all sections of the country generally rejected the idea of repaying the bonds in anything but gold, and party platforms in Maine, Wisconsin, Minnesota, and New York specifically opposed any form of repudiation. Supported by Secretary McCulloch, Republicans argued that the commitment made when the bonds had been sold was both legally and morally binding. They warned that any form of repayment other than gold would not only be inflationary, but would be more costly in the long run as it would destroy the national credit and drive up interest rates just when the government was engaged in refunding the national debt. There was, in fact, no requirement to pay the 5-20s at all at this time, so that the entire argument was pointless. The present generation had already paid a great price in order to save the Union and therefore was fully justified in leaving a debt to be assumed by future generations. There were two major dissenters from this position within the Republican Party: Thaddeus Stevens, who had consistently been a supporter of currency expansion and payment in greenbacks, and Benjamin F. Butler, who saw financial questions as the issues of the future. But neither was able to make his influence felt, as the party moved in the opposite direction.[23]

As the fall elections approached in 1867, each party was confident that the political strategies it had thus adopted on the major national issues would result in victory. The optimism of the Democrats was based on the results of elections in the spring in which they had halved the Republican majority in New Hampshire and elected the governor and three out of four Congressmen in Connecticut, the latter their first state-wide victory in the North since the end of the war.[24] While later defeats in New York and Rhode Island somewhat dampened their spirits, they still believed that their attacks on Negro suffrage, military reconstruction, the banks, and the bondholders would find strong support among the voters. The Republicans, for their part, dismissed the Connecticut results as depending on a very small change in votes and remained confident that their victories in 1865 and 1866 would be repeated.

The first fall elections occurred in September, with interest centering on gubernatorial contests in Maine, Vermont, and California. In Vermont the Republicans won by their usual three to one majority, but in California the Democrats elected their candidate and in Maine they reduced the Republican margin of victory by more than half. Democrats hailed these results as being even greater victories than they had anticipated, and they calculated that if the percentage change in Maine were duplicated in other states, they would once again be the majority party. On the other side, Republicans denied the national significance of the elections, blaming the loss in California on a division within the party there and their reduced majority in Maine on a reaction against a state prohibition law. The losses, Republicans claimed, would merely unify the party and strengthen it in the remaining contests.[25]

The October results, however, showed their 1866 vote undiminished only in the race for governor in Iowa. In the other elections, the Democrats won a state-wide race in Pennsylvania for chief justice of the supreme court and gained control of the Ohio legislature, defeating the Negro suffrage amendment there and only losing the governorship by a very narrow margin. Republicans now conceded that they faced an uphill fight in order to win in November. Their congressional committee, believing that the North still supported their southern policy, issued a statement warning that Democratic victories would encourage the renewal of sectional conflict and attempts to prevent the completion of reconstruction. Republican papers and speakers played on this charge, as well as the old issues of the war and Democratic Copperheadism.[26]

But it all proved futile as the Democrats again made major gains in November. The latter elected their candidate for secretary of state in New York, gained control of the New Jersey legislature, greatly reduced Republican majorities in Wisconsin, Minnesota, and Massachusetts, and defeated Negro suffrage amendments in Minnesota and Kansas. In comparison with their situation in 1866, therefore, when the Democrats had carried only part of the border states, they had in 1867 carried Pennsylvania, New Jersey, New York, and Connecticut in the East and shown the ability to carry Ohio and make serious inroads elsewhere in the West. The great significance of the 1867 elections, however, was not so much in the results themselves, as in how the parties would interpret them and adjust their preparations for the coming presidential election.

The Democrats saw in the October results the fulfillment of their most optimistic predictions and they were convinced that a revolution in northern politics had occurred which would restore them to national power. In Ohio the financial issue was given a large part of the credit for this, the Cincinnati *Enquirer* claiming that it was responsible for the fact that much larger gains were made there than in Pennsylvania. The gains in New York, however, where the financial issue had not been used, matched those in Ohio, supporting the view that the election had been much more of a referendum on reconstruction and Negro suffrage. Democrats who accepted this interpretation saw their victories as being a repudiation of Republican policies in the South, and they wondered whether Congress would now dare to carry those policies to completion. If it did, the New York *World* predicted, the 1868 elections would result in a Democratic House that would cut off support for the southern governments and, with a Democratic president, might even recognize a Senate composed of northern Democrats and southern conservatives.[27]

It was also significant that the victories had been won by regular Democrats running on regular Democratic tickets, reinforcing the lesson of 1866 that the party was strongest when standing on its own feet. Complimentary references to the President, which had been a standard feature of state platforms adopted in 1866 and early 1867, had been noticeably omitted by most state conventions in the summer and fall of the latter year. By that time Democrats had become increasingly convinced that the President was both inept and timid in action, with the fear of impeachment too much in his mind, and in early August the Chicago *Times* had actually urged him to resign. His activities later that month had seemed to promise a more vigorous policy. But by mid-September the Democrats had seen that his actions would bring no meaningful results and they had again attacked him for being weak, strongly disputing his view that he had no control over the district commanders.[28]

Nor had the Democrats received much in the way of patronage from the President, as while some of them had a degree of influence on appointments the necessity of obtaining Senate approval for many of the most desirable positions had meant that a large number of these had gone to moderate Republicans, acceptable to both the administration and Congress. The major Democratic papers, for their part, had made it clear that so long as Stanton and Secretary of State William H. Seward remained in the cabinet, they would consider the administration to be Republican, and they had argued strongly against any Democrat assuming a responsible position in it. Thus, as the fall results came in, the Chicago *Times* and the New York *World* insisted that the victories belonged only to the Democratic Party and not to Andrew Johnson. The Democratic press also seems to have reflected the majority opinion of the party leadership when it continued to oppose any closer identification with the administration, despite the fact that some Democrats wanted the President to change his cabinet in the light of the election results. The practice of dealing with the President at arm's length therefore continued, Washington McLean summing up the Democratic attitude by saying that they would take no stock in Johnson himself, but were interested in "administering on his estate." According to reports, these accumulated evidences of Democratic hostility to him convinced Johnson in turn not to attempt any remodeling of his administration.[29]

For their part, Republicans denied that the elections had the sweeping significance given them by the Democrats. They emphasized the influence of local issues and local party divisions and claimed that there had been a light vote, which always favored the Democrats. The Republican defeats, in their view, were momentary, and they recalled the losses their party had suffered in 1862 and the unbroken string of victories that had followed. But the defeats did indicate that the party would have to reform and make changes in order to recover its strength. On the nature of those changes there had been disagreement going as far back as the Connecticut elections. At that time the New York *Times* had claimed that the immoderation of Republican radicals had caused the shift in votes that had given the state to the Democrats, while the New York *Tribune* and the Philadelphia *Press* had insisted that if the Negroes had had the suffrage they would have cast enough Republican votes to reverse the result. As the fall results had been recorded this disagreement continued, part of the press calling for continued support of Negro suffrage until victory was won on that issue and others emphasizing the need for more tolerance in the party and the rejection of extremist leadership.[30]

By November, however, when the full extent of the losses was established, it became clear that the party had seriously misjudged the mood of the voters, particularly on the issue of Negro suffrage. A revealing incident was related by a party leader in Ohio, William H. Smith. In a certain district he had believed that only six Republicans were opposed to Negro suffrage and that he had managed to change all of their minds. Then in the election the "yes" vote on the suffrage amendment was crossed out on forty-three Republican ballots. For the state as a whole, analysis of the vote shows that about 5% of those who cast Republican ballots thus abstained on the suffrage proposal, while another 6% voted against it.[31] The failure to carry the full Republican vote in favor of Negro suffrage occurred wherever a referendum was on the ballot. Republican leaders also had to assume that, in addition to those who crossed party lines on this single question, many others were voting a straight Democratic ticket in response to the racial issue.

After the November elections, then, the prevalent mood in the party became clearly in favor of greater moderation in the future. An indication of this feeling came when Salmon P. Chase, who had been considered the radical candidate for the presidential nomination, was suddenly described by his supporters as one of the most conservative men in the country. Many moderates, in fact, welcomed the defeats just because they brought this reaction, feeling that it was just as well that the losses had come in a series of minor elections, giving the party time to make the changes necessary for victory in 1868.[32]

Such a victory would also require the strongest possible candidate, and to many this was obviously Ulysses S. Grant. The general had always been extremely popular with the party's rank and file, and since the end of the war many had considered him the most likely nominee in 1868. Despite this, those closest to him in the summer of 1867 testify that he had still been expressing a lack of interest in the presidency, not wanting to be identified as a partisan of either party, and complaining that each seized on every word he said as proof that he supported it.[33] These statements have led some historians to conclude that he was still equally available to either party in 1867, but this fails to recognize the extent to which Grant, despite his dislike for politics, had become involved in the struggle over reconstruction. Seeing it as a national rather than a party issue, he had supported the Republican policy even though it meant placing himself in opposition to his commander-in-chief. In common with most soldiers he had identified that policy with wartime loyalty and had felt that it was needed to protect the victory that had been won.

While he had not spoken out openly on these issues, the public had been given indications of his support for Republican reconstruction policies, the most obvious being a speech favoring that program which had been given in June, 1867, by John Rawlins, his chief of staff, in their mutual home town of Galena, Illinois. Moderate Republicans in fact had not questioned that his views were very close to theirs, and in mid-1867 he had been endorsed for the presidency by both the New York *Times* and the moderate faction of the party in New York City. However, radical elements within the party, such as Horace Greeley and his New York *Tribune*, had considered Grant too moderate for their liking and so had turned a deaf ear to all indications that he supported Republican policies. Instead they had demanded that he do the one thing he would not do under any circumstances, make a public statement of his political views.[34]

When the general had accepted the temporary appointment as secretary of war in August, 1867, he had opened himself up to further attack from this group, leading many Republicans of all views to feel that he had made a fatal political blunder. The radical press had charged that without Grant's cooperation the President would never have dared to suspend Stanton, and when the general had then acquiesced in the removal of Sheridan their protests had become even stronger.[35] It must be noted, however, that much of the party press had not shared this view, but had expressed continued confidence in Grant's motives and said that so long as he remained at the War Office the country was safe. When his letter to the President protesting Sheridan's removal had then been made public, even the radical press had approved, acknowledging that it was a clear and bold statement of Republican principles. In September the New York *Tribune* had admitted that it no longer doubted that

Grant supported the party's policies, but only questioned the strength of his will, fearing that he was "too ingenuous, too frank, too honest, too sincere and simpleminded," in his dealings with Johnson. By this time also both Democratic and southern papers were conceding that the general belonged with the Republican Party.[36]

By early fall, then, Grant's political position had no longer been in question, but Republican leaders of all persuasions had clearly still been hesitant to commit themselves to support his candidacy. There had been many other possible choices in the field, Benjamin F. Wade, Salmon P. Chase, Oliver P. Morton, and Schuyler Colfax being the most prominent, and with so much at stake it is understandable that the party heads would have preferred to nominate a man who had more political experience and with whom they were better acquainted than the general. Therefore, with almost a year left before the choice had to be made, even Republican leaders who had endorsed Grant, like Henry Wilson and Lyman Trumbull, had indicated that there were other candidates who were also acceptable to them.[37] This coolness on the part of the party's chiefs, however, had not changed the fact that Grant had been the most popular man available, and it seems reasonable to conclude that he was the leading contender for the nomination even before the elections of 1867.

After those elections, with the party turning toward moderation and facing possible defeat in 1868, it was difficult even to consider any other candidate. A few radical leaders attempted to stem the tide, arguing that with the southern electoral votes the party did not need Grant. But when Charles Sumner, at a secret meeting of Republican leaders in Washington, pleaded against bypassing the experienced political leaders of the party, he found no supporters.[38] Instead, as the election results came in they were followed by a wave of endorsements of Grant by such leading Republican newspapers as the Baltimore *American*, Toledo (Ohio) *Commercial*, Chicago *Tribune*, Washington *Chronicle*, Philadelphia *Press*, and Nashville *Press and Times*. He was also the choice of the only Republican state convention to meet, that in Maryland, and of numerous county conventions in Illinois. The press reported the organization of Grant Clubs and growing support for him in every section of the country, and it was widely assumed that the general was virtually assured of the Republican nomination.[39]

CHAPTER FIVE

RECONSTRUCTION AND IMPEACHMENT: THE CRISIS

The first test of how the 1867 elections would in practice affect the actions of the Republican Party came as Congress reconvened on November 21st with two pressing problems before it, the impeachment of the President and the future of the reconstruction program. In regard to the first, the election results had seemingly made it highly unlikely that the party would attempt such a bold measure as the removal of Johnson. Grant was said to be actively working against it, while even the usually radical New York *Tribune* opposed impeachment and Thaddeus Stevens stated that it was a dead issue. But, to the surprise of everyone, the Judiciary Committee reversed its previous decision against impeachment and now voted, five to four, that there were grounds for the removal of the President.[1]

This recommendation, however, which was based on the shift of a single vote, was obviously contrary to the dominant mood of the party, and after the initial surprise had worn off it was generally predicted that the impeachment resolution would be defeated by a large majority in the House itself. The overwhelming bulk of congressional mail was reported to favor this latter result, and in Boston an anti-impeachment Republican meeting was canceled on the grounds that the unanimity of opposition to the removal of Johnson made such efforts unnecessary. On December 7th, as expected, impeachment was defeated 57–108, with a majority of House Republicans voting against it, a result that was generally accepted without protest within the party.[2]

As has been seen, many northern Democrats and southern conservatives also believed that the new Republican mood of moderation established by the elections might extend to a willingness to surrender at least part of their reconstruction program. On the other side a public address by the President in mid-November seemed to indicate that he himself might be responding to the situation by a new willingness to be flexible in his position. Neither eventuality developed, however, as by the end of November the President, possibly provoked by the renewed threat of impeachment and emboldened by its evident approaching failure, was privately declaring that the time was now right for him to take the offensive.[3]

In his annual message in December, therefore, he vigorously denounced the congressional program as unconstitutional, blaming it for the continued division of the nation. The Republicans, he charged, were trying to give control of the South to blacks despite the clear evidence of history that the Negro was incapable of self-government. Only because of his fear of renewed civil war had he decided to enforce these laws even though he considered them to be unconstitutional. But, he warned, he would resist any law which would do immediate and irreparable damage and against which there was neither judicial remedy nor power in the people to protect themselves. Such an act would be an attempt to abolish a coordinate branch of the government, by which he undoubtedly referred to proposals to suspend a president from office as soon as impeachment was voted by the House, thereby denying him the use of his powers during the period of trial by the Senate.[4]

Congressional Republicans replied by indicating that they would not retreat from the measures already enacted. On December 16th, the House, by a strict party vote, passed a resolution declaring that the reconstruction program was a success and would be carried to completion. The Republicans completely ignored a compromise proposal, repeatedly offered by Senator James Doolittle of Wisconsin, which would have provided for only qualified Negro suffrage in the South. At the same time they continued to reject the idea of broadening the program for reconstruction, once again postponing consideration of Stevens' confiscation bill. But they did move to strengthen the existing laws where weaknesses had become apparent, the House passing a measure to change the requirement for majority participation in the southern elections to a simple majority of those actually voting.[5]

In the South, meanwhile, action on the congressional program was proceeding. The district commanders ordered the convening of constitutional conventions in all of the states except Texas, where the election to ratify the convention call and elect delegates would not be held until February, 1868. The first convention convened in Alabama on November 5, 1867, and the last in Florida on January 20, 1868. A recent comprehensive study of the delegates shows that of those that can be classified as to race and prewar residence by far the largest part, 53%, were southern whites, compared to 30% who were blacks and 17% whites who had lived outside of the Confederate states before the war. On a state by state basis the southern whites, who were especially strong in North Carolina and Georgia, were the largest single group everywhere except Florida, Louisiana, and South Carolina, where about 40, 45, and 60% of the delegates, respectively, were Negroes. Non-southern whites were generally the smallest group, varying from 7% in Georgia and Louisiana to 28% in Alabama and Florida, but their influence was often greater than their numbers, many of them having had more political experience than their southern counterparts.[6]

As the delegates had usually been elected on an individual basis, generalizations about the political compositions of the conventions are more difficult to make, except for the fact that those in favor of proceeding with reconstruction on the basis of the congressional terms were in a large majority everywhere. Based on voting patterns that were to develop in the conventions themselves, the same study of the delegates shows that of those whose political position can be clearly defined, almost 75% can be classified as radicals, with the large majority of blacks and non-southern whites falling into this group. According to these same figures the southern whites were about equally divided between radicals and conservatives, but these definitions are not as valuable as they might be as no differentiation is made within the latter group between anti-reconstructionists and conservative pro-reconstructionists.

The effect of the northern fall elections was evident as the conventions met. While some northern Republicans urged them to adopt radical measures of disfranchisement and confiscation, the overwhelming weight of advice they received seems to have favored the opposite course. The southerners were warned that they would be closely watched in the North, and in the interests of the party they were asked to act with moderation and speed. The same advice came from Pope, now considered the most radical of the commanders, while Ord privately stated that if the southern Republicans adopted extreme measures the constitutions would most likely be defeated.[7]

In addition, as the Republican-controlled constitutional conventions began their work, southern conservatives organized in opposition. The latter had been given a great psychological lift by the northern Democratic victories, and they now moved to convert what had been an individual and largely unorganized opposition to acceptance of the Reconstruction Acts into state-wide parties committed to defeating ratification of the new constitutions. A conference of conservative leaders in South Carolina in early November was followed by conservative state conventions in Georgia and Virginia in December and in Mississippi and Arkansas in January. Meanwhile, in Alabama, Louisiana, North Carolina, and Florida, conservative state committees became active, issuing addresses to the people and encouraging local organization.[8]

The platforms and addresses adopted by these groups were all very similar in content and tone. They accepted what they considered the "legitimate" results of the war and were prepared to grant the freedmen equal protection in person and property, but denounced the Reconstruction Acts as unconstitutional and refused to recognize the validity of the state constitutional conventions. Racial feeling was also strong, as they stated their belief in a "white man's government" and attacked any effort to establish political equality between the races. The southern conservative press reflected these same ideas, urging greater organization and unified action on the part of the white race and the rejection of the congressional program as unconstitutional.[9]

Conservative hopes for success in the South were increased by changes in the district commanders. Due to yellow fever in New Orleans in the summer and fall, Hancock did not actually take command in the Fifth District until late November. But then he quickly made his position clear by an order stating that as peace had been restored the civil authority should have precedence over the military. He applied this principle by reinstating state laws concerning jury selection, thereby revoking an order of Sheridan's that had opened the jury lists to blacks. He also reversed a number of removals made by the acting commander, General Joseph A. Mower, and took exception to Sheridan's interpretation of the disfranchisement provisions of the Reconstruction Acts. Johnson responded by urging that Congress commend Hancock for his devotion to the principles of constitutional liberty, an idea that found little favor in that body. But Democrats and conservatives joined the President in applauding Hancock's actions, and they expressed the hope that they would set the standard for a new policy in all of the military districts.[10]

That this might in fact happen seemed quite possible when, in late December, Pope, Ord, and Wager Swayne, the sub-district commander in Alabama, were all replaced. Ord was removed at his own request and the views of the new commander, Irvin McDowell, were not known, so that there does not seem to have been any political motivation behind this change. But until McDowell returned from his post in California, which would not be until June, the district was commanded by General Alvan C. Gillem, who immediately became involved in a number of disputes with the Republican majority in the Mississippi constitutional convention. In the Third District the changes were clearly the result of presidential dissatisfaction with the policies of the men removed, Pope and Swayne. The immediate reason given the press was that they had permitted registration frauds in Alabama and were preparing to reopen the rolls in that state in order to make the black majority even greater. Pope, in addition, was the last of the three original commanders who had been closely identified with the Republican policy and the newspapers had just printed an unofficial letter that he had written to Swayne in which he had spoken of the necessity for Republican victory in the South.[11]

To replace Pope, Johnson chose George G. Meade, who was considered one of the most conservative of the generals, and it was rumored that he had been ordered to adopt the same policies as Hancock. But Meade's appointment, which at first greatly raised conservative hopes in the South, in the end showed how little they could expect from the army, as Meade constantly sought Grant's advice and quickly made it clear that he considered it his duty to enforce the congressional acts without question. In practice the new commander followed a middle course, moderating orders issued by Pope concerning the jury lists and the placing of official advertisements in newspapers, but also removing the governor and treasurer in Georgia because they refused to honor requisitions from the convention and putting into effect stay laws requested by the conventions in all three states of the district.[12]

But, while Republicans could take some satisfaction in Meade's refusal to follow Hancock's example, they still had good reason to be concerned about the success of reconstruction as 1868 began. They could not be as sure as they had been the prior summer of the commanders' commitment to the effective enforcement of the Reconstruction Acts, and it should be noted that the list of commanders was now almost identical to that considered most acceptable to the South by the Chicago *Times* in March, 1867. Many Republicans, in fact, feared that they faced defeat in the South, while southern party members warned of the effects of renewed conservative activity and asked that the existing state governments be replaced.[13]

The situation in Alabama was particularly important as the convention there had convened before any of the others and completed its work in the shortest time. The draft constitution had been adopted on December 5th, and provision made for a vote on ratification beginning on February 4, 1868, with elections for state officers to be held at the same time. The most important clause of this constitution, that on disfranchisement, met the desires of neither the conservatives nor the radicals. The former had been defeated, 10–76, in an effort to have no disfranchisement at all, while radical proposals to disfranchise all registered voters who did not participate in the election and permit the legislature to extend disfranchisement had also lost, 42–53 and 28–54. In its final form the clause disfranchised all of those disqualified by the Fourteenth Amendment and the Reconstruction Acts, and, in addition, required an oath of all voters that they accepted the civil and political equality of all men.[14]

The conservatives in Alabama were well organized, and they

adopted a strategy of boycotting the elections in the hope of preventing participation by a majority of the registered voters. They seemed to have a good chance of success, as the oath and disfranchisement provisions of the constitution caused some moderate reconstructionists to break with the Republican Party. Although only two men considered to be conservatives had been elected to the convention, fifteen delegates signed a protest against the constitution because it went beyond the requirements of the Reconstruction Acts. The Montgomery Council of the Union League also recommended that it be defeated, while the Republican state committee felt it necessary to promise that Congress would revise any objectionable provisions. In addition, Governor Patton, who was favorable to congressional reconstruction, urged Meade to postpone the elections because he believed that the character of the Republican nominations made defeat of the constitution probable. There seems to have been some feeling among the army leaders that this might be a wise move, but the elections had already been authorized by Pope and it proved to be too late to make any changes in the provisions for them, beyond extending the time from two to four days.[15]

With the Republican plan for reconstruction facing growing opposition in the South, it was suddenly threatened from another direction, the Supreme Court. In November, 1867, Ord had ordered the arrest and trial by a military court of a Vicksburg, Mississippi, newspaper editor, William McCardle, for publishing articles attacking the military government. McCardle's petition for a writ of habeas corpus had been denied by the United States Circuit Court, and he had then appealed the decision to the Supreme Court under an 1867 statute designed to protect freedmen in the South. Republicans were well aware that in the obiter dictum in the Milligan case, five of the eight members of the Court had declared that Congress had no power to authorize military trials where the civil courts were open. Faced with reports that these same justices would now rule the Reconstruction Acts unconstitutional, Congress, in mid-January, moved to restrict the power of the Court. By an almost strict party vote a bill requiring the concurrence of two thirds of the justices before the Court could declare an act of Congress unconstitutional was passed by the House and sent to the Senate, where, however, no immediate action was taken on it.[16]

House Republicans also moved to meet the growing challenges to the success of their policy for reconstruction by attempting to strip Johnson of his remaining powers and place the South completely under the control of Grant. Under a bill passed on January 21st, the latter would have been given both the authority to appoint and remove the commanders and equal powers with them within their districts. It provided, in addition, that the existing provisional governments should not be recognized as valid by either the executive or judicial power of the United States. The Senate, however, again failed to act, as Grant restated his objection to any bill that would result in a direct struggle between himself and the President.[17]

The fact that in this situation the major solution that most Republicans saw was to place the future of their program entirely in the hands of Grant is a clear indication that events since the fall elections had, if anything, reinforced the certainty that he would be the party's presidential nominee. It is true that in the House debates Democrat James Brooks of New York had argued that the opposite was the case and that the new reconstruction measure was actually a maneuver to kill Grant's chances by making him responsible for whatever happened in the South. But this had been a partisan statement, which failed to account for the fact that the two leading anti-Grant Republicans in the House, Stevens and Butler, had made an unsuccessful attempt to give control of the southern states to their constitutional conventions rather than the commanding general.[18]

In fact, since November the list of Republican endorsements of Grant had continued to grow, and it now included the the influential Union League of Philadelphia, the Grand Army of the Republic, the governors of Massachusetts and Minnesota, a legislative caucus in California, and the first two northern Republican state conventions to meet, those in Connecticut and New Hampshire. Attention was beginning to focus on the choice for the second spot on the ticket, and those who wanted that nomination hastened to seek Grant's favor. Benjamin Wade denied reports that he had ever questioned Grant's Republicanism, while it was stated that Governor Reuben Fenton of New York had scheduled that state's convention for early February so that it could be one of the first to jump on the Grant bandwagon. Most significantly, the Republican National Executive Committee, meeting in December, called the national convention for Chicago on May 20th, both the place and the early date being favorable to Grant. In an informal straw poll, twenty of the twenty-three members of the committee declared themselves in favor of his nomination.[19]

Of all the other possible nominees the only serious contender remaining in the field was Chief Justice Salmon P. Chase. His strength was concentrated among more radical members of the party, who accepted Grant's position on reconstruction but still doubted his commitment to racial equality. There was, in particular, extensive activity on behalf of the chief justice in the South, but it must be recognized that the results were not great, and there were also reports of support for Grant in the same section. While the national council of the Union League did call on the Republican national convention not to nominate anyone who had not clearly declared himself in favor of equal rights, the only specific endorsements Chase obtained were from the Louisiana Union League and a caucus of delegates to the Georgia constitutional convention. But even if they had been unanimously committed to Chase, the southern Republican parties, which were not even sure of being seated at the national convention, could not have significantly influenced the nomination. In the North, despite individual support for Chase, there was not the slightest sign of an organized movement in his behalf.[20]

In the ranks of the opposition many Democrats now conceded, both publicly and privately, that Grant would, in all probability, be the choice of the Republican Party. Despite this, however, speculation continued that he might either refuse the Republican nomination or actually be chosen as the Democratic candidate also. Part of the reason for these recurring stories is revealed in a letter from Manton Marble, editor of the New York *World*, to Senator James Doolittle. Informed by Doolittle that Grant would accept the Republican nomination on a Negro suffrage platform and had authorized the pro-Republican speech by John Rawlins the prior June, Marble refused to print either of these facts. He would do nothing, he told Doolittle, to overcome the remaining radical doubts about Grant. Rather he hoped that it might still be possible to prevent the nomination of the general by the Republican convention, and he would therefore continue to publicize statements against Negro suffrage which Grant had made in 1865. Marble, in addition, believed that Grant had only moved to support the Republicans after the 1866 elections, and he wanted to leave the door open for the general to return to conservatism in response to the 1867 results. In the immediate reaction to the Democratic victories in the fall, others shared this hope that Grant might now come over to what seemed to be the winning side. This, however, was not a reflection of the real situation, but only of their own mistaken belief that the general's identification with Republican policy was based solely on political expediency.[21]

All of this lingering doubt as to the general's future course of action disappeared when the reinstatement of Stanton, on January 14, 1868, brought the public clash with Johnson that Grant had so long tried to avoid. Under the terms of the Tenure of Office Act, the President was required to submit his reasons for the suspension of Stanton to the Senate within twenty days of the beginning of the new session. Before Congress convened, there had been reports that Johnson would replace Grant with someone more favorable to his own views and then challenge the validity of the law by formally removing the suspended secretary of war. Johnson had, however, decided against this course, apparently after having received assurances from Grant on two points of major concern to the President. The entire cabinet, including the general, had promised Johnson its support if he refused to obey a congressional order suspending him from office during an impeachment trial. Grant had also promised the chief executive that he would either resist Stanton's reinstatement in office, forcing the latter to test the law in the courts, or inform the President beforehand of his decision not to do so. By the end of November, then, Grant had considered the situation in Washington stable enough that he might be able to leave the city for a few months during the winter, and he had written Sherman that the President would no longer want the lieutenant-general to serve in Washington.[22]

On December 12, 1867, Johnson had complied with the law by sending a message to the Senate in which he had defended his suspension of Stanton on the grounds that the latter was not in harmony with the administration, had been partly responsible for the 1866 New Orleans riot, and had himself declared that the Tenure of Office Act was unconstitutional. What the Republican response would be was not at all clear. Some believed that even if the Senate rejected the charges Stanton would have to seek a court order to regain his office, while a few even predicted that in their now more moderate mood Senate Republicans would take no action at all, letting Stanton go by default. According to reports, the secretary himself had stated that he would resign immediately following Senate action, desiring only the personal vindication of the rejection of the charges against him.[23]

All of these possibilities were not as unlikely as later events might make them seem. The very vagueness of the protection given Stanton by the Tenure of Office Act, compared to the way in which the removal of Grant had been forbidden, indicates that Republicans did not consider the retention of the former as secretary of war to be absolutely vital to the success of their program. But it was essential for them to prevent a situation in which the office would be left vacant, which would occur if the charges were not rejected or if Stanton resigned. In that case Johnson would be left free to appoint someone totally committed to defeat congressional reconstruction, having it within his power to evade the necessity for Senate consent by making temporary appointments so long as the Senate rejected his nominations. As the Republicans considered the situation, then, the tone of speculation about the action they contemplated began to change. By the time Congress returned from its Christmas recess, it was understood that a report was being prepared which would recommend non-concurrence in the charges and that Stanton was being urged not to resign as soon as he was reinstated.[24]

Yet, any attempt to force the reinstatement of Stanton threatened to place Grant in the difficult position of having to oppose the wishes of either the Republican Senate, whose policies he supported, or the President, who was his commander-in-chief. In addition, Stanton and Grant had never enjoyed close personal relations despite their political cooperation, and the latter had been very much upset by reports that the secretary had attacked him for accepting the war office from Johnson. The two men had also clashed previously over issues involving the authority of the secretary of war over the commanding general, questions that were still of great concern to Grant.[25]

For these reasons the general joined some conservatives and moderate Republicans in a last-minute effort to prevent what was obviously a potentially explosive clash between the executive and the legislature. They proposed to Johnson that he nominate Jacob Cox, a moderate Republican and ex-governor of Ohio, as secretary of war, promising that they would obtain confirmation by the Senate and the dropping of consideration of the charges against Stanton. The latter, then, would never gain the vindication that he desired, but Republicans would not have to fear that the powers of the war office would be used against them while the President would not be forced to reaccept a cabinet officer who was strongly objectionable to him. This effort came to nothing, however, as Johnson rejected the proposition.[26]

It would seem fairly clear that whereas Grant and the moderates feared the political effects of a struggle over the war office, the President welcomed them. In this decision he may have been influenced by the belief that Grant still felt himself committed by his promise of the prior fall to resist Stanton's reinstatement. If so, the President disregarded an interview with Grant on January 11th, in which the general informed Johnson that he would not attempt to retain possession of the war office if the Senate rejected the charges against Stanton because he had discovered that such action would make him liable to both fine and imprisonment. The President disputed this point, arguing that he had the constitutional right to remove the secretary of war and offering to assume any fine or jail term that might be imposed. According to Grant's version of events, this discussion in no way changed his mind, and he left the White

House after having made it clear that he would no longer act in accordance with the commitment he had made the prior fall. Johnson, however, claimed that the understanding was that Grant was still bound by the promise and would return on Monday to further discuss his intentions.

The question of whether or not the general had indicated that his decision was final on that Saturday cannot be definitively settled, as there were no witnesses to the interview other than the two men themselves. But while there is some support for Johnson's contention that another meeting was contemplated, the President clearly distorted the truth in his later accounts by making it seem that the major point of the discussion that Saturday was Grant's reaffirmation of his promise, rather than the general's desire to withdraw from that commitment. Certainly the President was made aware of the latter's intentions in that regard, and it is therefore strange that he made no further effort to determine what the general would do, even though Grant did not return to the White House on Monday. The most useful key to understanding the whole affair may be to recall what had happened in October, 1866, when Johnson had simply refused to hear Grant's repeated statements that he would not accept the Mexican mission.[27]

In any case on that Monday, January 13th, the Senate voted 35–6 to refuse to concur in the suspension of the secretary of war. The next morning Grant locked the doors to the secretary of war's offices and delivered the keys to Assistant Adjutant General Edward Townsend, who, in turn, gave them to Stanton. It was soon reported that the latter had decided to hold the office until a successor had been appointed and confirmed by the Senate. Grant, with the aid of General Sherman, continued to press for a compromise settlement based on Stanton's resignation and the nomination of a new secretary acceptable to congressional Republicans, but again his efforts were unsuccessful.[28]

Johnson then encouraged publication of reports of a cabinet meeting at which he had charged Grant with having acted in bad faith, and relations between the two men reached a breaking point. An exchange of letters followed in which each man developed his own version of what had occurred, charging the other with deliberate deception. A bitter personal hostility was thus established between them that lasted the rest of their lives. It was the publication of this correspondence that led Thaddeus Stevens to remark that he was now prepared to "let him [Grant] into the Church," thus ending even radical opposition to the nomination of the general to the presidency. However, that choice was already so close to being a certainty that the statement should not be taken as marking the point at which Grant became a Republican, but rather the recognition by the always pragmatic Stevens that it was time for him to join the Grant church.[29]

The specific questions argued in the Johnson-Grant correspondence have already been discussed, but in addition Johnson raised the broader charge that Grant had deceived him by taking the war office in order to oppose administration policies, rather than to support them. That this had been Grant's purpose cannot be questioned, but, as has been seen, Johnson should have been well aware of it. He had appointed Grant knowing that the general supported the congressional policy and had kept him in office even after it became clear that Grant would be the Republican presidential nominee. He had done this not because Grant had fooled him, but because he had hoped to use him as a shield against congressional attack for the removal of Stanton, undoubtedly anticipating that the general's political prospects would be damaged in the process. The President had little cause for complaint if Grant refused to be so used, and had instead turned the tables by waiting until the last moment to announce that he would not attempt to retain the war office.

In any case, Stanton's occupation of the secretary of war's office did not settle the question of his status, and it was at first expected that Johnson would refuse to recognize him. But authoritative statements were quickly printed denying that members of the administration would be ordered to ignore Stanton, and such speculation ended when the Treasury Department honored requisitions signed by him. Johnson did order Grant not to obey any order from the secretary of war unless he knew that it had the President's sanction, but the general replied that in the absence of contrary evidence he had to assume that all orders had such approval.[30]

Some urged Johnson to let the matter rest there, arguing that Stanton's presence in the cabinet against the wishes of the Chief Executive was a political liability for the Republicans, while further action might bring impeachment. But the President was determined to remove the secretary and thus persisted in his search for a possible successor. He turned, as he had before, to William T. Sherman, appointing the lieutenant general to the command of a newly created Department of the Atlantic and nominating him for the brevet rank of full general in mid-February. Sherman, however, had already indicated to the President that he did not want an assignment in Washington, particularly if it meant potential conflict with Grant. He now repeated his feelings to Johnson in very strong terms, at the same time asking his brother, John Sherman, to have the Senate reject his brevet promotion. Faced with Sherman's determination, Johnson withdrew his order, and the status quo was preserved for a short time.[31]

During this period Congress continued its search for countermeasures against the President. A Senate-passed bill would have removed all general and special agents of the government thirty days after it became law, with the President authorized to refill, with Senate approval, only those specifically authorized by statute. Another measure, which was also passed by the Senate but not the House, would have restricted the President's right to make temporary appointments to fill executive vacancies, limiting him to the choice of men who already held positions which had required Senate approval. Impeachment was also given renewed attention, although action on it did not get beyond the committee level. A bill by Senator George F. Edmunds to establish procedures for an impeachment trial, including possible suspension of the officer being tried, was defeated in the Judiciary Committee. In the House, Thaddeus Stevens obtained the transfer of the impeachment investigation to his own Committee on Reconstruction, but was defeated there, six to three, when he attempted to bring new charges based on Johnson's efforts to prevent the reinstatement of

Stanton.[32] By mid-February, therefore, despite the many problems they had considered since the start of the session, the Republicans in Congress had been unable to enact a single piece of legislation in relation to either reconstruction in the South or the relations between the branches of the federal government.

At just this time the Republicans received additional bad news from both the South and the Supreme Court. The threat to reconstruction from the Court had seemed to be reduced when, on February 10th, it had issued an opinion on the request by Georgia for an injunction against enforcement of the Reconstruction Acts, declining to take jurisdiction on the grounds that the questions involved were solely political in nature. Republicans had then hoped for a similar decision in the McCardle case, but instead their fears of adverse Court action were revived when, with hearings on the appeal scheduled for early March, a motion to dismiss it was denied. With a legal test thus rapidly approaching, Republicans also had to face the fact that southern conservatives had apparently found a way to delay completion of reconstruction until the courts could act. By the effectiveness of their boycott campaign conservatives were able to keep the turnout in the Alabama election, which was held on February 4th–7th, more than 13,000 votes short of the majority participation required by the law. Some Republicans wanted to admit the state despite this, while Meade recommended that the convention be reconvened to amend its work, but in any case it was clear that congressional reconstruction had suffered its first major defeat.[33]

This was the situation when, on the morning of February 21st, the President summoned Adjutant General Lorenzo Thomas to the White House and appointed him secretary of war *ad interim*, at the same time giving him an order removing Stanton from office. Although Johnson was later to claim that his only purpose was to test the constitutionality of the Tenure of Office Act, it seems clear that he was mainly driven by a desire to get rid of Stanton, with a possible secondary aim to impress the Democratic National Committee, then meeting in Washington, with the firmness of his action. None of these objectives, however, were to be accomplished as Stanton, after consultation with Grant, refused to surrender his position. Supported by strong words of encouragement from leading Republicans in Congress and a Senate resolution denouncing the attempted removal as illegal, the secretary of war remained in his office at the War Department day and night, protected by a body of armed supporters. At the same time in the House of Representatives, Thaddeus Stevens' Committee on Reconstruction, after considering no new evidence except the President's own orders, presented a report on February 22d recommending, "That Andrew Johnson, President of the United States, be impeached of high crimes and misdemeanors in office." On the 24th, after less than two days of debate, the 23d being a Sunday, the full House accepted this recommendation by a strict party vote of 126–47.[34]

This hasty action by the House, taken on what proved to be very shaky grounds, must be seen against the background of events since the November elections. With the Democrats suddenly showing surprising strength in the North, conservative resistance stiffening in the South, and the Supreme Court threatening to strike down their legislation, Republicans faced both the destruction of their reconstruction program and defeat in the presidential election. All of this could be changed by a president who supported their policies and who would use executive power to hasten rather than delay reconstruction and executive patronage to support the party rather than to oppose it. With so much at stake, therefore, it was not surprising that they used the grounds given them, however questionable, to attempt to remove the man who stood in their way. It is also evident that whereas rank and file Republicans had accepted the decision not to impeach the President in December, the feeling in the party now was that his removal was a necessity. On the other side, however, opponents of the congressional policy saw the impeachment as a revolutionary act, and men on both sides began to talk of the possibility of a renewal of armed conflict.[35]

CHAPTER SIX

RECONSTRUCTION AND IMPEACHMENT:
THE SETTLEMENT

The House quickly completed its action in preparation for the trial of the President, adopting nine articles of impeachment on March 2, 1868. The first eight of them dealt solely with charges directly related to the removal of Stanton and the appointment of Thomas, while the ninth accused Johnson of attempting to induce General William H. Emory, the commander in the District of Columbia, to violate the Command of the Army Act by accepting orders directly from the President. Seven Republican members, headed by Thaddeus Stevens, were then elected as managers to present the House's case before the Senate. On March 3d, the managers suggested two additional articles, which the House adopted that day. The new tenth article, which had been drafted by Benjamin Butler, charged that in speeches made in the summer of 1866 Johnson had attempted to "bring into disgrace, ridicule, hatred, contempt and reproach the Congress of the United States," in order to destroy its rightful power. The eleventh article, which would prove to be the most important, was basically a summation of all the others and accused the President of both disregard for the powers of Congress and the specific violation of the Tenure of Office Act.[1]

On the 4th of March, accompanied by the full House, the managers went to the Senate chamber to formally present the articles of impeachment. The next day Chief Justice Chase assumed his position as presiding officer of the Senate during the trial, and the President was summoned to answer the charges against him on March 13th. At that time he did not appear in person, nor was he ever to do so, but his lawyers responded for him and requested forty days in which to prepare an answer to the indictment. This the majority of the Senate considered excessive, but over radical objections ten days were granted. On March 23d the President's plea of "not guilty" was entered, his attorneys arguing that he had merely sought a court case to test the constitutionality of the law, which had not actually been violated as Stanton remained in the office, while, in any case, the tenure of the secretary of war was not protected by the terms of the Act. The next day the Impeachment Managers entered their replication, which merely denied the statements made in the answer, and the Senate scheduled the formal opening of the trial for March 30th.[2]

The fact that nearly a month was thus consumed by the Senate in the mere preliminaries of the trial is an indication of the extent to which both sides had drawn back from the extreme action threatened in late February. Johnson had ignored the suggestion of one Democratic congressman that he refuse to recognize the authority of a Congress from which ten states had been excluded. Instead, he followed the advice of conservative supporters who had suggested that in his choice of attorneys he pick conciliatory men who would not arouse the enmity of the Senate. Of the men he selected, William M. Evarts, Benjamin R. Curtis, Henry Stanbery, Thomas A. R. Nelson, and Jeremiah S. Black, only the latter might have been objectionable to Republican Senators and he was replaced by William S. Groesbeck before the trial began. The President's desire not to take any extreme measures was also evident in his decision not to have Lorenzo Thomas attempt to exercise any of the powers of the secretary of war. During the trial the President ignored Stanton, but he permitted other cabinet members to deal with him, and the secretary remained in complete control of the War Department.[3]

Another possible instrument for presidential control of the army in the South was eliminated as the result of a dispute between Grant and Hancock. In early February the latter had removed nine members of the New Orleans City Council, seven of them Negroes, for having voted to elect the recorder in one of the districts of the city, contrary to a standing order forbidding any election without the prior approval of the district commander. Grant had at first acquiesced in this action, but on February 21st he ordered that the councilmen be reinstated. While Hancock had no choice but to comply, he formally protested this decision to the Adjutant-

General and requested to be relieved of his post. On March 28th, then, Hancock was given the command of the Department of the Atlantic that Sherman had refused, the Fifth District being taken over by General Robert Buchanan, whose political views were not known.[4] While this might be considered an action designed to place Hancock, the leading general who supported the President's policies, in Washington at a critical time, his removal from the Fifth District was also an indication that Johnson had given up the effort to bypass Grant by placing generals loyal to himself in command in the South.

While the President was thus withdrawing from the bolder actions he had taken during the prior months, moderates on the Republican side were demonstrating that they rather than the radicals would control the action of the Senate. The very first roll calls taken, although only on procedural questions, showed that Republican Senators would vote as individuals rather than a solid partisan bloc. Thus, while the President's attorneys were not able to obtain the delays they desired, neither were the House managers able to speed up the trial as much as they wanted. Chief Justice Chase also made it clear from the first that he would not be guided by considerations of Republican policy in conducting the trial. Even before assuming his chair as presiding officer he wrote a letter concerning the trial rules to the Senate in which he made clear the judicial nature of that body when it sat as an Impeachment Court. As a result, while many still thought that the Senate would quickly find the President guilty, some of his supporters began to report a growing feeling among Republicans that impeachment had been a mistake and that there was a good chance for acquittal.[5]

But in order to fully understand both the trial and the result, it is necessary to turn away from the impeachment proceedings themselves and to consider the large number of other events that occurred in the more than two months during which the removal of the President was being considered. Even before the trial formally began, legislation was passed which removed the immediate threat of a clash between Congress and the Supreme Court. Opposition in the Senate prevented adoption of the sweeping House-passed measure, which would have required a two thirds majority of the Court to declare an act of Congress unconstitutional. But the Republicans did accomplish their immediate purpose by repealing the section of the 1867 Act that had provided the legal basis for McCardle's appeal by giving the Court appellate jurisdiction in habeas corpus cases. The justices, in turn, showed a desire to avoid conflict by voting six to two not to consider the case during the ten-day period in which Johnson would hold the bill for consideration. When the repealing act finally became law, over the usual presidential veto, the Court again satisfied congressional desires by postponing consideration of the effect of the repeal on the status of the McCardle case until the December term. Also put off until then were other cases affecting the constitutionality of the Reconstruction Acts in which the jurisdiction of the Court did not rest solely upon a plea for a writ of habeas corpus.[6]

In the South, meanwhile, with the threat to reconstruction from both the President and the Supreme Court virtually ended, major steps were being taken to complete the congressional program. Although Congress had been unable to agree on a bill to settle the status of Alabama following the election in that state, the Senate had taken action on the measure passed by the House in December which eliminated the requirement for majority participation in future southern elections. The bill finally adopted by both Houses, in March, in addition to making a simple majority of those actually voting all that was needed, also authorized the election of officers at the same time as the vote on ratification and permitted voters to cast their ballots in an election district other than the one in which they had registered. An additional indication of the change in Johnson's frame of mind came when he did not veto this measure, known as the Fourth Reconstruction Act, but allowed it to become law without his signature.[7] Southern conservatives were thus denied the use of the boycott tactic with which they might have been able to defeat almost all of the new constitutions which were just then being presented to southern voters for ratification.

By the end of March the constitutional conventions had completed their work in all of the states except Virginia, Mississippi, and Texas. The documents they produced generally brought the southern states closer to prevailing practices in the North in such areas as public education, the legal system, election procedures, and debtor relief. In addition to granting Negro suffrage as required by the federal law, all six opened with a general bill of rights, and the majority of them specifically guaranteed civil and political equality for all men without regard to race. But there had been a strong tendency to defeat measures which either prohibited or required any type of social equality, reflecting the balance between southern whites who were opposed to any form of integration, and non-southern whites who were unwilling to alter the social structure of the South but still sympathized with the strong Negro opposition to legally enforced segregation. Only in South Carolina and Louisiana, where Negroes were the largest single group in the convention, was segregation in schools outlawed, and the latter state additionally prohibited racial discrimination in public places.[8]

In no state were measures for confiscation of land or mass disfranchisement of ex-Confederates adopted. In Georgia, North Carolina, and Florida the conventions had voted down any disfranchisement at all, although in the latter this had been done only after a split in the convention and Meade's intervention to place the moderates in control.[9] South Carolina and Arkansas disfranchised those who were disqualified for office by the Fourteenth Amendment, while in Louisiana former Confederate supporters were required to sign a certificate admitting that they had been in error in order to regain the ballot. In addition, all voters in Arkansas and all candidates for office in Louisiana had to take an oath that they accepted the legal and political equality of all men.

Elections in these six states were held beginning with Arkansas in mid-March and ending with Florida in early May. They were for both ratification of the constitutions and the election of officers, with the disfranchisement provisions of the Reconstruction Acts, rather than those of the proposed constitutions, applying in the latter as well as the former. With the boycott no longer an effective weapon, southern conservatives were forced to try to win a clear majority at the polls in order either to prevent ratification of the constitutions or to win control of the new state governments. The relative importance given each of these goals varied from state to state, as the local situation dictated. In states like Georgia, where there was no disfranchisement clause and liberal provisions for debtors had widespread support among whites, there was little chance that ratification would be defeated and the major struggle was for control of the new government. In other states the opposite was true, as in South Carolina where the conservative nominee for governor declined to run because he thought his candidacy might distract attention from the effort to defeat the constitution.[10]

Conservatives expressed renewed confidence in their ability to split the black vote, despite their failure to do so in the prior fall elections. In South Carolina, where the black majority was overwhelming, they indicated their willingness to accept Negro suffrage, at least on a qualified basis, if they won power. But elsewhere the principal conservative reliance was obviously on their superior economic position, as they openly declared that they would not employ men who had voted for the Republican ticket. In addition there developed throughout the South secret organizations such as the Knights of the White Camelia in Alabama and Louisiana, the White Brotherhood in North Carolina, and, most notorious of all, the Ku Klux Klan in Tennessee. The latter had been founded in 1866, apparently more as a prank than anything else, but by 1868 it had developed into a well organized network which was reportedly responsible for a large number of outrages against both black and white Republicans. By that time also it had begun to spread to other states in the South. The district commander in Alabama felt it necessary to order it outlawed, while Meade, for the Third District as a whole, forbade the publication of Klan announcements, organized patrols to combat night-riders, and informed Washington that he urgently needed additional troops. The conservative and Democratic press belittled these stories of Klan activity, suggesting that the organization might even be a Republican invention, but they also warned those engaged in the movement that violence could only hurt the southern cause.[11]

The spring elections showed that these efforts at physical intimidation were not yet having a major effect, as the Negro vote did not drop significantly. But the results also made it strikingly clear that other types of conservative activity had become vastly more effective since the prior fall. In the very first election, in Arkansas, the Republicans claimed a questionable victory, the votes cast in two election districts exceeding the number of registered voters in them by a greater number than the state-wide plurality in favor of the constitution. Election officials claimed that this was due to people voting in the districts who had registered elsewhere, as permitted by the Fourth Reconstruction Act, and a very cautious General Gillem simply forwarded all of the papers, without comment, for congressional action. In the other states the constitutions were ratified and the Republican state tickets elected by generally comfortable, but not overwhelming majorities. The conservatives would be a very respectable minority in almost all of the state legislatures and on early returns had even threatened to gain control of one House in several states.[12] But even though opposition strength was increasing, all of the constitutions had been ratified and new state governments created based on an unbiased suffrage. Thus the requirements of the Reconstruction Acts had been complied with and the next step was up to Congress, which had to approve the constitutions and provide for formal readmission of the states.

Meanwhile, in Washington the impeachment trial was still the center of attention. From March 30th to April 20th the Senate had taken testimony, mainly centering on Johnson's attacks on Congress in the "swing around the circle," the events immediately connected with the removal of Stanton, and the legal questions involved in the tenure of cabinet officers. Then for two weeks each side had presented its closing arguments. Johnson's attorneys had basically reiterated their plea that no impeachable crime had been committed, as the President had the right to test the constitutionality of the law and had not actually removed Stanton, who in any case was not protected by the Tenure of Office Act. The managers had disputed all of these points, stating that the President's right to resist a law ended when his veto was overridden, that the law properly interpreted did cover Stanton, and that even without it the President had no power to remove an officer and make an *ad interim* appointment while the Senate was in session. Obviously sensing the weakness of the specific charge of violation of the Tenure of Office Act, they had also presented the attempted removal as one of a series of actions designed to subvert the constitutional powers of Congress, which they had argued was sufficient to justify removal even if no single act of the President constituted an indictable offense.[13]

On May 6th, John A. Bingham closed for the managers and the trial came to an end, with the outcome still very much in doubt. Despite charges that it had been an entirely partisan affair, with the Senate obeying the wishes of the House managers, at least a few Democrats were willing to concede that the proceedings had generally been fair. An examination of the record shows that the moderate Republicans had controlled throughout and normally taken a middle course. Thus, even though he was known to be moving away from the Republican Party on impeachment, the chief justice had been given the right to cast a tie-breaking vote and to rule on points of order, subject to appeal to the Senate. In addition, while evidence pertaining to cabinet discussion of the Tenure of Office Act had been excluded, the Senate had reversed a previous vote and permitted General Sherman to testify about Johnson's statements as to his intentions prior to the removal of Stanton.[14]

With fifty-four members in the Senate, the twelve Democrats and conservatives, who were sure to vote against conviction, had to be joined by only seven others for the President to be acquitted. By the end of the trial there were ten Republicans who had voted with the Democrats on procedural questions often enough that observers believed it possible that they might also vote against impeachment.[15] Republicans, on the other hand, denied the significance of the procedural votes and predicted the President's conviction with equal confidence, some of them even beginning to prepare for the start of a new administration. That such widely differing predictions were being made is in itself an indication of the closeness with which these Senators had guarded their views.[16]

Meanwhile, removed from the spotlight of the Senate chambers, pressure was being brought to influence the result. Almost all Republican state conventions endorsed the House vote for impeachment, although many of them also urged acceptance of whatever decision the Senate made after a fair trial of the law and the facts. At the same time southern Republicans warned that conservatives in their section would interpret acquittal to mean that the President was free to do as he wanted in the South, and influential northern leaders echoed their prediction that in that case reconstruction would be defeated and the November election lost. In addition the New York *Tribune* publicly revealed that Grant strongly desired the removal of Johnson, while the general privately brought his influence to bear on key senators.[17]

On the other side, there were rumors that Chief Justice Chase, who considered Johnson not guilty, was urging acquittal on a group of moderate senators, including his son-in-law, William Sprague of Rhode Island. Of more significance, one of the President's attorneys, William M. Evarts, was attempting to reach an understanding with the doubtful Republicans. According to reports, some of them were prepared to vote for acquittal, but were worried that given such a victory the President would immediately embark on further extreme measures. It was therefore suggested, on whose initiative it is not clear, that there be a prior understanding on a mutually satisfactory choice for secretary of war. The man selected was General John M. Schofield, who in an interview with Evarts agreed to accept the nomination on the understanding that he was acting at the request of the Republican senators and with the pledge that Johnson would make no effort to interfere with his enforcement of the Reconstruction Acts. These conditions were apparently acceptable, for on April 24th the nomination of Schofield was sent to the Senate.[18]

Other factors were also working towards acquittal. With reconstruction almost completed in the South, the crisis atmosphere of February was gone and the weaknesses of the case against Johnson became more evident. There were reports that even the managers were dissatisfied with the way the case had developed, which they blamed on the rules adopted by the Senate, and that Thaddeus Stevens favored withdrawing the action. There were also some doubts among Republicans about the wisdom of making the radical Benjamin Wade, who as president *pro tem* of the Senate was next in succession, president of the United States. To encourage this feeling, some Democratic papers suggested to Grant Republicans that if Wade were in the White House he would use the executive patronage to put his own supporters in office and Grant would be unable to remove them if he were elected in November.[19]

Prior to reaching a verdict, the Senate met on May 11th to give its members an opportunity to express their views, thereby ending much of the speculation and rumors about the probable vote. Four Republicans, Lyman Trumbull, William P. Fessenden, James Grimes, and John Henderson, on the basis of their statements seemed certain to vote for acquittal on all charges. With others considered doubtful on some or all of the articles, it now seemed probable that impeachment would fail. But Republicans gained an opportunity to bring pressure on the possible dissenters when the Senate decided to delay the vote from May 12th to the 16th, because of the illness of Senator Jacob M. Howard. During this period Republican leaders, newspapers, and meetings combined to urge conviction of the President, with especially strong pressure being brought to bear on those Senators who were thought to be still uncertain about their votes.[20]

When the Senate reconvened it was clear that the vote would be close, whatever the result. Johnson's chances seemed to be seriously reduced when the Senate decided to vote first on the article that had the most support, the all-encompassing eleventh which summarized and combined the other ten. But when the Chief Justice had completed what was probably the most drama-laden rollcall in American history, the vote was 35 "guilty" and 19 "not guilty," just one short of the number needed for conviction. Exactly the needed seven Republicans had broken with their party to acquit the President. Each of the dissenting votes may not have been as critical as it would seem, however, as rumors persisted that other senators had been prepared to vote for acquittal if it would have changed the result.[21]

Immediately after the vote the Senate adjourned for a week to permit the Republicans to attend the Chicago convention. There the stand to be taken on impeachment and the seven dissenting senators became a major issue. In the aftermath of the vote on the eleventh article there had been predictions that Chase and the Republicans voting for acquittal would be read out of their party and form a new National Union coalition. But, despite the party pressure that had been generated in favor of conviction, the most influential Republicans defended the right of each senator to vote as his conscience dictated. Many Republicans now saw no reason to force the dissenters out of the party just when it needed all of its strength, and one report of the first reaction of those gathering in Chicago indicated that feeling there was mainly directed against the impeachment managers for having led the party into defeat.[22]

The mood in Chicago changed briefly with the arrival of a trainload of men from Washington pledged to "Grant, Wade and vengeance." The supporters of the Ohio senator, disappointed in their expectation that he would be president, tried to build up feeling against the senators who had voted for acquittal in order to convince the delegates that the nomination of Wade for the vice-presidency would be the most effective way to rebuke them. Moderation prevailed, however, in the Resolutions Committee, which drafted a plank endorsing the action of those who had voted for conviction without making reference to those who had not. On the convention floor the delegates defeated an attempt to consider a set of resolutions adopted by the Union League, which attacked the seven senators, and the draft platform plank was adopted without objection.[23]

The two other major items of significance in the platform were the planks on Negro suffrage and the payment of the bonds. The financial question will be considered in greater detail later, and it will suffice here to say that the Republican convention avoided a strong commitment one way or the other, calling for the payment of the bonds according to both the letter and the spirit of the law without specifying whether that meant gold or currency. As for the suffrage issue, despite the reverses of 1867 and the defeat of every Negro suffrage referendum since 1865, some in the party refused to retreat on the question. A number of state conventions continued to endorse equal voting rights for all, and the Minnesota legislature put a referendum on the subject on the ballot for the third time. But others feared the political effect of taking a strong stand,

and the state conventions in New York, New Jersey, Ohio, and Wisconsin failed to readopt Negro suffrage planks, while in Pennsylvania the majority of Republican Assemblymen voted against an equal suffrage referendum.[24]

These latter forces prevailed in the convention, winning a close vote in the Resolutions Committee. The platform, while stating that Negro suffrage in the South was required for the safety of the nation, declared that it was solely a matter of state concern in the North, on which the national convention took no stand. This was an obviously weak and two-sided plank, which represented the victory within the party of those practical politicians who were most interested in keeping the support of both southern blacks and northern whites. However, it must be kept in mind that if anyone was deceived it was the whites and not the blacks, as the most important action taken by the lame-duck congressional session after the election was the proposal of the Fifteenth Amendment to the federal constitution which required equal suffrage everywhere.

The presidential nomination, as long expected, went unanimously to Grant on the first ballot. The vice-presidential choice, in contrast, came only after a spirited and open contest, with a large number of men considered. The principal contenders, other than Wade, were Governor Reuben Fenton of New York, Speaker of the House Schuyler Colfax, Senator Henry Wilson of Massachusetts, and ex-Governor Andrew Curtin of Pennsylvania. But both Curtin and Fenton were weakened by opposition within their own state delegations, while Wilson was unable to muster the unanimous support of New England. Wade was the early leader, but he was a man who also stirred strong opposition and it soon became clear that he could not win. In contrast, Colfax, whose nickname was "Smiler," was a popular figure, not strongly identified as either a radical or a moderate, and he seems to have been the second choice of almost everyone. Over the first four ballots his strength continually rose as other contenders fell out of the running, and he was finally nominated on the fifth ballot despite the objection that he came from the same section as Grant.[25]

The fact that the advocates of "Grant, Wade, and vengeance" had been able to influence the party's action so little, meant that

there was little expectation of a different verdict on the other articles of impeachment when the Senate reconvened after the convention. Voting on the second and third articles, which were considered the strongest ones remaining, ended in exactly the same
result as the prior week, and the Court then adjourned *sine die*. In
the aftermath of the trial, the House authorized an investigation
into charges that corrupt methods had been used to obtain the results, while a Republican Senate caucus broke up when three of
the dissenting senators entered. But the party leadership seems to
have quickly decided that the best course was to end the affair as
quickly as possible and try to forget it. The House investigation
produced no immediate useful results, and was ended over the
objection of Benjamin Butler, while attempts to bring new impeachment charges in July were simply buried. In the Senate no
further question was raised as to the regular party status of the
seven dissenting senators, and there were even reports of com-
plaints that they were gaining greater influence over Grant than
anyone else. In general, the bitter feelings aroused by the trial
seem to have died quickly, and it was seen that in the long run the
acquittal of the President by a single vote may have been the best
result possible.[26]

As for the War Department, Stanton immediately resigned after
the adjournment of the impeachment court and Schofield was confirmed as secretary of war. During the few days in which the Senate was ironing out difficulties in the wording of the confirming resolution, the President did not permit Lorenzo Thomas to act as
secretary *ad interim*, which was taken as an indication that Johnson would not again attempt to control the army. Additional evidence of this came when Johnson bowed to Schofield's wishes in
the selection of a new commander for the First District, rather
than appointing one of the conservative generals available to him.
According to his own testimony, Schofield was also strengthened in
the maintenance of his independent authority when the Senate refused to confirm the reappointment of Stanbery, who had resigned
in order to act as one of the President's attorneys in the trial, and
William M. Evarts then became attorney-general.[27]

With the trial ended, Congress resumed its work on Reconstruction, contrary to Democratic predictions that the southern states would be kept out because the Republicans now feared that they could not carry them in November. Ignoring the irregularities in the Arkansas vote, the House had already, on May 8th, passed a bill to readmit that state on the condition that no citizen or class of citizens then enfranchised ever be deprived of the vote. In the Senate a proposal to delete this condition was defeated by a single vote, but other minor disagreements between the Houses caused some delay so that it was not until June 22d that the essential features of the House bill became law, again over a presidential veto. The Arkansas Act set the pattern for an omnibus bill under which the other six states were readmitted. The major issue in this bill was the inclusion of Alabama, which was adopted by votes of 74–60 in the House and 22–21 in the Senate. After another veto, the Omnibus Bill became law on June 25th.[28]

Under the procedures established by Congress, it was first necessary for the state legislatures to meet and ratify the Fourteenth Amendment. After some discussion, it had been decided that men disqualified under the Amendment could not be seated, but that the legislators were not officers in the provisional governments and so did not have to take the ironclad oath required by the Third Reconstruction Act. Even this ruling did not avoid all difficulties, however, as troops had to be called out to prevent violence when Republicans in the Louisiana legislature tried to make all members take an oath of wartime loyalty. At the other extreme, Meade was criticized for refusing to review the decision of the Georgia legislature to seat all of its members even though the eligibility of some of them under the Fourteenth Amendment was subject to question. Despite these problems, the legislatures of all seven states quickly ratified the Amendment, and the military turned authority in all of them over to the new state governments by the end of July. Over Democratic protests that the whole process had been unconstitutional, representatives of all seven states were then admitted to Congress before the adjournment of the session.[29]

In the remaining three states the completion of reconstruction was to be delayed for another year. The great distances involved in Texas, and its relatively less developed state, had kept it lagging behind the rest of the South since 1865. Its constitutional convention did not meet until June 1, 1868, and then disputes within the Republican ranks and a long recess would keep it from completing its work until 1869. The Virginia convention, in contrast, had met before most of the others, but had also turned out to be one of the longest, remaining in session until mid-April, 1868. Its proposed constitution contained one clause that aroused particularly strong opposition. Although the convention only disfranchised those covered by the disqualification clause of the Fourteenth Amendment, it required an ironclad oath of all officeholders. Schofield warned that this provision would make it totally impossible to find enough qualified men to run the state, and he strongly urged the convention to rescind it. But the delegates refused to take his advice, and he retaliated after the convention adjourned by refusing to hold an election, giving as his grounds the fact that neither the convention nor Congress had voted the necessary funds. He then attempted to obtain permission to submit the disqualification clause to the voters as a separate item, while Virginia Republicans persuaded the House to pass a bill setting a definite date for an election. But neither action was successful, moderate Republicans in the Senate refusing to accept the House bill apparently because they feared either that ratification would be defeated or the Democrats would carry the state in November.[30]

That fears of defeat were well founded was proven in Mississippi. The convention there, the last to adjourn except for that in Texas, provided for disfranchisement and disqualification provisions very similar to those in Virginia. An election to ratify this constitution was held on June 22d, and despite the fact that the state had the second highest percentage of black population in the South, the conservatives won their only clearcut victory there. The constitution was defeated by over 7,000 votes and the Democratic candidate elected governor by an even larger margin. Republicans charged that this unexpected result was the product of widespread violence and intimidation in the interior portions of the state, and some credence is given this accusation by the fact that there were 20,000 less votes cast in favor of ratification than there had been for the calling of the convention.[31]

In the closing days of the session, Congress attempted to deal with these three states, the Senate passing a bill to require the ironclad oath of all officials in Virginia and Texas, while a House-passed measure would have given control of all three to their constitutional conventions. There was no time for final action, however, and thus the three remained under the control of their district commanders. The only step taken in relation to them was the passage of a law prohibiting the counting of their votes in the Electoral College. In these last weeks Congress also passed a concurrent resolution declaring the Fourteenth Amendment ratified and forcing its promulgation by Seward. After providing for another session on September 21st, if needed, Congress adjourned on July 27th.[32]

CHAPTER SEVEN

FINANCIAL QUESTIONS

While the issues of reconstruction and impeachment dominated the second session of the Fortieth Congress, there was also a growing awareness of the importance of dealing with the financial problems facing the country. As Congress met in December, 1867, there was particular urgency in demands for action on economic measures, as the long business decline that had begun at the end of the war reached its nadir in that month.[1] But although many measures were considered on a wide range of subjects related to the economy, only a few were passed. The main result of the session was to indicate the areas of conflict on these issues, leaving their resolution to the future.

The most immediate demand was for the repeal of the contraction policy which many blamed for the downturn. As has been seen, early in 1867, the House had declared itself against that policy in principle, but it had gone no further as the representatives had been unable to agree on a bill. Before a week of the new session went by, however, a measure forbidding further reduction in the currency was passed, 127–32. Republican leadership in the anti-contraction movement was again evident, as they supported the bill 103–17, while the Democrats divided 24–15 in favor of it. The sectional division was now also extremely clear as westerners supported the bill nearly unanimously, the opposition votes coming almost entirely from the Northeast. The Senate, on January 15th, passed a similar measure by the equally one-sided vote of 33–4, all of the opposing votes coming from New England and New York. There was some speculation that Johnson would veto the bill, on the grounds that it was the opening wedge for currency expansion and debt repudiation, but instead the President let it become law without his signature.[2]

His decision not to sign it was a reflection of the continued commitment to rapid specie resumption of Secretary of the Treasury

McCulloch, who still hoped that the greenbacks could be made fully redeemable in gold by mid-1869 at the latest. This was a goal that was also supported by an influential part of the eastern business community, but Congress gave virtually no consideration to various measures which were introduced to accomplish this purpose. The same was true in regard to bills proposed by those who were not satisfied with just ending contraction, but wanted, in addition, a degree of currency expansion. The plans of the latter varied from relatively minor expansion, to be achieved by forcing the Treasury to reduce the amount of money it was holding in its vaults, to more serious measures involving an increase in the authorized circulation of the national bank notes or the greenbacks. They had equally little success in obtaining congressional action, however, and the policy of maintaining existing levels of currency, without either expansion or contraction, prevailed.[3]

This Congress, as had its predecessors, also dealt with the complex tax structure that had been created during the war. Revenue acts in 1866 and 1867 had eliminated many excise taxes and reduced the income tax to a uniform 5% on all incomes over $1,000. At this session a special tax on cotton was repealed and almost all of the remaining taxes on manufacturing were replaced by a .2% tax paid by manufacturers on sales over $5,000. Later in the session the tax on whiskey was also reduced from $2.00 to $.50 a gallon, a reform urged by Special Revenue Commissioner David Wells on the grounds that the prior high tax had encouraged widespread evasion and corruption. Action proved impossible, however, on a bill to consolidate the internal tax laws, which was put off until the next session. Also postponed was any attempt to revise the wartime tariff, a particularly complex and controversial problem which Congress had been attempting to resolve since mid-1866, with no result except passage of the protectionist Wool and Woolens Act of 1867.[4]

But the major financial issue in both the congressional session and the political campaign that followed was the national debt. The subject was introduced into Congress at the very beginning of the session when Republican Senator George F. Edmunds of Vermont proposed a resolution promising repayment of the bond principal in gold, and Democrat Thomas A. Hendricks of Indiana offered an amendment favoring payment in currency. Congress, however, took no action on these general resolutions, turning instead to specific proposals for the refunding of the debt. A variety of plans was offered, including one by Secretary McCulloch, but attention focused on the report of the Senate Finance Committee made by its Republican chairman, John Sherman of Ohio, in February. Sherman was a major western spokesman on financial questions who had been one of the earliest opponents of the contraction policy. In addition he had close relations with Jay Cooke and agreed with the latter that it was desirable to refund the debt prior to contraction or resumption, in order for the government to obtain the benefit of the gold premium in the sale of the new bonds. Responding to growing pressure from his own section, Sherman had also publicly stated his belief that payment of the 5–20s in greenbacks might be both legal and justifiable. But he hoped to avoid the necessity for such action, which some would view as partial repudiation, by his proposed funding plan.[5]

The essential feature of the committee bill was the issuance of a new 5% bond, redeemable in ten years and payable in forty, with the principal tax exempt and both interest and principal payable in gold. The new bonds were to be used solely for the redemption of the existing debt and the 5–20s could be exchanged directly for them, but this conversion privilege had to be exercised within six months of the time the 5–20 bond became redeemable. The proposal was thus an effort to avoid entirely the issue of how the 5–20s should be paid by convincing the bondholders to give up their 6% bonds, which might be paid in currency, in return for 5% bonds, with gold repayment guaranteed. After much discussion, however, the Senate was unable to agree on this bill, and the subject was then dropped until after the national party conventions. Nor was action taken at this time on a proposal by Republican Congressman John A. Logan of Illinois that a 2% tax be put on the bond principal, an oblique way of reducing the government's interest expense by one third. But support for such a measure was so great that Secretary McCulloch, while attacking any tax on the existing debt as a breach of faith with the bondholders, incorporated in his own refunding plan a 1% tax on any new bonds, to be levied by the federal government and turned over to the states.[6]

While Congress considered specific legislative proposals to deal with these financial questions, their political importance continued to grow. As has been seen, they had already begun to influence the parties in 1867, with westerners more likely to respond to them than easterners and Democrats more likely to favor repayment of the bonds in greenbacks than Republicans. As these trends continued through the beginning of 1868, the movement in favor of the latter proposal became almost irresistible within the Democratic Party in the West. Immediately after the November elections, the Chicago *Times* had seemed to be moving away from its carefully maintained neutrality into opposition to any plan for payment of the bonds in greenbacks. It linked such plans with radical Republican extremism and stated that Benjamin Butler and the "Cincinnati Plan" proposed simply to keep the presses going "so long as rags and lampblack hold out." But the paper withheld final judgment on the greenback payment issue, maintaining that it was one of policy and not principle, on which the public had not yet made up its mind. Then, on December 31st, following endorsement of the Pendleton Plan by local meetings throughout the Midwest, it declared that the Democrats of the section were almost unanimous in support of the proposal. In a letter that reveals much about the thinking of those western Democrats who now shifted their position, Wilbur Storey of the *Times* explained to Manton Marble of the New York *World* that they could worry about sound economics after the fall elections, the only important thing now was to win.[7]

The strength of this trend became clear during the first part of 1868, as Democratic state conventions in the great majority of the western states came out in favor of paying the bonds in greenbacks. But whereas Pendleton had originally emphasized the emission of just enough greenbacks to redeem the bonds that were securing the bank notes, only in Ohio and Minnesota did the platform planks make this qualification. Elsewhere, there was an evident willingness to accept a degree of currency expansion in response to the popular feeling that prosperity and paper money were interrelated, even though it meant moving that much further away from hard money principles. Thus the Chicago *Times* said that the war had shown that the country could absorb more money than had previously been thought feasible, while Wilbur Storey expressed the fear that Congress might actually authorize more currency and deprive the Democrats of a valuable issue. The Democratic candidate for governor of Illinois saw no danger to the economy in issuing enough greenbacks to redeem all of the bonds as quickly as they matured, and a Democratic Congressman thought that the country could use double the amount of currency that it had. At the same time in Ohio both the Cleveland *Plain Dealer* and the Cincinnati *Enquirer* were calling for repayment of the debt as quickly as possible without "too great" an inflation, and the Democratic convention in Iowa endorsed redemption of the bonds "as rapidly as they become due, or the financial safety of the country will permit." [8]

Although the East continued to be the center for the opposition to these proposals within the Democratic Party, support for them existed in that section also. Democratic state conventions in Maine and Pennsylvania endorsed taxation of the bonds and their payment in currency, while there were even reports that many delegates in the New York convention favored such planks and Democratic members of the New York state assembly voted overwhelmingly for a resolution supporting both measures. On the other hand those opposed to these planks couched their position in less than absolute terms. The legality of payment in greenbacks seems to have been conceded even by August Belmont, the Democratic national chairman and leading New York banker who personified the ties between the party and the financial community. The New York *World* also took basically the same stand, opposing greenback payment on policy grounds, but stating that the issue was not one of principle. Reflecting these views the Democratic state convention in New York voted to take no stand on financial issues, leaving all such questions to the national convention. The same was done in Massachusetts, while Democrats in Connecticut opposed repudiation, but favored paying the debt "in the manner provided by law." It was only in New Jersey that the wording was used, calling for maintenance of the national debt "inviolate," which normally indicated strong opposition to the payment of the debt in greenbacks.[9]

This failure of the eastern state parties to take a strong stand also seems to reflect recognition by those who favored payment in gold that they would be a minority at the national convention. Therefore, rather than pressing for a plank embodying their own views on the issue, they argued that the party should be silent on it and turn to other financial questions. The New York *World* and Horatio Seymour developed in detail the type of financial platform they would like to see. The latter, in speeches to the New York state convention and a mass meeting in Cooper Institute, tried to make economy in government, rather than the debt, the focus of the Democratic financial policy. He charged that reconstruction and extravagance were costing the taxpayers far more than was involved in the bond payment question. If the federal budget were reduced and financial responsibility shown, he contended, it would be possible to return to a specie basis without contraction. There would then be no fall in prices, but one currency, in the form of gold, would be established for both the bondholder and the ordinary citizen. The *World* agreed that there was no need for the party to adopt a platform on the bond issue as the country would not be prepared to pay the debt for another fifteen to twenty years, and it warned that the plank desired by the westerners would needlessly cost the party many votes in the East.[10]

The easterners argued that the differences within the party on financial questions were small, and they hoped that in the interest of harmony the westerners would not ask for a specific endorsement of the greenback plank. The westerners were equally anxious to maintain party harmony by minimizing the significance of the split, but they were convinced that they needed a greenback plank in order to carry their own states in the fall. At the national convention in New York City in July the latter, as expected, controlled the Resolutions Committee by a wide margin as they had the support of the South and each of the western states cast the same single vote as the far more populous eastern states. They therefore defeated a noncommittal financial plank and proposed a greenback platform which was adopted by the convention without debate or objection. It called for the repayment of all bonds in currency unless the law specified payment in gold, the taxation of bonds equally with other property, and one currency for all.[11]

On the other side, Republicans in general continued to be less receptive to the demand for repayment of the bonds in greenbacks, as has been discussed previously. During the 1867 campaign the Pendleton Plan had been almost unanimously opposed by even western Republicans. But after the elections the latter, in particular, were subject to continuing pressure from constituents warning them of the strength of demands for relief from financial burdens. The point was given added emphasis in January, when the Republican candidate in a special congressional election in Ohio endorsed payment of the bonds in greenbacks and won a larger victory than had been expected. One response to the mood of the West was the decision of Speaker Colfax to appoint Robert Schenk chairman of the House Committee on Ways and Means, rather than James Garfield who was still in favor of contraction and specie resumption. The influence of the popular mood was also seen in the statements by John Sherman on payment of the bonds in currency, which have already been discussed, and the endorsement of such a method of repayment by the Republican state conventions in Indiana and Ohio, which met on February 20th and March 4th, respectively.[12]

But this was as far as the movement went among western Republicans prior to the national convention. The major Republican paper in the section, the Chicago *Tribune,* took a firm and unwavering stand against payment in greenbacks, and no other state platform copied the example of Indiana and Ohio. Rather, they tended to be silent on the question or to contain general statements in favor of maintaining the public credit. In the East, Stevens and Butler continued to favor the greenback plan, but they still found little support. Strong pressure was brought on the other side by the bankers, who threatened to call in all of their loans if Congress acted on the Pendleton Plan, and in particular by Jay Cooke, a heavy contributor to the Republican Party who not only had a financial interest in the bonds, but who also felt that his personal integrity was at stake. For these and the reasons previously discussed those eastern state platforms that dealt with the issue contained strong planks calling the national debt a "sacred obligation" which must be held "inviolate" and paid in full good faith, according to the spirit of the contract.[13]

The relative weight of the opposing opinions in the party was accurately reflected in the national platform, which was largely based on resolutions adopted by the Illinois state convention. While not specifically endorsing repayment in gold, it did denounce all forms of repudiation and call for repayment of the debt "in the utmost good faith . . . , not only according to the letter, but the spirit of the laws under which it was contracted." The platform in addition stated that redemption of the debt should be spread out over a number of years, thereby lessening the importance of the issue, and warned that any form of repudiation would be more costly in the long run as the government would have to continue paying high rates of interest. While clearly a defeat for those in the party who favored redemption in greenbacks, it was still possible for the latter to live with these planks as they could argue that their proposals did not involve repudiation but were consistent with the spirit of the contract.[14]

After their national convention some Republicans evidently felt that they could not enter the campaign solely on the basis of the national platform and the laws already passed. Joseph Medill of the Chicago *Tribune* strongly urged that a small tax be put on the bonds, and the House of Representatives, by a 92–54 vote, actually instructed the Committee on Ways and Means to report a bill for a 10% tax on bond interest. But this measure, which had been supported by all but one Democrat and the large majority of western Republicans, was not acted on when reported. The reasons for this are not altogether clear, but it would seem that in the interim the forces opposing the tax had had a chance to organize, and wavering members were probably influenced by a strong statement against the bill by the Ways and Means Committee itself. In the Senate, meanwhile, a bill was under consideration to raise the limit on total national bank note circulation by $20 million in order to aid the southern and western states that had not received a fair share in the original allocation. Objections were raised to even this

degree of currency expansion, however, so that the final form of
the Senate bill provided for an equal amount of notes to be taken
from the states that had an excess of the distribution, and the
House took no action at all on the measure.[15]

In the closing weeks of the session, both Houses did manage to
agree on a funding bill. Based on a new proposal made by John
Sherman, the final version of the bill, as approved by both Houses
on July 25th, provided for new 30 and 40 year bonds, paying 4½
and 4% interest, respectively, both interest and principal payable
in gold. They were to be exempt from all taxes, except the normal
income tax on the interest, and were to be used solely for the redemption of the 5–20s, par for par. There was no threat that the existing bonds might be paid in greenbacks, although the legality of
such an action was left open, but the bondholders were offered security and a long term bond in return for accepting a much reduced interest rate. However, there was little chance that the
bondholders would take advantage of the offer at the time, so that
there was little stir created when Johnson killed the bill by a
pocket veto. His action, reportedly based on opposition to the ex-
emption from taxes, also had the effect of leaving the debt an open
question for the presidential campaign.[16]

CHAPTER EIGHT

THE DEMOCRATIC NOMINATION

In contrast to the Republican presidential nomination, for which a serious contest never developed, the Democratic selection was made only after a wide-open struggle, with a large field of contenders and the result uncertain until the very moment at which the choice was made. The contest over the nomination reflected divisions within the party as to the best strategy to follow in the campaign. Democratic hopes for victory, which had been kindled by their gains in 1867, flared even higher in the spring of 1868 when they again carried Connecticut and reduced the Republican plurality in New Hampshire even though it was now clear that Grant would head the Republican national ticket and his name had been used liberally by that party in both state campaigns. The Democrats received further encouragement in June when they captured the state legislature and congressional seat in Oregon and elected the mayor in Grant's hometown, Galena, Illinois.[1]

But despite these victories, which showed a continuing general trend in their favor, Democrats still faced the problem of adopting a specific platform and ticket that would maximize their support and gain a majority of the popular votes in states that cast a majority of the electoral votes. The only states they were certain to win were Delaware, Maryland, and Kentucky, with a total of twenty-one electoral votes. In addition, they had a reasonable chance in those states where they had elected their state-wide ticket or captured the legislature within the last year, Connecticut, New York, Pennsylvania, Ohio, New Jersey, Oregon, and California. But even if they managed to win all of these, they would still have only 122 votes, which would be two short of the number required if the southern states were excluded from the count. However, if the Republicans were sure of carrying the South they would readmit those states, with their seventy electoral votes, prior to the election, increasing even further the number of votes the Democrats would have to gain elsewhere.

As that base figure of 122 votes included all of the mid-Atlantic states, while New England was safely Republican and it was assumed that the South would only be counted if it were also, the only place for the Democrats to pick up votes was in the Midwest. On this basis, midwestern Democrats urged that both the nominee and the issues be chosen with a view to gaining the greatest strength in their section. Soon after the Ohio election the Cincinnati *Enquirer* suggested that the man be George H. Pendleton, on a platform stressing financial questions. The Ohio convention, meeting on January 8, 1868, instructed its delegation to vote for him, while that of Indiana, on the same day, stated that he was a "true and consistent Democrat . . . who has our entire confidence and preference." In the succeeding months the Pendleton movement grew rapidly, as many western and border conventions either endorsed him or selected delegations known to be in his favor. His position as the leading contender was soon commanding, as through the end of May no other candidate was able to obtain an official endorsement from any Democratic state convention. Sentiment for Pendleton was even reported in Maine, Massachusetts, New Hampshire, and Pennsylvania, while he and his supporters made a major effort to reach an understanding with the Democratic leaders in New York.[2]

The latter effort failed, however, as the East remained the center of opposition to Pendleton's nomination, with the powerful New York party taking the lead in the effort to find another candidate. Those who rejected Pendleton's financial theories, of course, played an important role in the effort to defeat him, but there were also other reasons for objecting to his candidacy. In Pennsylvania, for example, the convention had substantially accepted the western financial proposals but the state party had its own favorite sons for the presidency. Pendleton's opponents also made much of his position during the war, as he had been identified with the peace wing of the party and had been given the second spot on the ticket in 1864 in order to balance the pro-war stand of George B. McClellan. The basic argument they used against him was that he was a sure loser, because while he might pick up western votes with his financial policy that very program, in addition to his war record, would cost the party those eastern states that it had won in 1867.[3]

Rather than adopting a strategy designed solely to gain votes in the Midwest, eastern leaders, therefore, argued in favor of concentrating on securing the 122 electoral votes that the party was most likely to win, hoping that the South would either not be readmitted or that it would split. Only a small additional gain would then be necessary, which they hoped would be accomplished by simply permitting the reaction in their favor to continue unchecked. The nomination of a candidate with an acceptable war record, on a platform that did not deal with the divisive financial issues, would, they thought, encourage the continued conversion of Republican voters without alienating anyone already voting the Democratic ticket.

The anti-Pendleton group won a major victory when the National Executive Committee, meeting in February, chose New York as the convention site and July 4th as the opening day, over a western city at an earlier date. But finding a strong alternative candidate to Pendleton proved to be a very difficult task, even with the extra time available. One of the most likely choices was Horatio Seymour of New York, the ex-governor of that state and a major figure of long standing in national Democratic politics, who had some support in every section of the country. But whereas Pendleton had been the first to enter the race, Seymour was the first to declare himself out, stating both publicly and privately in November, 1867, that there were personal reasons why he could not be a candidate for the nomination. Despite this declination, which was repeated in February, 1868, Seymour's name remained prominent in all speculation about the possible Democratic choice. He had a history of publicly declining to be a candidate for nominations which he actually desired, and some thought that this would be the case again.[4]

A second man who had to be given some consideration was Andrew Johnson. As has been seen, the Democrats had no great regard for the President, feeling that he had shown both weakness and political ineptness since 1865. But he still controlled the vast executive patronage and he retained a potential for influencing southern events, so they could not afford to alienate him entirely. Thus, they had applauded his annual message and the changes in military personnel in the South, while faulting him for not having made better appointments in the first place. The impeachment might have upset this policy of keeping the President friendly but at arm's length by making him a hero to the Democratic rank and file. But this did not happen as the Democratic leadership, even further enraged by Johnson's failure to consult them before removing Stanton, made it clear that they were defending him as a matter of principle and not because they supported him politically. The National Executive Committee, which was meeting at the time of the removal, refused to make any comment on the situation or even extend its session to await developing events. While Democratic state conventions in the months that followed attacked impeachment and complimented the President, he was given serious consideration as a candidate only in his native Tennessee. Elsewhere in the North the Democratic press continued to oppose too close an identification with the administration.[5]

With Grant obviously slated to be the Republican nominee, other military men were considered by the Democrats. William T. Sherman and Admiral David G. Farragut, the other major heroes of the war, were both mentioned, but neither became a serious contender. Winfield Scott Hancock, however, became a strong and apparently willing candidate as the result of his actions as commander of the Fifth District. As has been seen, these had won him the plaudits of southern and Democratic papers and had resulted in a presidential message in December, 1867, recommending that Congress commend him for his devotion to constitutional liberty. At the same time there had been reports that Johnson would support him for the presidential nomination, and while these had proven to be untrue Hancock had developed great popularity in the South. A native of Pennsylvania, he was also expected to have the support of that state, and he had the additional advantages of both an excellent military record and clear-cut opposition to Republican reconstruction policies. But his candidacy had to struggle against a wide-spread preference in the North for the nomination of a regular Democrat who had remained within the party during the war. A military man seems to have been particularly objectionable to western Democrats, while it was felt that those voters who would be attracted by a military record would vote for Grant in any case.[6]

A dark horse possibility was Senator Thomas Hendricks of Indiana, to whom some New York leaders turned when Seymour eliminated himself. A westerner, from a state that would be crucial in the election, Hendricks was not as closely identified as Pendleton with either western financial policies or the Peace Democracy. While the endorsement of Pendleton by the Indiana convention kept Hendricks from entering the field openly as a candidate, his brother-in-law corresponded privately with Marble and Samuel J. Tilden, the Democratic chairman in New York state, and there were reports of increasing dissatisfaction with Pendleton among Indiana Democrats. It is unclear, however, whether the New Yorkers supported Hendricks as the eventual nominee, or simply as one means of stopping the Pendleton movement. During this same period, Tilden was also maintaining close relations with yet another contender, ex-Union General Frank Blair, Jr. of Missouri, and the two leading Democratic papers in New York, Marble's *World* and the Albany *Argus*, refrained from officially endorsing any of the men available.[7]

This was the situation in May when, with less than two months to go before the convention, no strong alternative to Pendleton had yet been developed. In the meantime, as has been seen, Chief Justice Chase had fallen out of favor with the Republican Party because of his handling of the impeachment trial. As early as March, some Republican papers had suggested that the Democrats were considering him as a presidential nominee, and Tilden seems to have made indirect approaches to him at about this time. But nothing further had been done and the suggestion had found little support in the Democratic press, which had been happy enough to have Chase split with his party, but had seen no reason to put him at the head of theirs.[8]

In April the possibility of Chase's accepting the Democratic nomination had again been raised, this time in private letters to the chief justice from Alexander Long, an Ohio Democrat of somewhat irregular standing who had bolted the party in 1865 in order to run for governor on a state sovereignty ticket. Chase had replied that he had absolutely no desire for the presidency, but he said if the Democratic Party would adopt a platform of universal suffrage, universal amnesty, and hard money, "I should not be at liberty to refuse the use of my name." Then, in May, public interest in the Chase candidacy was suddenly rejuvenated when the New York *Herald* endorsed him, and Horatio Seymour urged a meeting of upstate Democratic leaders to give serious consideration to the nomination of the chief justice. The possibility of such an action quickly became the subject of intense political discussion, with the major argument in favor of it being that Chase would draw large numbers of votes from moderate Republicans and southern Negroes, giving the Democrats the best chance to capture both the presidency and the House of Representatives.[9]

But despite the furor it provoked, the Chase movement was much less substantial than it appeared. The New York *Herald* was an independent paper, which had supported Lincoln in 1864 and Johnson after the war, and it reflected the views of no one but its publisher, James Gordon Bennett. The principal Chase organization, a committee of 100 formed at a meeting in Philadelphia, was composed of men of similar political standing. A list of those present at the organizational meeting shows no prominent Democrats, the two most notable men being Senators James Dixon of Connecticut and James R. Doolittle of Wisconsin, both of whom had been elected as Republicans during the war and then supported Johnson after it.[10]

Within the Democratic Party the main interest in Chase's candidacy came from New York. There some leaders of Tammany Hall, who were already planning to run Mayor John T. Hoffman for governor in November, hoped that the chief justice would help bring large numbers of voters to the state ticket. To other, more nationally minded men, including Seymour and August Belmont, Chase's nomination seemed to offer not only the best chance to win the presidency, but also a way to do it on the basis of policies they supported, moderation on racial issues and reconstruction and opposition to payment of the bonds in greenbacks. But at the same time Chase failed to win the support of two of the most important men in New York, Peter Cagger, who was particularly influential among upstate Democrats, and Samuel J. Tilden, who had inherited the state chairmanship from Dean Richmond in 1866 and was probably the most important single Democratic leader in the state. In no sense, therefore, was the New York Democratic Party as a whole committed to support Chase, and private correspondence shows that even major upstate leaders who were supposedly prepared to endorse his candidacy were actually mainly interested in stopping Pendleton and not in nominating the chief justice.[11]

But whatever the complications and hidden motivations involved in the New York situation, it proved impossible to create a significant national movement in favor of Chase as a strong reaction against his nomination developed. The chief justice, like Hancock, was subject to the objection that a regular Democrat should be nominated, and some threatened to bolt the party if he were chosen, stating that it would be a retreat from the principles they had defended throughout the war. Chase was, in addition, particularly objectionable to some because he had been an outspoken supporter of Negro suffrage for many years. August Belmont, seeking an accommodation on this issue, wrote the chief justice soliciting a new statement of his views. But Chase's reply, while making clear his opposition to disfranchisement and the use of military governments in the South, restated his support for the Congressional action requiring political equality in the reconstructed states.[12]

Those favoring at least the consideration of Chase's candidacy argued that the Democratic Party could accept this position, in essence returning to the suggestion that these same men had advanced in the spring of 1867 that the party not make a major issue of reconstruction and equal suffrage. The New York *World*, supported by the Chicago *Times*, suggested that with Congress about to admit the southern states neither their future form of government nor the Negroes' right to vote were any longer matters of national concern, and the platform therefore did not have to contain planks on either. But the reaction to this proposal within the party was somewhat similar to that of the prior year, as Democratic leaders in Ohio again took the lead in opposing it. The *World*, therefore, quickly withdrew from its position, stating that the disapproval it had provoked showed that the party did not agree with it.[13]

The editorials, said the *World*, had been a trial balloon to see whether Democrats were prepared to accept even the minimum change in their suffrage position that would be required if Chase were to be the nominee. As the party was obviously not prepared for such a change, the paper did not believe that he had a chance for the nomination, an assessment in which most observers concurred by late June. Another indication of the decline in the Chase movement was the failure of Seymour to include an anticipated public endorsement of the chief justice in a speech delivered in New York on June 25th.[14]

Objections to Chase had been particularly strong from the southerners, who stood in a special relationship to the Democratic Party. In that section the conservative state conventions of the winter and spring, in addition to organizing for their own elections, had also voted to affiliate with the Democratic Party and send delegates to the national convention. However, southern leaders and newspapers made it clear that they would not play an active role in New York, but would leave the choice of candidates to the northern delegates. Their main concern was that the Democrats win the election and then destroy, or permit to be destroyed, the new reconstruction governments. Among the Democratic contenders Pendleton seems to have been the popular favorite in the South because of his identification with the Peace Democracy, but they were quite ready to accept the eastern argument that just because of his war record he could not be elected. The essential thing, they felt, was to find the man who could win and as such a victory depended on carrying the northern states, they would accept the judgment of the delegates from that section with regard to candidates.[15]

But the flexibility of the southerners as to candidates did not extend to the question of the platform plank on reconstruction. If the Democratic Party did not expressly support the overthrow of the reconstruction governments, they warned, the South would see no

difference between the two national parties. They reacted vigorously against the suggestion of the New York *World* and the Chicago *Times* that congressional reconstruction was now a *fait accompli* which the Democrats would be powerless to change. In
South Carolina, where a Democratic convention in April had accepted qualified Negro suffrage, protests led to another convention
in June, which called for a white man's government and the restoration of the southern states as they had been before the passage of
the Reconstruction Acts. Many southerners, therefore, made it
clear that their stated willingness to support any Democratic candidate did not include Chase, whose selection they would view as
the abandonment of the South to Negro control. Others, while prepared to accept the chief justice if the northerners thought he was
the only man who could win, indicated that they would be much
happier if someone else were chosen.[16]

This was the situation as the delegates gathered in New York
for the opening of the convention. Pendleton had a very large
lead, but it was still felt that he could be stopped, especially if,
as expected, the convention retained the two thirds rule. With a
total of 317 votes in the convention, 205 would then be needed
to secure the nomination. Put another way, this meant that a block
of 113 votes was all that was needed to deny the nomination to
any man, with the eastern states alone controlling 105. As Pendleton would get very few of these votes, he would need virtually
unanimous support from the other sections if he were to win. These
figures also show the importance of the large states, New York
with 33 votes, Pennsylvania with 26, and Ohio with 21, inasmuch
as a combination of any two of them could supply roughly half
the votes needed to prevent a nomination.

As might be expected, the pace of events, and of speculation
about them, greatly increased in the few days preceding the convention. The pressure on Seymour to allow his name to be used
had greatly increased as other contenders had failed to develop
strength, and some believed that a speech he gave on June 25th
marked his entry into the field. But when the New York delegation
caucused on July 2d, he again positively declined to run, and it
then decided to vote for a favorite son, Sanford E. Church. Hen-

dricks had also been increasingly mentioned in pre-convention speculation, but he was removed from immediate contention when the Indiana delegation announced that it would continue to support Pendleton so long as the latter had a chance. It was denied, however, that Hendricks had positively refused to permit the use of his name, so that some continued to consider him a likely compromise choice while both the Detroit *Free Press* and the New York *Herald* predicted that Seymour would be selected.[17]

At the same time, Chase's supporters were actively pressing his name, despite initial reports from many sources indicating that he had little popularity among the delegates. An address was presented to the convention urging his selection as the man best able to unite all those opposed to unconstitutional tyranny, while statements by him endorsing state control of suffrage and promising to support the ticket chosen were circulated among the delegates.[18] The other candidates were not inactive either. Andrew Johnson, who also had men in New York working in his interest, wrote a letter indicating that he would accept the nomination if offered, and on the day the convention opened, issued a new amnesty proclamation which extended the executive pardon to everyone but Jefferson Davis. At the same time a letter from Hancock's private secretary was published, stating that although the general did not want his name used in antagonism to that of any other Democrat, he too would take the nomination. Frank Blair, Jr., who was something of a more remote possibility, also made his views known in a letter to a Missouri delegate, James Brodhead, that was to play an important role in later events. Supporting the southern position in full, Blair declared that it would be the duty of a Democratic president to declare the Reconstruction Acts null and void and to disperse the newly created southern governments, permitting southern whites to organize and regain control of their states.[19]

Before acting on nominations, however, the convention decided to adopt its platform, the Pendleton men undoubtedly hoping that a greenback platform would smooth the way for a greenback candidate. As they had the support of a clear majority of the convention on this point they had no trouble, as has been seen, in getting the financial planks they desired. On the major issues in other

areas, the platform demanded amnesty for all, the immediate restoration of all the states "to their rights in the Union under the Constitution," and state control of the suffrage, the last a noncommittal
plank which did not specifically attack Negro suffrage as some had
wanted. Another section, which was added at the insistence of the
southerners, characterized the Reconstruction Acts as "usurpations
and unconstitutional, revolutionary and void." While this statement satisfied southern desires, the New York *World* found it
equally acceptable, pointing out that it came as part of a general
condemnation of what had already been done without any promise
as to future Democratic action. The rest of the platform was rou-
tine, calling on all patriots to unite to prevent the destruction of
liberty and constitutional government that would follow a Republican victory in November.[20]

Then, on July 7th, balloting began for the presidential nomina-
tion, with the result still very uncertain. The first ballot showed
Pendleton leading with 105 votes, mainly from the Midwest and
border. Andrew Johnson was second, with 65 southern and border
votes, in what seems to have been mainly a complimentary gesture.
Well behind were Winfield Scott Hancock, with 33½ votes from
Massachusetts, Louisiana, and Mississippi, and the favorite sons,
Sanford E. Church of New York, Asa Packer of Pennsylvania, Joel
Parker of New Jersey, James English of Connecticut, and James R.
Doolittle of Wisconsin. Between them the latter group received 96
northern votes that were essentially being held until an acceptable
alternative to Pendleton developed. A total of six ballots was taken
the first day, during which Pendleton gained only 17½ votes. The
major loser was Andrew Johnson, who was quickly eliminated as a
serious contender. At the same time Thomas A. Hendricks began
to show scattered strength, having a total of 30 votes on the last
ballot, mainly from Vermont, Michigan, North Carolina, and Florida. On the fourth ballot Horatio Seymour received the nine votes
of North Carolina, but the ex-governor of New York, who had been
chosen president of the convention, again declined in absolute
terms.[21]

On July 8th the convention took ballots seven through eighteen.
Although again no decision was reached, the voting proved to be

decisive in one way, as it resulted in the elimination of Pendleton from the race. The chances of the Ohioan, which had already been hurt by his failure to receive any support from Michigan or Wisconsin in his native Midwest, were dealt an irreparable blow when the bulk of Indiana's delegates shifted to Hendricks on the very first ballot of the day. Despite this, his managers refused to concede, and he remained the leading candidate through the fifteenth ballot. During this long series of votes the Pendleton and anti-Pendleton forces in the north remained locked in a head to head confrontation in which neither budged an inch. On the fifteenth ballot Pendleton still had 92 of the 100 non-southern votes with which he started the day, while only 5 of the other 137 votes from the same area were cast for him on any of the ballots taken.

The major movement in the convention came from the southern delegations, who had no strong commitment to any candidate. A majority of their votes, therefore, slowly shifted to Pendleton as the leader, giving him a high at one time of 156½. But this was less than half of the convention's strength, and as it became clear that there was no place from which he could gain the additional votes needed for a two thirds majority the southerners drifted away again. By the sixteenth ballot Pendleton was reduced to the core of his northern supporters and a new leader, Winfield Scott Hancock, emerged. The latter remained the leader on the final two ballots of the day, reaching a high of 144½ votes on the last one. By that time almost half of Pendleton's northern and border votes had also deserted him, and Hendricks had moved into second place with 87 votes.[22]

Thus the final ballots on the second day represented the breaking of the stalemate and the third day would see an almost entirely new contest. Superficially Hancock seemed to have the best chance as he was far ahead of Hendricks, but an analysis of the strength each man had results in a somewhat different picture. Hancock had emerged as the leader essentially because he was extremely popular in the South, and as those delegations had moved away from Pendleton there had been no other strong candidate to attract them. The southern and border states had therefore gone to Hancock in very large numbers, providing him with almost two thirds of his votes on the eighteenth ballot. He had, in addition, an original base of about 18 votes in New England and since the fifteenth ballot had been receiving the 26 votes of his native Pennsylvania. But he had shown no ability to gain votes elsewhere in the North, and the value of his southern support was dubious as those delegates had repeatedly stated that they would permit the North to control the nomination.

Hendricks' strength, on the other hand, was concentrated in the North and was just beginning to develop. He had been supported by New York since the eighth ballot, after a caucus of that state's delegation had again rejected Seymour's advice to support Chase.[23] In addition, he had most of the votes of Vermont, Illinois, Indiana, Michigan, Kansas, and West Virginia, and he had received the support of Arkansas, Florida, and North Carolina in earlier ballots. But, most significantly, he had picked up most of the votes that had deserted Pendleton in the Midwest, and thus could hope to fall heir to the remainder of the Ohioan's strength there, which had just begun to break away.

Another key to the nomination would be the action of the three large delegations, New York, Pennsylvania, and Ohio. The efforts of Chase's friends had been heavily concentrated on the New York delegation, where, as has been seen, the chief justice had the support of influential leaders. However, an attempt to enlist Sanford Church in the Chase movement by a promise to recognize him as the Democratic leader in New York had failed, and the delegation caucus, as has been seen, had voted to support Hendricks. Despite this, Horatio Seymour continued to press for an endorsement of Chase, aided by reports that the chief justice regarded the platform as acceptable. Finally, on the evening of the 8th, the caucus agreed that if Hendricks' vote began to decline, New York would present the chief justice's name to the convention.[24]

An attempt was made to get Ohio to join this movement, but most of the leaders of that state raised strong objections. Not only was Chase a native of their state and an old political enemy, so that the argument that he could be elected probably scared them more than anything else, but they were also the very men who had objected most vigorously to the type of change in the party's posi-

tion that would be required if he were to be the head of the ticket.
The Ohio men were equally opposed to Hendricks, who they felt
had deserted Pendleton at a critical moment. In addition it would
seem that they still hoped to secure the nomination for Pendleton
in 1872, and believed that if they now cooperated with either New
York or Pennsylvania in the selection of an eastern candidate the
favor would be returned four years later. They thus first attempted
to create an alliance with New York in support of Seymour, but the
latter again refused to enter the race. Then, after formally withdrawing Pendleton's name when the convention reconvened on
July 9th, they voted unanimously for Asa Packer, the original favorite son of Pennsylvania. After this failed to bring the latter back
into the race, 11 of Ohio's 21 votes went to Hancock, the split in
the delegation apparently indicating the extent to which some
were still opposed to anyone but a regular Democrat.[25]

However, while Ohio was looking for an eastern candidate, the
rest of Pendleton's midwestern strength went almost entirely to
Hendricks, who jumped to a total of 107½ votes on the nineteenth
ballot. The contest now settled down to a two man race, with Hancock retaining a slim 135½ to 132 lead on the twenty-first ballot.
Considering the northern vote alone, however, Hendricks was
leading 104½ to 53½, and if the southern delegates would now
shift to him to the same extent that they had supported Pendleton
he would be only inches away from the nomination.

But it is hard to say whether the various floor leaders were
aware of this or whether they were more conscious of vote totals
that seemed to indicate a new stalemate. In any case, speculation
about a movement towards Chase continued, with some pressing
the New York delegation to nominate him even though Hendricks'
vote was still increasing. On the twenty-first ballot four Massachusetts votes went to the chief justice, bringing a storm of approval
from the galleries but no similar response from the floor. On the
next ballot Massachusetts passed in the initial roll call, while Hendricks continued to gain, picking up Nevada, Oregon, most of Missouri, and, most importantly, all of North Carolina. Then, whether
to prevent a move by the southerners to Hendricks or by New
York to Chase, Ohio suddenly cast its entire vote for Seymour. He

declined again, but was ignored this time, and in a sudden wave of enthusiasm state after state changed its vote in his favor until he was finally nominated unanimously.[26]

On the very first day of the convention the New York *Herald* had predicted that Seymour would remain aloof from the struggle, watching the other candidates eliminate each other while he himself remained on good terms with all, until he would emerge as the only available man and would permit the convention to force the nomination on him.[27] With the prediction so exactly fulfilled, and the New York delegation maneuvering in the convention in a way that could have been designed to prevent any choice at all from being made, it is quite plausible to suggest that the result had been planned from the start. But while many of the New York leaders undoubtedly desired Seymour's nomination, there is no available evidence that any of them actually expected that he would receive it. Rather, they seem to have operated on a day-to-day basis, working to prevent Pendleton's nomination while themselves remaining friendly with all, in the hope of coming out as best they could. It hardly seems likely that they could have anticipated and planned for the long three-day struggle, in which one major faction or another had objected to each of the other candidates.

Nor is there any reason to doubt the sincerity of Seymour's repeated declinations, which had gone far beyond the usual coyness of candidates for a presidential nomination. He had prevented his own endorsement by the New York state convention by insisting that he be elected as a delegate to the national convention, and had seemingly completely eliminated himself from the competition by accepting the presidency of the latter body. Before he could be nominated it had then been necessary to force him to leave the hall, and according to reports Seymour had cried out to a friend, "Pity me, Harvey, pity me," as he left. This strange reluctance to take a nomination that so many other men were fighting to get may in part reflect Seymour's conviction that he could not win. However, this explanation cannot be considered fully sufficient, as he had first declined in November, at a time when the political situation had contained hopeful elements. It therefore seems reasonable to conclude that there was an element of truth in the repeated rumors that there were medical reasons why he could not run, particularly as Seymour had suffered from ill health through much of his life. Without accepting the Republican claim that hereditary insanity was the problem, it must be noted that stories of a physical disability circulated among Democrats also, and that the New York correspondent of the Charleston *Courier*, who apparently had access to the inner circle of the Democratic leadership, stated that Seymour was under doctor's orders not to participate in politics.[28]

After the long struggle over the presidential nomination, the convention settled the vice-presidential race rather quickly. The executive committee of a Conservative Soldiers' and Sailors' Convention, which had met just before the Democratic convention, had urged the selection of General Thomas Ewing, Jr., of Kansas. But the South launched a campaign for another ex-Union general from the West, Frank Blair, Jr., undoubtedly because of his pre-convention letter to James Brodhead on reconstruction policy. Blair was endorsed by seven border and southern states, with speeches made in his favor by two ex-Confederate generals, William Preston of Kentucky and Wade Hampton of South Carolina. When, in addition, the New York delegation seconded his nomination, all other candidates quickly withdrew, and Blair received the nomination unanimously on the first ballot. The convention then adjourned and the stage was set for the opening of the presidential campaign.[29]

CHAPTER NINE

THE ELECTION OF 1868

By tradition a presidential candidate took no active part in the campaign, and this custom exactly suited Grant's own inclinations. The general left Washington late in June and he did not return until November, as president-elect. He spent part of this time at his home in Galena and the rest touring the West, where he made short and entirely nonpolitical speeches to the crowds that greeted him. During this period he took no part at all in shaping political strategy and cut himself off from communications on all but the most urgent army matters, enjoying what he described as "the most quiet, pleasant time . . . that has fallen to my lot since the opening of the rebellion." But before leaving Washington Grant produced one political document, his letter accepting the nomination. In it he endorsed the Republican national platform as both moderate and wise, but refused to deal with specific issues on the grounds that a presidential candidate should not make commitments which might limit his freedom to respond to changing conditions and the will of the people. Then he closed with a phrase that was to become the keynote for the Republican campaign, "Let us have peace." [1]

Again and again through the summer and fall, Republican orators returned to this theme, as they charged that Democratic victory would bring renewed civil war, while the election of Grant would finally end the eight-year-old conflict.[2] On the basis of the admission to Congress of representatives from eight of the eleven ex-Confederate states, Republicans declared that their program for reconstruction had been a success and was now almost completed. Renewed resistance to federal authority in the South had been encouraged by the recent revival of Democratic strength, but if the hopes of southerners for a Republican defeat were disappointed, they would be forced to recognize the futility of further opposition to the congressional terms for reconstruction. With the man who had defeated Lee in the White House, there would be no question of the will and the ability of the national government to enforce its demands and southerners would give up the struggle, permitting the readmission of the remaining three states and the complete restoration of peace and unity to the nation.

A Democratic victory, on the other hand, would reopen all of the issues that had been settled since the war and encourage extreme actions by the southerners. Blair's Brodhead letter, the Republicans claimed, showed that the Democrats were prepared to take revolutionary steps in order to restore the defeated rebels to power in the South. This charge was given additional weight when prominent southerners stated that the northern delegates at the New York convention had been prepared to give the South anything it wanted, while Wade Hampton told a New York audience that if Seymour proved to be the choice of the white voters of the country he should, if necessary, be inaugurated by force.[3]

Republicans insisted that the refusal of the Democrats and southerners to accept the conditions of peace made the issues of the war still relevant. They recalled the Democratic peace platform of 1864, saying that the Democrats had then declared the war a failure and favored peace, while they now declared the peace a failure and wanted war. The Democratic record of treason was compared to the Republican record of loyalty, and voters were urged not to permit the results of the war to be lost. This was particularly the theme of the innumerable soldiers' and sailors' committees organized throughout the North, who recalled the events of the war and urged veterans to "fall in" again behind their old commander and "vote as we shot."[4] Again the Republicans were aided by a number of ill-advised speeches by leading ex-Confederates, who identified the Democratic Party with the Confederate cause and made threats against northern carpetbaggers and southern Republicans. While the northern Republican press quoted extensively from these speeches, the independent New York *Herald* warned that they would cost the Democrats the election.[5]

There were also many personal attacks on Horatio Seymour, his wartime record in particular becoming an issue of the campaign. Republicans charged that as governor of New York he had not been vigorous enough in his prosecution of war measures, and a speech in which he had addressed the New York draft rioters of 1863 as "My friends" was much quoted. In addition, he was attacked for the circumstances under which he had received the Democratic nomination, it being claimed that he had either used Chase and then betrayed him or had shown extreme weakness in permitting his name to be offered when he had previously stated that he could not, with honor, be a candidate. There was also much speculation about why he had resisted the nomination for so long, with some claiming that it was because his health was so poor that he could not survive a year in the White House, while others revived stories that he had been afraid to take the office because of a history of hereditary insanity in his family.

The Democrats vigorously denied these charges of ill health, possible insanity, and misbehavior in obtaining the nomination, and they produced letters from Lincoln, Stanton, and other Republicans praising Seymour's contribution to the war effort.[6] But even as they denounced attacks against their candidate as underhanded, Democratic speakers and newspapers were engaged in an equally personal campaign against Grant. The old stories of drunkenness were revived, as was the charge that Grant had misused his influence in connection with his father's wartime trading in cotton. A specific appeal for Jewish support was made on the basis of Grant's order in 1862 expelling all Jews from the Department of the Tennessee. Nor were the Democrats prepared to concede Grant's role as the great military hero of the war, a series of articles in the New York *World* claiming that he had been a poor general who had defeated Lee only by throwing away the lives of thousands of Union soldiers. Military leaders, the Democrats warned, were becoming too powerful, and they quoted an unnamed high-ranking officer who predicted that if elected president, Grant would attempt to establish a dictatorship within a year.[7]

This charge of military despotism was also a major part of the Democratic campaign on the issue of reconstruction. They continued to attack the use of military governments and the change in the basis of suffrage in the South as unconstitutional, commonly referring to the new governments as "pretended" or "bogus." At the

same time they denied that the congressional program had succeeded in restoring peace to the South, charging, in the words of
Wade Hampton, that the Republicans offered only the peace of the
wolf to the lamb. Final restoration of the Union could only be obtained on the basis of the constitution, and the Republicans bore
sole responsibility for the failure to achieve this as soon as hostilities ended. In an exchange of letters between Union General William S. Rosecrans and a number of ex-Confederate generals,
headed by Robert E. Lee, the latter stated that the South had no
desire either to reestablish slavery or oppress the Negroes, but had
been willing since the end of the war to resume peacefully its
place in the government, if given its constitutional rights.[8]

Frank Blair, campaigning in the West, placed particularly great
emphasis on the issue of reconstruction. But it was less widely used
in the East, where some leaders were obviously anxious to disasso-
ciate the party from the doctrines of Blair's Brodhead letter. Seymour, in particular, avoided extreme statements on reconstruction,
stating in his letter of acceptance that a Republican Senate would
keep a Democratic President and House from making sudden or
violent changes, even if the latter wanted to. Similarly, Seymour
made no mention of racial issues, while Blair and other Democrats
made strong appeals to racist feeling, calling for "a white man's
government" and indicting the Republicans for favoring Negro
equality. These latter Democratic speakers also warned that black
voters would control the balance of power in the nation, claiming
that twenty senators from the southern states would be elected by
three million ignorant freedmen and have twice the power of the
senators chosen by the more than thirteen million whites of the five
most populous northern states.[9]

The campaign in the South was particularly vigorous, as conservative leaders urged their people to make every effort to secure the
election of a Democratic administration which would redress all of
their grievances. The Democrats showed particular strength in
Georgia, where they had united with moderate Republican members of the legislature to prevent the election of the regular Republican candidates to the United States Senate and to expel Negro
legislators on the grounds that the constitution did not specifically

extend the right to hold office to all. Conservatives could also be encouraged by victories in local elections in South Carolina and the defeat of the constitution in Mississippi, both in June. Their confidence was reflected in the demand by Democratic state committees in Virginia, Texas, and Mississippi that they be allowed to participate in the presidential election. In this they were rebuffed by the military commanders, who acted in accordance with the recently passed Electoral College Act.[10]

But Democratic hopes remained high in the other states, where they would be aided by the fact that the disfranchisement provisions of the Reconstruction Acts no longer applied. As has been stated, the state constitutions of Georgia, North Carolina, and Florida did not disfranchise anyone, while in Louisiana the only requirement was that certain classes of ex-Confederates take a recantation oath. This latter seems to have had little effect as Democratic leaders strongly urged their people to sign the necessary statement. The same was true where a promise to accept the political equality of all men was required, as Democrats were told that this meant only for so long as the present constitutions were in effect. In addition, the Alabama legislature voted to remove all disfranchisements in that state, while election officials in South Carolina were forced to admit that a close reading of the disfranchisement clause there showed that no one was affected by it. Florida Republicans responded to this growing Democratic strength by having the legislature choose the presidential electors, thereby avoiding the dangers of a popular contest. But a similar bill in Alabama was vetoed by the governor, so that there and elsewhere in the South the decision would rest with the voters.[11]

In their efforts to carry the southern elections, Democrats again tried to gain Negro support. Black Democratic clubs were organized throughout the South, and conservatives expressed confidence that this time they would be able to split the black vote. They appealed to Negro voters not to follow the lead of strangers and warned them that they had better seek the friendship of southern whites, who would regain power sooner or later. In return they promised the blacks equal protection of the laws, but generally not voting rights. In addition, whites were again urged not to employ anyone known to be a Republican. At the same time official Democratic statements uniformly condemned the use of force or violence. With an obvious awareness of the effect on northern opinion, Democratic leaders insisted that they wanted only a fair and peaceful test of the issues, and they warned their people not to give the Republicans a campaign issue like the New Orleans riot of 1866.[12]

Despite this, violence continued in the South, leading to the organization of militias in certain states and appeals for federal aid from others. With the readmission of the seven southern states the special powers exercised in them by the military commanders had ended, and the army in the South was again completely under Johnson's control. At the end of July the Department of the South, encompassing the states of the Second and Third Districts, had been created under the command of Meade, while Arkansas and Louisiana had been placed in the Department of Louisiana, to be commanded by Lovell Rousseau, an outspoken conservative. According to the federal constitution intervention to preserve domestic order could now be authorized only if requested by the state legislatures or, in emergencies, by the governors.[13]

As Johnson had already characterized the new governments as "illegitimate and of no validity whatever," Republicans at first feared that he would ignore requests for aid from them. But this threat did not materialize as he continued to let Schofield and the commanders in the field control the army's actions. Republicans received their first reassurance on this point when the President responded to a request for aid from the Louisiana legislature by issuing orders which had reportedly been drafted by Schofield without the consultation of the other members of the cabinet.[14] The local commander was instructed to keep himself informed of developments in his area while holding his troops in readiness to act, and the relevant sections of the constitution and federal statutes on the use of the army to preserve domestic order were quoted to him.

On August 25th, a copy of this letter was sent to all of the commanders in the South, along with an opinion by Attorney General Evarts that federal marshals could call on troops for assistance in the performance of specific duties, but not for the general preservation of order. The accompanying instructions stated that every request for aid should be sent to the President, if possible, but in an emergency situation the highest commander who could be reached in time was responsible for determining whether action was necessary. It was the obvious intent of these instructions to establish only the broadest outline of when action was permissible, leaving it to the local commanders to decide whether it was advisable in each particular case. In September the commanders were specifically told that the President wanted them to use full discretion, and Schofield further advised George Thomas, commanding the Department of the Cumberland, that in ordinary cases he could anticipate the President's order, as it was "only a formality required by the law." [15]

During this period federal troops were sent into Middle Tennessee to maintain order there, while Meade ordered the redistribution of the forces in the Department of the South, following requests for aid from Alabama, Florida, North Carolina, and South Carolina. The governors of Arkansas, North Carolina, South Carolina, and Georgia also issued proclamations asking their people to preserve the peace. But violence continued, the best known single incident occurring in Camilla, Georgia, where a number of blacks were killed when a crowd going to attend a Republican rally was attacked because it refused to surrender its arms. Tension was also high in New Orleans and the surrounding parishes, where there were sporadic racial clashes in late September.[16]

Although the President was making no effort to interfere with army affairs in the South, southern Republicans did feel, with some justification, that because of the conservative views of the major commanders the Republican state governments were not receiving the type of support to which they were entitled. Federal aid was particularly needed as the War Department was refusing to send arms to the state militias because of the section of the Army Appropriations Act of March 2, 1867, forbidding such organizations in the states then still unreadmitted. Some southern Republicans felt that the situation was serious enough to require the reconvening of Congress on September 21st to pass additional reconstruction legislation. But national Republican leaders, in the middle of the presidential and congressional campaigns, apparently felt that there was little to be gained and much to be lost by another session of Congress. The two Houses, therefore, convened only long enough to make provision for another session on October 16th, at which time it was again decided that there was no need for Congress to meet.[17]

While the Republicans concentrated on reconstruction as the greatest issue of the campaign, many Democrats, including Seymour himself, insisted that financial questions were of equal or even greater importance. Within the latter party there was general acquiescence in the greenback plank of the national platform, which was specifically endorsed by both a New York state convention and such major eastern leaders as Joel Parker of New Jersey and Sanford E. Church and John T. Hoffman of New York. Immediately after the national convention Seymour himself had pointedly stated his full approval of the entire platform, while Pendleton had come East to play a major part in the always important campaign in Maine in September. Some sectional differences on this question were still evident, however, as westerners continued to support currency inflation in order to repay the bonds, which easterners were not prepared to accept. There was also a marked contrast in the way the issue was used in the campaign, as easterners quoted those Republicans who favored greenback payment to show that it was not a party question, while westerners insisted that it was because the Republican Party was fully committed to payment in gold.[18]

In addition to the bond payment question, Democrats also made a major campaign issue of the charges of extravagance and fiscal mismanagement which Seymour had developed in his Cooper Institute speech on June 25th. The candidate himself, in his letter of acceptance, attacked congressional reconstruction principally on the grounds that it meant continued high military spending and delay in the restoration of normal business conditions, and he hinted at "wrongs in the financial management [of the country] which have been kept from public knowledge." Other Democrats quoted figures on government expenditures since the end of the war to show that Republican spending, even in peacetime, was many times greater than that of previous administrations, especially for the military services. As a result the national debt had actually risen by thirty-five million dollars between May and September, despite the unbearable burden of taxes the people were paying.[19]

Within the Republican Party the split on the question of repayment of the bonds continued. In July the Kansas Republican convention joined those few western states advocating payment in greenbacks, while Thaddeus Stevens said that he would vote Democratic if he thought that his party was committed to payment in gold. On the other hand Jay Cooke threatened not to give a cent to the party if it accepted the greenback proposal, and he seems to have represented the majority of Republican opinion which still tended to make it a moral issue of honesty versus dishonesty in dealing with the public creditors.[20] But, perhaps because of this split and a feeling that they were relatively weaker on this issue, Republicans generally emphasized problems related to reconstruction in their campaign, insisting that economic questions were a secondary matter.

The major Republican statements on the finances tended to be defensive, therefore, being concerned not so much with the debt as with the refutation of Democratic statistics on the budget and taxation. Relying heavily on figures supplied by Special Revenue Commissioner David Wells, they claimed that the Democrats had lumped many war-related expenses in with current Army expenditures in order to arrive at a greatly inflated figure for the cost of reconstruction. The Democratic Party, they charged, had brought on the war by its antebellum policies, and was therefore responsible for both the war debt and the more than $500 million spent since the war for bounties, pensions, and other war claims. On the other hand, the Republican Party, by astute management, had already paid a significant portion of the cost of the war, while it had reduced the financial burden on the people to a limited number of excise taxes and an income tax that was paid by relatively few.[21]

From the beginning the Republicans expressed complete confidence that their campaign would end in victory. They welcomed the nominations of Seymour and Blair, feeling that the Democratic ticket was weak and easily subject to attack, while they were sure that the New York convention had alienated those conservative voters whom the Democrats needed for victory. Their expectations on this latter point proved to be well grounded, as a number of men who had supported National Union in 1866 now publicly endorsed Grant, including the most prominent War Democrat in New York, John A. Dix. The Republican press claimed that this reflected an almost unanimous movement of conservative voters back into the Republican Party, and their belief in victory never faltered as the campaign progressed.[22]

On the Democratic side the immediate reaction to the New York nominations was decidedly mixed, except in the South, where both Seymour and Blair were considered sound on reconstruction policy. But in other areas there were many who thought that the ticket had little hope for success, midwesterners being especially disappointed at the failure of their own favorite sons. In addition, supporters of both Johnson and Chase charged that there had been trickery and bad faith in the convention, and for a short time there was even talk of organizing a third party. Although this threat did not materialize, as no prominent conservative supported it, Chase did remain neutral throughout the campaign, while the Democrats were able to mollify the President only with great difficulty. Even then the party received little benefit from administration support as certain members of the cabinet were known to favor Grant, and it was the Republicans rather than the Democrats who assessed federal officeholders for campaign contributions. Seymour himself delayed writing his official letter of acceptance for more than three weeks, apparently still hoping that the ticket might be changed. He alternated between conviction that success was impossible and faith that they would win a victory which, he said, he feared more than defeat.[23]

Through all of this, Democratic newspapers continued to profess optimism, and by August there seems to have been a genuine lifting of hopes in the party. By that time the situation in the reconstructed states was much more promising than could have been anticipated earlier in the year, and a victory in Kentucky by an unprecedented majority seemed to indicate that the South could at

least be split. If the Democrats could then do just slightly better in
the North than they had in 1867, victory was still possible. Dis-
counting the endorsements of Grant by conservative leaders, the
Democratic press insisted that large numbers of northern Republican voters were being converted, and the private correspondence
of Democratic leaders shows that at least some of them genuinely
thought that Seymour could be elected. They could be encouraged
in this belief by the fact that two independent observers, the
Round Table and the New York *Herald*, both of which had predicted a Republican victory in July, now gave Seymour a better
than even chance.[24]

As state elections in Vermont and Maine approached, however,
Democratic predictions became more cautious. The expected one-
sided Republican victory in Vermont on September 1st was dismissed as "the Dutch taking Holland," and Democrats insisted that
the significant fact was the drop in the Republican majority compared to 1864, rather than its increase since 1867. The Maine
election, two weeks later, was generally considered a much more
important test, and there some Democratic observers had at first
thought that their ticket might even be elected. But later reports
were gloomier, and Democratic papers again declared that they
would consider it a victory if the Republican plurality fell below
the average for prior presidential and congressional years.[25]

The Democrats therefore professed to see no reason for concern
when the election resulted in a Republican victory that was much
larger than that in 1867, but somewhat smaller than those in 1864
and 1866, insisting that the Republican majority of 1867 could not
be used as a basis of comparison because it had been greatly reduced as the result of local issues. By saying this, however, they
were acknowledging the incorrectness of the assumption that had
been basic to all of their predictions of victory in November, the
belief that the 1867 results had represented the start of a still continuing reaction against the Republican Party on national issues. A
better gauge of the true significance of the September results was
the reaction of the New York *Herald*, which had seen Grant's election as certain as soon as the Vermont results came in.[26]

Elections in Ohio, Pennsylvania, and Indiana on October 13th provided the next testing ground, all three being states in which both parties were strong and extremely hard fought campaigns had been conducted. In 1867 the Democrats had won major victories in October, electing their state-wide ticket in Pennsylvania and carrying the legislature in Ohio. But now Republican predictions in all three were very optimistic, while Democratic statements were much more cautious. The latter conceded that the Republicans had an edge in Ohio, while some Democratic leaders warned that either Seymour or George B. McClellan would have to tour Pennsylvania if they were to win there.[27]

On election day the worst fears of the Democrats were realized as the Republicans swept all three states, although the majority in Indiana was so small that both parties claimed victory for days and the Democrats charged that Pennsylvania had been carried by fraud. The critical point, however, was that the Democrats had lost in three states that they had to have in order to win in November, while it was now also clear that the 1867 reaction against the Republican Party had been reversed in every section of the country. The Republicans now considered the election virtually over, and they began to speculate about the division of the offices. Democratic papers, for their part, tried to put the best face they could upon the results, taking some consolation from a net pick-up of seven House seats and again emphasizing their gains since 1866 rather than their losses since 1867.[28]

But some within the party recognized that defeat was certain unless a drastic change was made. Since September a few Chase supporters had been insisting that the chief justice should be substituted for Seymour at the head of the ticket, and the October elections converted a number of leading Ohio Democrats to this view, including Washington McLean and Clement Vallandigham. At the same time the New York *World,* acting independently, made a thinly veiled suggestion that Frank Blair resign from the ticket in order to counteract the effect of Republican warnings of renewed civil war if the Democrats won. Coming as it did from a paper that was the spokesman for the New York Democratic Party, the latter proposal was taken as semi-official and received great attention. The evidence indicates, however, that the other New York leaders did not know of it beforehand. The Albany *Argus*, which was very close to Seymour, hastened to oppose it in order to make clear that the latter was not trying to get rid of his running mate, and Seymour himself declared that any change made in the ticket would have to include him. Both candidates also declared that they were willing to step down if the party thought it best.[29]

In this situation the question of dropping Blair was quickly lost sight of, and the only effect of the *World* editorial was to start an open public discussion of a replacement for Seymour. The movement for a new head of the ticket gained momentum quickly, as supporters of Johnson, Hancock, and Hendricks rushed forward to press the claims of their own favorites. But speculation continued to center on the chief justice. It was revealed that even before the publication of the *World* editorial, a private meeting of Democratic leaders in Cincinnati, at which Frank Blair had been present, had recommended the nomination of Chase, and the Cincinnati *Enquirer* now gave substantial status to the proposal by stating that the latter was acceptable to the mass of Democrats while the present ticket was sure to lose.[30]

It is possible to view this surge of support for this almost unprecedented suggestion as a measure of Democratic desperation and despair. But this is not fully sufficient, as other parties have gone into November divided and facing certain defeat without thinking of changing their tickets. There seems rather to be in the Democratic reaction more of an air of combined hope and frustration, as they had been beaten in October by a small margin and continued to think that if they could only put the right political combination together they would be restored to national power.

In any case the furor died as quickly as it had arisen. A part of the party press had from the first attacked the proposal as a virtual admission of defeat, and a study of letters written to Manton Marble shows that while there was general approval of his course for the first few days after the *World* editorial, a strong reaction against it appeared thereafter. In addition, while Chase was indicating to some that he might be willing to take the nomination on an independent ticket and with his own platform, he authorized one of his chief supporters in New York to tell the leaders there that under no conditions could he accept the Democratic nomination as the party was too strongly committed to a reconstruction policy which he found totally unacceptable. Indeed, with the national election only three weeks away there was scarcely time to reorganize the campaign, while such a sudden switch in political strategy might do irreparable damage to the party's unity. The New York leaders therefore moved to quickly end the discussion by coming out against any change in the ticket, a position also taken by the majority of the Ohio Democratic state committee. Seymour, saying that he had no desire to shift the burden of defeat to someone else, then agreed to stay on and make one last effort to revive the Democratic campaign by a personal speaking tour through western New York, Ohio, Indiana, Illinois, and Pennsylvania.[31]

Beginning on October 21st, the candidate traveled through election day, making a major speech in a different city almost every day. On financial issues he endorsed the party position on the bond payment question, but did not spend much time discussing it. Rather he repeatedly delivered a speech in which he attacked the Republicans for their extravagance, the heavy burden of taxation borne by workingmen, and the maldistribution of the national bank notes, which he blamed for most of the economic difficulties of the West. In addition, he denounced the congressional reconstruction policy, claiming that the violence occurring in the South showed that it had totally failed. In the latter stages of the trip he also returned to wartime issues, claiming that it had been the unconstitutional policies adopted by the Lincoln administration which had kept the North divided and thus made peace impossible as soon as the fighting ended.[32]

While the Democratic press claimed that their party was stronger than ever and that the Republicans feared the effect of Seymour's speeches, the tone of their own editorials as election day approached indicates that they were prepared for defeat. This was particularly true in the South, where the emphasis of conservatives shifted from dependence on a national Democratic victory back to the need to carry their own states. Within days after the October elections, Democratic state committees in both South Carolina and

Georgia attempted to increase their party's appeal to Negro voters by promising to retain Negro suffrage if they were given power.[33]

At the same time in Louisiana violence again flared, leading the governor to ask for military intervention on the grounds that the civil authorities could not maintain order. Instead General Rousseau banned political processions and arranged for James B. Steedman, a Democrat and former Union general, to become head of the city's police force. As a result the largely black force was replaced by one consisting of "stout, courageous white men," as Rousseau described them, and by election day the streets of the city were being patrolled by armed members of Seymour and Blair clubs. The state then went Democratic by a large margin, with the election itself relatively peaceful as Republicans advised Negroes not to attempt to vote, despite Democratic promises of safety. Elsewhere in the South great violence at the polls seems to have occurred only in South Carolina and Arkansas, Governor Powell Clayton of the latter state declaring martial law in ten counties the day after the election.[34]

In general, however, the November 3d election caused no great excitement, Grant winning an easy victory as expected. Seymour carried only New Jersey, New York, and Oregon in the North; Kentucky, Maryland, and Delaware in the border; and Georgia and Louisiana in the South, for a total of 80 electoral votes to Grant's 214. In addition, there is strong evidence that the Democratic victory in New York was the result of wholesale naturalization frauds, while sharp decreases in the Republican vote in certain areas of the South indicates that large numbers of Negro voters had been kept from the polls by force or intimidation.[35]

But on closer examination as shrewd an observer as James G. Blaine was impressed with the closeness of the vote, considering the year and the candidates, and it may be noted that three years after the successful conclusion of the war, the hero of Appomattox received just 52.7% of the popular vote compared to the 55% cast for Lincoln in 1864. The congressional races also showed a decline in Republican strength, as the Democrats made a net gain of twenty-five seats in the House, reducing the Republicans to less than a two thirds majority in that body. However, these figures may also be misleading, and to properly assess the meaning of the vote it is necessary to turn from the national results to a sectional breakdown.[36]

In the North, defined as the non-slaveholding areas of 1860, the most compelling fact is the stability of the party vote. In both the presidential election of 1864 and the elections of 1866, these states had given just over 55% of their popular votes to the Republican ticket, and Grant now received a 54.7% majority in them. Table 1, which shows the Republican percentage of the northern vote in 1864, 1866, and 1868, section by section, illustrates this fact. A significant change in party strength occurred only in the Pacific states, where the population was small and an influx of ex-Confederates seems to have taken place after the war, and in New England in 1866, almost solely as the result of a sharp drop in the Republican vote in Massachusetts in that year. The fluctuation in party strength does increase as figures are broken down to the state level, where a smaller number of votes are involved and local factors make themselves more evident. Still, in eleven of the twenty states, there was less than a 3% change in the Republican percentage of the vote from one election to the next, and most of the other nine states were in lightly populated frontier areas that were still receiving large numbers of immigrants.

TABLE 1   REPUBLICAN PERCENTAGE
OF VOTE 1864, 1866, 1868, BY SECTION

	1864	1866	1868
New England	63.3	59.0	63.9
Mid-Atlantic	50.6	51.2	50.5
Midwest	56.3	57.3	55.9
Pacific	58.2	52.2	50.6
Total	55.1	55.0	54.7

A comparison of the counties carried by each party in 1864 and 1868 results in the same conclusion. Of the 213 counties in the northeastern states, 142 voted Republican in both elections and 58 voted Democratic. No county moved from the Republican to the Democratic column, and just 13 counties, 6% of the total, switched from Democratic to Republican control, all but one of these being

counties that had been Republican in 1860. The same was true in
the midwestern states, where of 559 counties, 359 voted Republican
in both 1864 and 1868, and 157 voted Democratic. Thus only 43
counties, just under 8%, changed their party allegiance, the great
majority of them being counties going from Democratic to Republican majorities, with again most of the latter having voted Republican in 1860.

A study of county by county voting percentages in Ohio and
Pennsylvania also shows that what voter fluctuation did exist, occurred with a great degree of consistency throughout all parts of
these states. In Pennsylvania, the Republican percentage of the
vote decreased by .2% between 1864 and 1866, and then rose by
.8% in 1868. With 66 counties in the state, the change in the Republican vote varied by more than 3% from the state-wide average
in only 5 counties for the first period and 2 counties for the second.
In Ohio, where there were 88 counties, the vote fluctuated somewhat more as the Republicans lost 1.9% between 1864 and 1866,
and an additional .5% between 1866 and 1868. But the change
was again fairly uniform throughout the state, as only 12 counties
varied from the average by more than 3% in 1864–66, and 7 did
so in 1866–68. In both states these nonconforming counties were
varied both politically and geographically, so that there are too
few of them for us to attempt meaningful generalizations about
them.

This general political stability, however, could be broken under
certain circumstances. This becomes evident when the 1867 results are used as an additional basis of comparison, as Republican
strength in those northern states that held elections that year
dropped to 50.5% of the popular vote. As has been seen, this Republican decline occurred in every section of the North and virtually every state. Therefore, while the Democrats did benefit from
their use of economic issues in the midwest, this cannot be the sole
explanation for their resurgence. The party actually did best in the
mid-Atlantic states, carrying all three of the latter with an over-all
majority of more than 54% of the popular vote. It would seem reasonable, therefore, to relate the defection of Republican voters to
discontent with the advanced position taken by their party on is-

sues of race and reconstruction and to the fact that the 1867 elections involved state and local offices in which national political considerations would have their smallest influence.

The similarity of the Republican vote in 1868 to those in 1866 and 1864, however, shows that the party had succeeded in meeting the challenge of the 1867 results and recapturing the allegiance of those voters it had lost. With control of the presidency at stake, Republican leaders spared no effort to rally their full voting strength by invoking all of the war-related symbols available to them. The party, in addition, had consciously adopted a more moderate direction, recognizing the need to unify its own ranks as much as possible. At the same time there is some evidence that public opinion was becoming more favorable to the advanced Republican position, as in 1868, for the first time, equal suffrage referendums were adopted in two states, Iowa and Minnesota.

Another obvious factor in the Republican recovery was the vote-getting power of Ulysses S. Grant. As voting was done by a printed party ballot, all Republican candidates received essentially the same vote and it is difficult to measure Grant's coattails with accuracy. But Table 2, which compares the Republican vote in Ohio and Pennsylvania in October, 1868, with that in November,

TABLE 2   REPUBLICAN PERCENTAGE OF VOTE, OHIO AND
PENNSYLVANIA, 1867, OCTOBER AND NOVEMBER, 1868

	1867	O'68	Change	N'68	Change
Pennsylvania	49.9	50.8	+ .9	52.2	+1.4
Ohio	50.3	51.7	+1.6	54.0	+2.3

shows that the Republicans made a partial recovery in the earlier election and then much larger gains in November. The general feeling at the time was that there was a bandwagon effect which automatically increased the November vote of the winner in October, but this had not occurred in 1864 when Lincoln's vote had not been appreciably greater than that of the Republican tickets in the October states. Again the increase in the Republican vote between October and November in 1868 was remarkably consistent in both states, as the Republican percentage of the vote did not decrease in a single county, while their gain exceeded 4% in only two counties in Pennsylvania and seven counties in Ohio.

It is also difficult to assess the effect of economic issues on the relative strength of the parties, except to say that voter shifts in both 1867 and 1868 were similar in the East and the West, indicating that they were not primarily a response to financial questions. In addition, by the fall of 1868 the economy was moving up from the low point of the prior December, so it might be expected that voters were less responsive to appeals to economic interests. At this same time, as Robert Sharkey states, the farmers were still enjoying wartime prosperity and the relative position of the workers was actually improving as wages caught up with wartime price increases.[37]

In summary, the northern political system showed the overriding influence of the war. The Republican strength, however, contained soft spots and the party was not assured of the full support of all parts of its wartime coalition, as shown by the lower vote in October, 1868, and the loss of nine northern House seats in elections during 1868. But even with these declines the Republicans were still the normal majority party of the North, and under the right circumstances could equal their wartime high of about 55% of the vote. At the same time victory had clearly not added strength to the Republican coalition or destroyed the effectiveness of the Democratic Party. On reflection this is not surprising as the successful conclusion of a war has generally not brought great political benefits to the party that conducted it.[38] Men who had remained loyal to the Democratic Party through the difficulties of the war years were not likely to desert it now, especially as the issues, race relations and the powers of the federal government, were the same ones as had dominated politics since the antebellum period.

In the southern and border states, in contrast, the situation was much more fluid and political change was taking place at a much more rapid pace. Despite the fact that Grant carried the majority of these states, this was also the area of greatest Democratic success as the party gained sixteen congressional seats and Seymour received 51.5% of the popular vote in the border and 58.7% in the South. In addition there was every indication that this Democratic strength would continue to grow. In Missouri, Tennessee, and West Virginia Republican victory still depended on the continued disfranchisement of ex-Confederates, which was becoming increasingly difficult to justify or enforce. At the same time Republican dependence on black voters in the South was shown to be an unsure base for control of those states as whites in portions of Louisiana, Georgia, South Carolina, and Tennessee demonstrated their ability to systematically exclude black voters from the polls.[39]

If all of the southern and border states, including the three excluded from the election, had voted Democratic, as they were to do at every election from 1880 to 1892, Seymour would have won.[40] This has been taken as another indication of Republican weakness, but again it should cause no surprise. Just because the North had won the war, the ex-Confederate states were prepared to resume their place in the national government. If this area and the border states, where there were also large numbers of ex-Confederates, came under the control of the Democratic parties, it would mean that 117 electoral votes would be cast by those to whom Appomattox represented not victory, but defeat. Only forty-two additional votes would then be needed to elect a President, which was part of the reason why Congress had adopted its reconstruction program in the first place. Republicans knew that if their effort to develop a base for their party in the South failed, as of course it did, they would once again be a sectional party depending for success on their ability to win just over 50% of the popular votes in states casting just over 50% of the electoral votes.

But whatever the basis for Grant's victory, his election meant the end of one phase of reconstruction. Both Democrats and southerners now gave up their efforts to contest the validity of congressional reconstruction and accepted, however reluctantly, the authority of the new southern governments. Before the end of 1868 Virginia conservatives were moving towards acceptance of a modified version of their proposed state constitution. Elections in all three of the still unreadmitted states in 1869 resulted in the adoption of their constitutions by almost unanimous votes. On Grant's orders the disqualifying and disfranchising provisions in Virginia and Mississippi were submitted as separate items and the voters defeated them.[41]

The process of reconstruction mandated by Congress in March of 1867 had, therefore, been completed, with all that the Republicans had required accomplished. The result, however, was not the beginning of a period of harmony and understanding. The conflict for control of the South changed from a question of who would establish the basis for reconstruction to a series of struggles for political control within each state. But it continued to be as bitter and violent as ever, and in the eight years of his presidency Grant was to be unable to fulfill his promise to restore peace to the nation.

NOTES

Introduction

1. Eric L. McKitrick, *Andrew Johnson and Reconstruction* (Chicago, 1960); David Donald, *The Politics of Reconstruction, 1863–1867* (Baton Rouge, 1965); LaWanda and John Cox, *Politics, Principle, and Prejudice, 1865–1866* (New York, 1963); W. R. Brock, *An American Crisis: Congress and Reconstruction, 1865–1867* (London, 1963); Charles H. Coleman, *The Election of 1868: The Democratic Effort To Regain Control* (New York, 1933). A perceptive analysis of some of the historical problems involved is Larry Kincaid, "Victims of Circumstance: An Interpretation of Changing Attitudes Toward Republican Policy Makers and Reconstruction," *Journal of American History*, LVII (June, 1970), 48–66.

2. Howard K. Beale, *The Critical Year: A Study of Andrew Johnson and Reconstruction* (New York, 1930), p. 406.

3. The process of first deadlock and then compromise is described fully in Donald, *Reconstruction*, pp. 53–82; McKitrick, *Reconstruction*, pp. 449–60, 473–85; Larry G. Kincaid, The Legislative Origins of the Military Reconstruction Act, 1865–1867 (unpublished PhD dissertation, Johns Hopkins University, 1968).

4. Avery Craven, *Reconstruction: The Ending of the Civil War* (New York, 1969), p. 275.

5. Benjamin P. Thomas and Harold M. Hyman, *Stanton: The Life and Times of Lincoln's Secretary of War* (New York, 1962), pp. 471–565, *passim* (the quotation is from p. 534).

6. See discussion below, pp. 35, 67–70.

7. See Thomas and Hyman, *Stanton*, pp. 533–34, and discussion below, pp. 24, 34.

8. Craven, *Reconstruction*, p. 213; McKitrick, *Reconstruction*, pp. 486–91. An excellent recent survey of the literature on impeachment is James E. Sefton, "The Impeachment of Andrew Johnson: A Century of Writing," *Civil War History*, XIV June, 1968), 120–47.

9. In this I find myself in disagreement with Hans L. Trefousse, "The Acquittal of Andrew Johnson and the Decline of the Radicals," *Civil War History*, XIV (June, 1968), 148–61, who argues that the acquittal marked the beginning of the decline of radical influence on Republican policy.

10. Felice A. Bonadio, *North of Reconstruction: Ohio Politics, 1865–1870* (New York, 1970), *passim*. It is my opinion that Bonadio has taken the normal grumbling and poor-mouthing of politicians too seriously. Bonadio presents remarkable detail on the factionalism, in-fighting, and patronage struggles within the Republican Party, but errs in seeing these things as peculiar to the era rather than as a normal part of American politics.

11. The theme of northern racial prejudice has been fully developed in Leslie H. Fishel, Jr., "Northern Prejudice and Negro Suffrage, 1865–1870," *Journal of Negro History*, XXXIX (January, 1954), 8–26, and C. Vann Woodward, "Seeds of Failure in Radical Race Policy," in *New Frontiers of the American Reconstruction*, ed. Harold M. Hyman (Urbana, Ill., 1966). The motives of the Republican leadership are discussed in LaWanda and John Cox, "Negro Suffrage and Reconstruction Politics: The Problem of Motivation in Reconstruction Historiography," *Journal of Southern History*, XXXIII (August, 1967), 303–30; Glenn M. Linden, "A Note on Negro Suffrage and Republican Politics," *Journal of Southern History*, XXXVI (August, 1970), 411–21; Forrest G. Wood, *Black Scare: The Racist Response to Emancipation and Reconstruction* (Berkeley, 1968), pp. 92–93; and discussion below, pp. 11–12, 52–53.

12. For this view of the Democratic Party I am indebted to Professor Joel Silbey of Cornell University for a paper read at the 1968 Southern Historical Association Convention in New Orleans.

One: The Problem of Reconstruction

1. Text in Edward McPherson, *The Political History of The United States of America during the Period of Reconstruction* (Washington, D. C., 1871), pp. 121–22.

2. *Ibid.*, pp. 8–12, 18–25; Michael Dale Pierce, Andrew Johnson and the South, 1865–1867 (unpublished PhD dissertation, North Texas State University, 1970), pp. 15–23, 38–61, 113–47. Mississippi and South Carolina did not repudiate their debt, Georgia reserved the right to ask for compensation for emancipated slaves, and Mississippi did not ratify the 13th Amendment. In addition, action was not feasible in Texas until 1866.

3. A good recent survey of the debate on economic determinism is B. P. Gallaway, "Economic Determinism in Reconstruction Historiography," *Southwestern Social Science Quarterly*, XLVI (December, 1965), 244–54.

4. *A Compilation of the Messages and Papers of the Presidents, 1789–1897*, James D. Richardson, comp. (10 vols., Washington, D. C., 1896–99), V, 3343; James G. Randall, *Constitutional Problems under Lincoln* (rev. ed., Urbana, Ill., 1951), pp. 513–15.

5. On this subject see V. Jacque Voegeli, *Free But Not Equal: The Midwest and the Negro during the Civil War* (Chicago, 1967), *passim;* Hans L. Trefousse, *The Radical Republicans: Lincoln's Vanguard for Racial Justice* (New York, 1969), esp. chaps. v, vi, vii; David Donald, "Devils Facing Zionward," in *Grant, Lee, Lincoln and the Radicals: Essays on Civil War Leadership*, ed. Grady McWhiney ([Evanston, Ill.], 1964), esp. pp. 79–82; P. J. Staudenraus, "The Popular Origins of the Thirteenth Amendment," *Mid-America*, L (April, 1968), 108–15; C. Vann Woodward, *The Burden of Southern History* (rev. ed., Baton Rouge, 1968), pp. 69–77.

6. On Democratic activity during the war see esp. William G. Carleton, "Civil War Dissidence in the North: The Perspective of a Century," *South Atlantic Quarterly*, LXV (Summer, 1966), 390–402; Richard O. Curry, "The Union as It Was: A Critique of Recent Interpretations of the Copperheads," *Civil War History*, XIII (March, 1967), 25–39; Forrest G. Wood, *Black Scare*, chaps. ii, iii, iv, *passim;* Voegeli, *Free But Not Equal*, pp. 13–15, 54–55, 125–26, 141–44.

7. On the question of Republican motivation and response to southern events see George M. Blackburn, "Radical Republican Motivation: A Case History," *Journal of Negro History*, LIV (April, 1969), 109–26; McKitrick, *Reconstruction*, pp. 175–86; Kenneth Stampp, *The Era of Reconstruction, 1865–1877* (New York, 1965), chaps. 3, 4, *passim.*

8. For this view of the relations between the President and the southerners I am indebted to Pierce, *Johnson and the South*, esp. pp. 63–76, 83–89, 98–99, 104–7, 113–40.

9. See text of Johnson's speech on Feb. 22, 1866, in McPherson, *Reconstruction*, pp. 58–62. My own thinking on Johnson's motivation has been most influenced by Stampp, *Reconstruction*, chap. 3, although my emphasis is somewhat different. Pierce reaches the same conclusion in *Johnson and the South*, pp. 7–14.

10. The votes and the texts of the bills and veto messages are in McPherson, *Reconstruction*, pp. 69–81. See also McKitrick, *Reconstruction*, pp. 274–325, and Cox, *Politics, Principle, and Prejudice*, pp. 172–211.

11. For development of the Republican policy see McKitrick, *Reconstruction*, pp. 326–63; Joseph B. James, *The Framing of the Fourteenth*

Amendment (Urbana, Ill., 1965), pp. 37–152, 169–77; Benjamin B. Kendrick, *The Journal of The Joint Committee of Fifteen on Reconstruction* (New York, 1914), pp. 221–353. Party platforms are in *American Annual Cyclopaedia,* 1866, under state headings.

12. The best treatment of the relation between Johnson and the parties in 1865–66 is in Cox, *Politics, Principle, and Prejudice,* esp. chap. v. Also see Beale, *The Critical Year,* chap. iv.

13. The reaction of the Democrats to the President's policies is dealt with in Cox, *Politics, Principle, and Prejudice,* esp. chap. iii, and Edward L. Gambill, Northern Democrats and Reconstruction, 1865–1868 (unpublished PhD dissertation, University of Iowa, 1969), pp. 15–148, *passim.*

14. *Ibid.,* pp. 148–55; McKitrick, *Reconstruction,* pp. 410–16.

15. Martin E. Mantell, New York and the Elections of 1866 (unpublished MA thesis, Columbia University, 1962), pp. 49–79; Erwin S. Bradley, *The Triumph of Militant Republicanism: A Study of Pennsylvania and Presidential Politics* (Philadelphia, 1964), pp. 238–41; George H. Porter, *Ohio Politics during the Civil War Period* (New York, 1911), p. 232; Arthur C. Cole, *The Era of the Civil War, 1848–1870,* Vol. III of the *Centennial History of Illinois,* ed. C. W. Alvord (Springfield, Ill., 1919), pp. 397–98; Edith E. Ware, *Political Opinion in Massachusetts during Civil War and Reconstruction* (New York, 1916), pp. 163–64; Walter C. Woodward, *The Rise and Early History of Political Parties in Oregon* (Portland, Ore., 1913), pp. 251–54.

16. For the best general treatment of the campaign see McKitrick, *Reconstruction,* pp. 421–47.

17. Gambill, Northern Democrats, pp. 164–65, 175–84, 204–10; J. Cochrane to Johnson, October, 1866, J. A. Dix to Johnson, Nov. 8, 1866, Andrew Johnson Mss, Library of Congress; O. H. Browning to Doolittle, Oct. 13, 1866, James R. Doolittle Mss, State Historical Society of Wisconsin; Bonadio, *North of Reconstruction,* pp. 173–75.

18. Richard O. Curry, ed., *Radicalism, Racism, and Party Realignment: The Border States during Reconstruction* (Baltimore, 1969), pp. 17–19, 51–56, 93–94, 116–22, 161–69, 194–99, 228–32.

19. Party divisions from *Tribune Almanac,* 1867, p. 23. This is as of November, 1866 and does not include a full Congress. As the 40th Congress would normally not have met until December, 1867, elections in New Hampshire, Rhode Island, Connecticut, Kentucky, Tennessee, and California were not held until the spring and summer of 1867. On the defeat of moderate Republicans see Donald, *Reconstruction,* p. 60; Mantell, New York and the Elections of 1866, p. 88.

20. Gambill, Northern Democrats, pp. 210–14; Pierce, Johnson and the South, pp. 224–30; New York World, Nov. 16, 1866; statements in Arkansas and Georgia legislatures in American Annual Cyclopaedia, 1866, pp. 27, 352–53; New Orleans Picayune, Nov. 11, 16, 29, 1866; Charleston Courier, Nov. 13, 24, 28, 1866.

21. Chicago Times, Jan. 5, 27, 1867; Washington National Intelligencer, Dec. 15, 1866, Jan. 3, 29, 1867; New York World, Nov. 8, 9, 14, 17, 19, 30, Dec. 1, 7, 1866; Johnson to L. Parsons, Jan. 17, 1867, Johnson Mss, LC. Out of roughly 1,000 votes in southern legislatures, only 33 were cast in favor of the Amendment (McPherson, Reconstruction, p. 194).

22. 4 Wallace 2 (1866), 277, 333 (1867). The decision in the Milligan case had been handed down the prior spring, but the basis for it was not known until the opinions were given. Chief Justice Chase and Justices Swayne, Miller, and Wayne dissented on the question of Congress's power. In the test oath cases the dissenters were Chase, Swayne, Miller, and Davis.

23. The text of the compromise proposals is in McPherson, Reconstruction, pp. 258–59. Also see "Notes of Colonel W. G. Moore, Private Secretary to President Johnson, 1866–68," St. George L. Sioussat, ed., American Historical Review, XIX (October, 1913), 104–5; Charleston Courier, Feb. 8, 1867; New York World, Feb. 13, 1867; excerpts from southern press in Chicago Times, Feb. 15, 1867; Pierce, Johnson and the South, pp. 243–49.

24. For the process by which the Act was written see the references in introduction, n. 3. The texts of the original bill and the Sherman amendments are in Congressional Globe, 39th Congress, 2d Session, pp. 1037, 1459. Discussion of presidential powers in ibid., pp. 1099, 1208, 1319–20, 1330, 1369–70, 1462, 1562.

25. Ibid., pp. 1340, 1733, 1976; U. S. Statutes at Large, XIV, 428. The disfranchisement only applied until the states were readmitted.

26. Ibid., 430, 485; Thomas and Hyman, Stanton, pp. 525–28.

27. U. S. Statutes at Large, XV, 2.

28. Cong. Globe, 40th Cong. 1st Sess., pp. 308, 316, 319, 334, 389, 441, 454.

Two: Grant, Johnson, and Reconstruction

1. When the Sherman amendments were added to Steven's military bill another House passed measure was pending in the Senate which would have created a new government for Louisiana consisting of a governor

and a nine-man council, appointed by the President with the consent of the Senate (*Cong. Globe*, 39th Cong. 2d Sess., pp. 1128–29).

2. James W. Garner, *Reconstruction in Mississippi* (New York, 1901), pp. 97–98; William T. Alderson, The Influence of Military Rule and the Freedmen's Bureau on Reconstruction in Virginia, (unpublished PhD. dissertation, Vanderbilt University, 1952), p. 71; John Porter Hollis, *The Early Period of Reconstruction in South Carolina* (Baltimore, 1905), pp. 45–47; James E. Sefton, *The United States Army and Reconstruction, 1865–1877* (Baton Rouge, 1967), pp. 25–59; "Report of the Joint Committee on Reconstruction," *House Reports*, 39th Cong., 1st Sess., no. 30 (Cong. ser. #1273), part I, 108–11, part II, 141–44, part III, 26–28, 100–2, part IV, 122–24; Thomas and Hyman, *Stanton*, pp. 449, 465, 472–77; John Robert Kirkland, Federal Troops in the South Atlantic States During Reconstruction, 1865–1877 (unpublished PhD dissertation, University of North Carolina, 1967), pp. 52–59, 75–77, 84–86, 103–4, 331–41.

3. Adam Badeau, *Grant in Peace* (Hartford, Conn., 1887), pp. 25–30, 32–34; Albert D. Richardson, *A Personal History of Ulysses S. Grant* (Hartford, Conn., 1868), p. 378. Both reports are in "Condition of the South," *Senate Executive Documents*, 39th Cong. 1st Sess., no. 2 (Cong. ser. #1237).

4. "Removal of Hon. E. M. Stanton and Others," *House Executive Documents*, 40th Cong. 2d Sess., no. 57 (Cong. ser. #1330), pp. 57–60; Richardson, *Grant*, p. 521; McPherson, *Reconstruction*, pp. 122–24.

5. *Ibid.*, pp. 15–17, 194–96.

6. Leon B. Richardson, *William E. Chandler: Republican* (New York, 1940), p. 80; William B. Parker, *The Life and Public Services of Justin Smith Morrill* (Boston, 1924), pp. 229–30; Philip Kinsley, *The Chicago Tribune: Its First Hundred Years* (3 vols.; New York, 1943–46), II, 42–44; William B. Hesseltine, *Ulysses S. Grant: Politician* (New York, 1935), p. 63.

7. New York *Times*, Aug. 30, 31, Sept. 4, 5, 17, 29, 1866; New York *Tribune*, Sept. 14, 1866; Grant to Julia Dent Grant, Sept. 9, 1866, Ulysses S. Grant Mss, Library of Congress.

8. "Removal of Stanton," pp. 63–68; Badeau, *Grant in Peace*, pp. 49–52; William S. Myers, *The Self-Reconstruction of Maryland, 1864–1867* (Baltimore, 1909), pp. 67–76.

9. "Removal of Stanton," pp. 69–73; *The Sherman Letters*, Rachel Sherman Thorndike, ed. (New York, 1894), pp. 279–82; Badeau, *Grant in Peace*, pp. 53–54; "Notes of Col. W. G. Moore," pp. 99–102.

10. Sefton, *US Army*, pp. 101–2; Badeau, *Grant in Peace*, pp. 44–45, 65; New York *Times*, Jan. 14, 1867; Jesse R. Grant, *In the Days of My Father: General Grant* (New York, 1925), p. 49; *General Grant's Letters to a Friend*, James Grant Wilson, ed. (New York, 1897), pp. 52–54.

11. Chicago *Times*, Mar. 27, 1867; New York *Tribune*, Mar. 14, 26, 1867; New York *Times*, Mar. 15, 1867. Sherman, Winfield S. Hancock, George Meade, and Irvin McDowell had been suggested as more conservative choices (Chicago *Times*, Mar. 12, 1867). The districts and commanders were: 1st District (Virginia)–Schofield; 2d District (North and South Carolina)–Sickles; 3d District (Georgia, Alabama, and Florida)–Thomas (replaced by John Pope when he declined); 4th District (Mississippi and Arkansas)–Ord; 5th District (Louisiana and Texas)–Sheridan.

12. Badeau, *Grant in Peace*, pp. 60–61, 65–66; Grant to Pope, Apr. 21, 1867, Grant Mss, LC; "Correspondence Relative to Reconstruction," *Senate Executive Documents*, 40th Cong. 1st Sess., no. 14 (Cong. ser. #1308), pp. 15, 20, 96–104, 148–50, 193, 240, 244–46.

13. *Ibid.*, pp. 205–7, 211, 212, 214, 242–46; King to Johnson, May 2, 1867, Johnson Mss, LC; "General Orders-Reconstruction," *House Executive Documents*, 40th Cong. 2d Sess., no. 342 (Cong. ser. #1346), pp. 166–67.

14. Dated May 24 and June 12, 1867, "Correspondence Relative to Reconstruction," pp. 262–87.

15. Thomas and Hyman, *Stanton*, pp. 539–45; "Interpretation of the Reconstruction Acts," *House Executive Documents*, 40th Cong., 1st Sess., no. 34 (Cong. ser. #1311).

16. "Correspondence Relative to Reconstruction," pp. 9–12, 57–59, 107, 143, 237; Sheridan to Grant, June 22, 1867, Johnson Mss, LC.

17. Sickles to Johnson, June 10, 1867, Sheridan to Grant, June 22, 1867, Johnson Mss, LC; "Correspondence Relative to Reconstruction," p. 107.

18. *U. S. Statutes at Large*, XV, 14.

19. The provision that they were not bound by anyone else's opinion could not be taken to apply to orders from the commander-in-chief. In the Senate both Thomas Hendricks (D–Ind.) and Lyman Trumbull (R–Ill.) stated that the section was meaningless, *Cong. Globe*, 40th Cong. 1st Sess., pp. 626–27.

20. New York *Times*, July 10, Sept. 16, 1867; Philadelphia *Press*, Aug. 30, 1867; Charleston *Courier*, Aug. 20, 1867; "Correspondence Relative to Reconstruction," pp. 69–71.

21. McPherson, *Reconstruction*, p. 261; New York *Herald*, Aug. 3, 1867.

22. See discussion of Grant's action in New York *Tribune*, July 13, 1867, and New York *Times*, Aug. 19, 1867. Also see "Removal of Stanton," pp. 1–2; "Notes of Col. W. G. Moore," p. 109; *Diary of Gideon Welles*, Howard K. Beale, ed. (3 vols.; New York, 1960), III, 176–81; Apr. 5, 1867, W. G. Moore's "Small Diary," Johnson Mss. LC, ser. 9a, p. 32 of typed transcript. In October, 1867, Johnson again stated his belief that Grant was completely with the radicals, Welles, *Diary*, III, 232.

23. "Removal of Stanton," pp. 4, 7; McPherson, *Reconstruction*, pp. 314, 345; Badeau, *Grant in Peace*, pp. 566–69; Welles, *Diary*, III, 188–89; "Notes of Col. W. G. Moore," pp. 111–13; Hesseltine, *Grant*, pp. 95–96. It may seem strange that Grant could have so misunderstood the meaning of the law, but this error was common in newspapers at the time and has survived to recent years; see New York *Tribune*, Aug. 30, 31, 1867; Chicago *Times*, Aug. 22, 1867; Francis B. Simkins, *The South Old and New* (New York, 1947), p. 186.

24. J. G. de Roulhac Hamilton, *Reconstruction in North Carolina* (New York, 1914), p. 232; McPherson, *Reconstruction*, pp. 342–45. The proclamation extended full pardon to all Confederates except Jefferson Davis, Alexander Stephens, cabinet members, foreign agents, officers above the rank of brigadier general in the army and captain in the navy, governors of states, persons actually in confinement or on bail, and persons involved in the assassination of Lincoln.

25. Badeau, *Grant in Peace*, pp. 60–68, 102–5, 371; Thomas and Hyman, *Stanton*, pp. 534–35; Sefton, *US Army*, pp. 101–2; George K. Leet to O. E. Babcock, Aug. 29, 1867, Grant Mss, LC; Boston *Post*, Sept. 28, 1867; Hamilton, *North Carolina*, p. 234.

26. Chicago *Times*, Sept. 21, 1867; Philadelphia *Press*, Sept. 20, 1867.

Three: Reconstruction in the South

1. Thomas B. Alexander, "Persistent Whiggery in the Confederate South, 1860–1877," *Journal of Southern History*, CXXVII (August, 1961), 308–17; Walter L. Fleming, *Civil War and Reconstruction in Alabama* (New York, 1905), pp. 358–59; William C. Harris, *Presidential Reconstruction in Mississippi* (Baton Rouge, 1967), pp. 43–51; C. Mildred Thompson, *Reconstruction in Georgia* (New York, 1915), pp. 148–56; Hamilton, *North Carolina*, pp. 120–22; William W. Davis, *The Civil War and Reconstruction in Florida* (New York, 1913), pp. 354–68, *passim;* Richard Grady Lowe, Republicans, Rebellion, and Reconstruction: The Republican Party in Virginia, 1856–1870 (unpublished PhD dissertation, University of Virginia, 1968), p. 210.

2. New York *Times*, Mar. 1, 1867; Hamilton J. Eckenrode, *The Political History of Virginia During the Reconstruction* (Baltimore, 1904), p. 52; Charleston *Courier*, Mar. 20, 21, 23, 1867.

3. *Ibid.*, Apr. 1, 3, 15, 1867; Mobile *Advertiser and Register*, Mar. 24, 1867; Richmond *Whig*, Mar. 5, 1867; New York *World*, Mar. 26, 28, 30, 1867; Richard L. Zuber, *Jonathan Worth: A Biography of a Southern Unionist* (Chapel Hill, N. C., 1965), p. 254; Joseph T. Durkin, *Stephen R. Mallory* (Chapel Hill, N. C., 1954), pp. 399–400; *Recollections of Alexander H. Stephens*, Myrta L. Avery, ed. (New York, 1910), pp. 546–47; John William Jones, *Personal Reminiscences, Anecdotes and Letters of Gen. Robert E. Lee* (New York, 1876), pp. 225–27; New York *Times*, Mar. 1, Apr. 21, 29, May 9, 13, June 15, July 11, 1867; New Orleans *Picayune*, Mar. 31, 1867; Harris, *Mississippi*, p. 241.

4. "Correspondence Relative to Reconstruction," pp. 56, 57, 92–93, 199; Mobile *Advertiser and Register*, Mar. 31, Apr. 3, 1867; Richmond *Whig*, Mar. 15, 1867; Charleston *Mercury*, in Cleveland *Plain Dealer*, Mar. 29, 1867; Charleston *Courier*, Apr. 8, 9, 15, 17, 22, 1867; New Orleans *Picayune*, Mar. 28, 1867.

5. This discussion reflects my own impression of southern thinking at this time, based largely on reading of southern newspapers.

6. Mobile *Times*, Richmond *Dispatch*, and Atlanta *New Era*, in Chicago *Tribune*, Aug. 9, 1867; Richmond *Whig*, June 17, 1867; Mobile *Advertiser and Register*, May 8, 1867.

7. The New Orleans *Picayune*, Mar. 17, 1867, estimated that Negro population of the state had decreased by a third since 1860, when in fact it had increased.

8. Mobile *Advertiser and Register*, Apr. 20, 1867; Richmond *Whig*, Apr. 16, 17, 22, May 29, 1867; Raleigh *Sentinel*, Apr. 23, 1867; Vernon Lane Wharton, *The Negro in Mississippi, 1865–1890* (Chapel Hill, N. C., 1947), pp. 142–44; Joe M. Richardson, *The Negro in the Reconstruction of Florida, 1865–1877* (Tallahassee, Fla., 1965), pp. 150–51.

9. Willie M. Caskey, *Secession and Restoration of Louisiana* (University, La., 1938), pp. 179–80; Otto H. Olsen, *Carpetbaggers' Crusade: The Life of Albion Winegar Tourgée* (Baltimore, 1965), pp. 39–41, 63; Lowe, *Virginia*, pp. 210–3, 218–23, 228–30, 244–45; Sarah Woolfolk Wiggins, "Unionist Efforts To Control Alabama Reconstruction, 1865–1867," *Alabama Historical Quarterly*, XXX (Spring, 1968), p. 59; Thomas S. Staples, *Reconstruction in Arkansas, 1862–1874* (New York, 1923), pp. 101–2; New York *Times*, Sept. 4, 7, 8, 1866.

10. John R. Ficklen, *History of Reconstruction in Louisiana (through 1868)* (Baltimore, 1910), pp. 113–14, 142–43; Francis B. Simkins and

Robert H. Woody, *South Carolina During Reconstruction* (Chapel Hill, N. C., 1932), pp. 53, 82–83; Richardson, *Florida*, pp. 148–49; Garner, *Mississippi*, p. 180; Hamilton, *North Carolina*, pp. 241–42; Ernest W. Winkler, ed., "Platforms of Political Parties in Texas," *Bulletin of the University of Texas*, Sept., 1916, no. 53, p. 100; Elizabeth Studley Nathans, *Losing the Peace: Georgia Republicans and Reconstruction, 1865–1871* (Baton Rouge, 1968), pp. 18–31, 35–36; Fleming, *Alabama*, pp. 510–11; Lowe, *Virginia*, pp. 203–5, 251–53; Clement Mario Silvestro, None But Patriots: The Union Leagues in Civil War and Reconstruction (unpublished PhD dissertation, University of Wisconsin, 1959), pp. 252–83; John A. Carpenter, *Sword and Olive Branch: Oliver Otis Howard* (Pittsburgh, 1964), pp. 139–44; Boston *Post*, Aug. 8, 1867; New York *World*, Aug. 6, 1867. Compare, for example, the Mobile *Advertiser and Register*, July 11, 23, 1867 with Aug. 7, 21, 1867.

11. Richard L. Hume, The "Black and Tan" Constitutional Conventions of 1867–1869 in Ten Former Confederate States: A Study of Their Membership (unpublished PhD dissertation, University of Washington, 1969), pp. 661, 664–65; Nathans, *Georgia*, pp. 38–40; Harris, *Mississippi*, pp. 243–44; Simkins and Woody, *South Carolina*, pp. 82–83; Lillian A. Pereyra, *James Lusk Alcorn, Persistent Whig* ([Baton Rouge], 1966), pp. 87–97.

12. *American Annual Cyclopaedia*, 1867, under state headings; Winkler, "Texas," pp. 100–2; New York *Times*, Apr. 15, June 22, July 10, Aug. 7, Sept. 19, 1867; New York *Tribune*, July 26, 1867; Chicago *Tribune*, Aug. 1, 1867; Eckenrode, *Virginia*, pp. 68–79; Raleigh *Sentinel*, Oct. 11, 1867; John Allen Meador, Florida Political Parties, 1865–1877 (unpublished PhD dissertation, University of Florida, 1964), pp. 71–72.

13. See n. 3, above, and Wiggins, "Alabama Unionists," pp. 60–62. Three of the most prominent opponents of cooperation, Charles Jenkins and Benjamin H. Hill of Georgia, and Benjamin F. Perry of S. C., all fit this pattern (*Appleton's Cyclopaedia of American Biography* (6 vols., New York, 1887–1889), III, 203, 426, IV, 734).

14. "Correspondence Relative to Reconstruction," pp. 93–94, 97–101; *Mississippi* v. *Johnson*, 4 Wallace 475 (1867).

15. Letters in Charleston *Courier*, Apr. 19, 1867, and New York *Times*, May 9, 22, June 3, July 7, 1867.

16. New York *Tribune*, Mar. 27, 1867; Philadelphia *Press*, May 17, July 22, 1867; New York *Times*, May 25, 31, 1867; Mobile *Advertiser and Register*, May 1, 9, 15, 16, 30, June 19, 1867; New Orleans *Picayune*, Apr. 25, 1867; Richmond *Whig*, June 17, July 8, 1867; Char-

leston *Courier*, July 10, 27, Aug. 29, 1867; Benjamin H. Hill, Jr. *Senator Benjamin H. Hill of Georgia* (Atlanta, 1891), pp. 294–307, 730–811.

17. New Orleans *Picayune*, May 11, Aug. 25, Sept. 29, 1867; Mobile *Advertiser and Register*, June 2, 21, 22, July 7, 1867; Richmond *Whig*, June 27, 1867; Raleigh *Sentinel*, July 24, 1867; New York *World*, July 22, 1867; Chicago *Times*, July 25, Aug. 6, 1867.

18. Registration figures are from "Registered Voters in Rebel States," *Senate Executive Documents*, 40th Cong. 2d Sess., no. 53 (Cong. ser. #1317), except figures for Alabama, which were taken from "Report of the Secretary of War, 1867," *House Executive Documents*, 40th Cong. 2d Sess., no. 1 (Cong. ser. #1324), p. 356, and figures for Arkansas and Mississippi, taken from *American Annual Cyclopaedia*, 1867, pp. 53, 1517. To arrive at 1867 population figures I extrapolated from 1870 and 1880 census totals, rather than using 1860 and 1870, in order to avoid the war years. The figures are from U. S. Bureau of the Census, *Ninth Census of the United States: 1870. Population*, I, 618–19, and *Tenth Census of the United States: 1880. Population*, I, 646–47. A reasonable figure for disfranchisement would seem to be 10–15% of the white voters, or 85–125,000 in the South as a whole. This is also the figure suggested in Forrest G. Wood, "On Revising Reconstruction History: Negro Suffrage, White Disfranchisement, and Common Sense," *Journal of Negro History*, LI (April, 1966), 105–7.

19. Texas was the only state where turnout exceeded 100% and, of course, statistics and projections are least reliable there because of its unsettled state and more rapid growth. Population figures are derived in the same way as in n. 18 above, except that 1870 figures have been increased by 9% to compensate for an estimated undercount of the Negro population by that amount in that year; see Francis A. Walker, "Statistics of the Colored Race in the United States," *Publications of the American Statistical Association*, II (1890), 91–106.

20. Eckenrode, *Virginia*, p. 83; Sefton, *US Army*, pp. 165–66.

21. Fleming, *Alabama*, pp. 512–13; *American Annual Cyclopaedia*, 1867, p. 516; New York *Times*, Sept. 30, 1867; Ralph L. Peek, "Military Reconstruction and the Growth of Anti-Negro Sentiment in Florida, 1867" *Florida Historical Quarterly*, XLVII (April, 1969), 396–97; Richmond *Whig*, June 22, Aug. 10, Sept. 23, 25, 1867; Raleigh *Sentinel*, July 25, Aug. 10, 29, Sept. 3, 1867.

22. New Orleans *Picayune*, Oct. 9, 11, 26, 1867; Charleston *Courier*, Sept. 13, Oct. 3, 11, 1867; Mobile *Advertiser and Register*, Sept. 27, Nov. 8, 1867; Richmond *Whig*, Oct. 15, Nov. 7, 1867; quotes from

Southern press in Chicago *Times,* Oct. 15, 1867; Raleigh *Sentinel,* Oct. 10, 31, Nov. 7, 1867.

23. Mobile *Advertiser and Register,* Oct. 1, 6, 26, 1867; Charleston *Courier,* Nov. 2, 1867; New Orleans *Picayune,* Oct. 16, 25, 1867; Raleigh *Sentinel,* Oct. 31, 1867; Richmond *Enquirer,* in Chicago *Times,* Oct. 15, 1867; Staples, *Arkansas,* p. 174. Statewide election returns are from "Registered Voters in Rebel States." The election in Texas, which was held in February, 1868, is not considered here.

24. In addition to Virginia, the commanders in the 2d and 3d districts estimated the racial breakdown of the vote, indicating that in these six states 82% of the registered Negroes voted, almost all for the convention. Assuming the same to be true for the other states, then 20% of the registered whites in Arkansas, 13% in Louisiana, and 7% in Mississippi voted for the convention. Obviously these figures, except for Virginia, are at best educated guesses which only give a rough approximation of the character of the vote.

25. County returns from *Tribune Almanac,* 1868, pp. 62–65, 68–69.

26. Georgia Lee Tatum, *Disloyalty in the Confederacy* (Chapel Hill, N. C., 1934), pp. 38, 62–63, 155; W. Dean Burnham, *Presidential Ballots, 1836–1892* (Baltimore, 1955), pp. 223–25. Counties were classified politically according to how they voted in a majority of the four elections.

Four: Northern Politics and the Elections of 1867

1. *Cong. Globe,* 40th Cong. 1st Sess., pp. 203–8; Republican Party platforms in *American Annual Cyclopaedia,* 1867, under state headings; Winfield J. Davis, *History of Political Conventions in California, 1849–1892* (Sacramento, Calif., 1893), pp. 248–49; Chicago *Tribune,* Sept. 12, 1867; New York *Times,* Aug. 14, 1867.

2. *Cong. Globe,* 39th Cong. 2d Sess., pp. 320–21, 40th Cong., 1st Sess., p. 565; New York *World,* Aug. 26, 1867; Chicago *Tribune,* Aug. 21, 1867; Philadelphia *Press,* Aug. 15, 16, 1867; New York *Times,* Aug. 14, 16, Sept. 7, 13, 20, 1867.

3. Philadelphia *Press,* May 14, 24, June 4, 1867; New York *World,* Mar. 28, 1867; New York *Times,* Apr. 28, May 7, 8, 12, 1867; *Letter of Horace Greeley to . . . members of the Union League Club* (New York, 1867).

4. *Cong. Globe,* 40th Cong. 1st Sess., pp. 480, 498; New York *Tribune,* June 28, 1867; New York *Times,* July 4, 1867; Philadelphia *Press,* July 1, 6, 1867.

5. Also see Eric Foner, *Free Soil, Free Labor, Free Men: The Ideology of the Republican Party Before the Civil War* (New York, 1970), pp. 261–300; and James McPherson, "A Brief for Equality: The Abolitionist Reply to the Racist Myth, 1860–1865," in Martin Duberman (ed.), *The Antislavery Vanguard: New Essays on the Abolitionists* (Princeton, N. J., 1965). The relationship between support for black equality and Free Soil and Republican votes is dealt with in Tom LeRoy McLaughlin, Popular Reactions to the Idea of Negro Equality in Twelve Nonslaveholding States, 1846–1869: A Quantitative Analysis (unpublished PhD dissertation, Washington State University, 1969), pp. 77–82, 84–86.

6. McKitrick, *Reconstruction,* pp. 444–45; Gambill, Northern Democrats, pp. 158–63; Cole, *Era of the Civil War,* p. 388; *American Annual Cyclopaedia,* 1865, pp. 304, 577, 823; 1866, p. 404. In March, 1866, the Wisconsin Supreme Court ruled that equal suffrage had been adopted by a referendum in 1849, even though it had been considered defeated because it did not get an absolute majority of all the votes cast at the election, Leslie H. Fishel, Jr., "Wisconsin and Negro Suffrage," *Wisconsin Magazine of History,* XLVI (Spring, 1963), 195–96.

7. *American Annual Cyclopaedia,* 1866, 1867, *passim; U. S. Statutes at Large,* XIV, 375, 379, 391; *Cong. Globe,* 40th Cong. 1st Sess., pp. 345, 466, 615; New York *Times,* Aug. 23, 1867. I am not counting those states, New Hampshire and Rhode Island, which already had Negro suffrage and in which the 1867 Republican conventions did not mention the issue.

8. Gambill, Northern Democrats, pp. 197–204, 216, 254, 256–58, 350–70; George T. McJimsey, *Genteel Partisan: Manton Marble, 1834–1917* (Ames, Iowa, 1917), pp. 113–15; Chicago *Times,* Feb. 22, Mar. 12, 18, 1867; Boston *Post,* Feb. 25, Mar. 21, 26, Apr. 3, 1867; New York *World,* Feb. 23, Mar. 4, 8, May 14, 1867; Washington *National Intelligencer,* Apr. 20, 1867; Cleveland *Plain Dealer,* June 21, 1867; *Cong. Globe,* 39th Cong. 2d Sess., p. 1973; McPherson, *Reconstruction,* p. 245.

9. New York *World,* May 6, July 25, 31, Aug. 6, 17, 1867; New York *Tribune,* July 12, 1867; Boston *Post,* July 27, 1867; Charleston *Courier,* Sept. 14, 1867; Detroit *Free Press,* June 12, 1867; Chicago *Times,* June 30, Aug. 21, 1867; Cleveland *Plain Dealer,* May 6, June 4, July 24, Aug. 6, 1867. The Cincinnati *Enquirer* was an exception, insisting that Grant was a Republican and the Democrats wanted no part of him, June 15, 27, July 13, 1867.

10. Boston *Post,* Nov. 16, 19, 1866; New York *World* Nov. 19, 1866; summaries of press response in Chicago *Times,* Nov. 12, 15, 17, 19, 21, Dec. 6, 1866; Gambill, Northern Democrats, pp. 257–59; Philadelphia

Press, Apr. 4, 15, 1867; New York *Times,* Apr. 6, 1867; G. H. Parker to Mason, July 3, 1867, J. P. Cook to Mason, July 2, 1867, Charles Mason Mss, Iowa State Department of History and Archives.

11. Gambill, Northern Democrats, pp. 46–50, 259–61; Wood, *Black Scare,* pp. 21–23; Voegeli, *Free But Not Equal,* pp. 1–9; Cincinnati *Enquirer,* Mar. 31, Apr. 15, Sept. 2, 1867; Cleveland *Plain Dealer,* Apr. 4, Aug. 6, 1867; New York *Times,* Aug. 14, 1867. State platforms in *American Annual Cylopaedia,* 1867, *passim;* and New York *Times,* June 22, July 16, 1867; New York *World,* Sept. 23, 1867.

12. Gambill, Northern Democrats, pp. 204–9, 159–60; Cincinnati *Enquirer,* Apr. 9, 16, 27, 1867; New York *Times,* Apr. 15, 1867; Boston *Post,* Apr. 23, 1867; Washington *National Intelligencer,* Mar. 18, July 10, 1867; Chicago *Times,* July 15, 1867; Cleveland *Plain Dealer,* May 28, 1867; New York *World,* May 17, 21, 24, 1867.

13. See n. 11, above, for sources of platforms, and Cincinnati *Enquirer,* July 17, 1867; New York *Times,* Aug. 14, 1867; Cleveland *Plain Dealer,* Aug. 6, 1867; New York *World,* Nov. 1, 1867.

14. "Report of the Secretary of the Treasury, 1865," *House Executive Documents,* 39th Cong. 1st Sess., no. 3 (Cong. ser. # 1254), pp. 3–14; Robert P. Sharkey, *Money, Class, and Party: An Economic Study of Civil War and Reconstruction* (Baltimore, 1959), pp. 56–94, 267–71; Irwin Unger, *The Greenback Era* (Princeton, N. J., 1964), pp. 60–64; *Cong. Globe,* 39th Cong. 2d Sess., p. 992.

15. Chicago *Times,* Mar. 15, Apr. 12, 1867; Unger, *The Greenback Era,* pp. 77–79; Cincinnati *Enquirer,* Mar. 13, 1867; *American Annual Cyclopaedia,* 1866, pp. 400, 405, 468, 536, 762; Max L. Shipley, The Greenback Issue in the Old Northwest, 1865–1880 (unpublished PhD dissertation, University of Illinois, 1929), pp. 334–39.

16. New York *Times,* June 1, 1863, May 24, 1864; Ellis P. Oberholtzer, *Jay Cooke, Financier of the Civil War* (2 vols.; Philadelphia, 1907), I, 257; *Cong. Globe,* 37th Cong. 3d Sess., p. 388, 38th Cong. 1st Sess., p. 3213.

17. Cincinnati *Enquirer,* editorials, May–June, 1867, *passim;* Chicago *Times,* Feb. 27, 1867; Cleveland *Plain Dealer,* May 30, 1867.

18. Chester M. Destler, *American Radicalism, 1865–1901* (New London, Conn., 1946), pp. 32–40; Cleveland *Plain Dealer,* Sept. 19, Nov. 6, 1867; Unger, *The Greenback Era,* pp. 68–76; Sharkey, *Money, Class, and Party,* p. 106.

19. New York *Times,* Aug. 14, Sept. 2, 1867; Cleveland *Plain Dealer,* Aug. 8, 9, Sept. 19, 1867; Cincinnati *Enquirer,* Aug. 16, 22, 1867;

R. R. Harbour to Mason, Aug. 12, 1867, Dean to Mason, Aug. 16, 1867, Mason Mss, Iowa Dept. of Hist.; New York *World*, Sept. 23, 1867.

20. New York *World*, Sept. 6, Oct. 4, 5, 1867.

21. New York *Times*, Sept. 14, 1867; Chicago *Times*, July 28, Aug. 23, Oct. 1, 1867; Cincinnati *Enquirer*, Aug. 22, Sept. 18, 1867; Cleveland *Plain Dealer*, Oct. 7, 1867.

22. Walter T. K. Nugent, *Money and American Society, 1865–1880* (New York, 1968), pp. 107–9; Oberholtzer, *Cooke*, I, 232–55, 317.

23. *American Annual Cyclopaedia*, 1867, pp. 472, 544–45, 771; Chicago *Tribune*, Aug. 22, Sept. 12, 1867; New York *Times*, Aug. 23, Sept. 5, 8, 14, 20, Oct. 3, 6, 7, 8, 11, 25, 1867; Philadelphia *Press*, Jan. 24, Aug. 24, Oct. 15, 1867; New York *Tribune*, Aug. 23, 1867.

24. These and following election results are from *American Annual Cyclopaedia*, 1866, 1867, under state headings. National Union totals in 1866 will be listed as Democratic.

25. Chicago *Times*, Sept. 10, 1867; New York *World*, Sept. 11, 1867; Boston *Post*, Sept. 11, 12, 1867; Chicago *Tribune*, Sept. 8, 1867; Philadelphia *Press*, Sept. 10, 14, Oct. 1, 1867; New York *Times*, Sept. 11, Oct. 3, 1867.

26. New York *Times*, Oct. 28, 1867; Philadelphia *Press*, Oct. 10, 17, 26, 1867; New York *Tribune*, Oct. 25, 29, 1867; speeches at New York meeting and by S. Colfax in *ibid.*, Oct. 17, 24, 1867.

27. Cincinnati *Enquirer*, Oct. 18, 22, 1867; New York *Times*, Oct. 16, 1867; Chicago *Times*, Oct. 9, 11, 16, 1867; Washington *National Intelligencer*, Oct. 11, Nov. 6, 1867; Boston *Post*, Oct. 14, 23, 1867; Cleveland *Plain Dealer*, Nov. 7, 1867; Charleston *Courier*, Nov. 2, 1867; New York *World*, Oct. 12, 21, Nov. 8, 1867.

28. New York *World*, Sept. 12, 1867; Chicago *Times*, June 15, Aug. 13, Sept. 10, Oct. 4, 1867; Boston *Post*, July 8, 1867; Cincinnati *Enquirer*, Apr. 14, Sept. 10, 1867; Cleveland *Plain Dealer*, June 29, 1867; *Cong. Globe*, 40th Cong. 1st Sess., p. 538; S. E. Church to Tilden, Mar. 8, 1867, Samuel J. Tilden Mss, New York Public Library.

29. Washington *National Intelligencer*, Sept. 2, 1867; Detroit *Free Press*, Aug. 29, 1867; Boston *Post*, Aug. 15, 27, 1867; New York *World*, Aug. 14, 26, Oct. 10, 17, 1867; Chicago *Times*, Aug. 25, Oct. 12, 1867; letters to Johnson, Mar.–Apr., 1868, *passim*, Johnson Mss, LC; T. O. Howe to H. Ruplee, Apr. 13, 1867, Timothy O. Howe Mss, State Historical Society of Wisconsin; *Cong. Globe*, 40th Cong. 1st Sess., p. 846; Welles, *Diary*, III, 147–48; New York *Times*, Oct. 10, 1867; Cleveland

Plain Dealer, Oct. 18, 1867; Philadelphia *Press,* Oct. 18, 22, Nov. 4, 1867; W. McLean to Barlow, Oct. 11, 1867, Samuel L. M. Barlow Mss, Henry E. Huntington Library.

30. Chicago *Tribune,* Oct. 10, Nov. 7, 1867; New York *Times,* Apr. 3, Oct. 10, 13, 14, 21, Nov. 7, 1867; New York *Tribune,* Apr. 3, Sept. 12, Oct. 10, 1867; Philadelphia *Press,* Apr. 3, Sept. 18, Oct. 9, 11, 15, 1867; Washington *National Intelligencer,* Oct. 18, 1867.

31. Smith to R. B. Mussey, Oct. 21, 1867, William Henry Smith Mss, Ohio Historical Society, letterbooks. At this time voting was done by means of ballots printed by each party. In this case on the suffrage issue the Republican ballot had a "yes" on it and the Democratic a "no." The analysis of the vote is based on the assumption that an insignificant number of Democrats would have altered their ballots on the referendum.

32. New York *World,* Oct. 22, Nov. 7, 1867; New York *Tribune,* Nov. 7, 1867; G. Tichenor to Dodge, Oct. 19, 1867, Grenville M. Dodge Mss, Iowa State Dept. of History and Archives; Gaillard Hunt, *Israel, Elihu, and Cadwallader Washburn* (New York, 1925), p. 121; William Gillette, *The Right To Vote: Politics and the Passage of the Fifteenth Amendment* (Baltimore, 1965), pp. 35–37.

33. Badeau, *Grant in Peace,* pp. 73–74; Sherman, *Letters,* pp. 292, 294–95; *Home Letters of General Sherman,* M. A. DeWolfe Howe, ed. (New York, 1909), pp. 359–60.

34. James H. Wilson, *The Life of John A. Rawlins* (New York 1916), pp. 470–502; Chicago *Tribune,* July 30, 1867; New York *Times,* May 24, June 11, July 24, Aug. 4, 17, 18, 1867; New York *Tribune,* June 27, July 30, Aug. 15, 1867.

35. Wilson, *Rawlins,* p. 344; John Bigelow, *Retrospections of an Active Life* (5 vols., New York, 1909–13), IV, 94; *Intimate Letters of Carl Schurz, 1841–1869,* Joseph Schafer, ed. (Madison, Wisc., 1928), p. 388; H. White to Washburne, Aug. 18, 1867, Elihu B. Washburne Mss, Library of Congress; Philadelphia *Press,* Aug. 16, 1867; New York *Times,* Aug. 29, 30, 1867; New York *Tribune,* Aug. 13, 21, 23, 1867.

36. New York *Tribune,* Aug. 14, 27, 29, Sept. 4, 7, 21, 1867; Philadelphia *Press,* Aug. 15, 27, 1867; New York *Times,* Aug. 14, 29, 30, 1867; Boston *Post,* Aug. 22, 30, 1867; Chicago *Times,* Aug. 28, 1867; Washington *National Intelligencer,* Aug. 28, 1867; New Orleans *Picayune,* Aug. 17, 1867; Mobile *Advertiser and Register,* Aug. 6, 1867; Charleston *Courier,* Aug. 8, 1867.

37. Richard Henry Abbott, Cobbler in Congress: Life of Henry Wilson, 1812–1875 (unpublished PhD dissertation, University of Wisconsin,

1965), pp. 330–31; Willard H. Smith, *Schuyler Colfax: The Changing Fortunes of a Political Idol* (Indianapolis, 1952), pp. 270–71; Sherman, *Letters,* pp. 292–94; Z. Chandler to Greeley, Aug. 19, 1867, Horace Greeley Mss, New York Public Library; New York *Times,* Aug. 16, 1867; New York *Tribune,* July 28, 1867.

38. *Ibid.,* Oct. 15, Nov. 7, 1867; New York *Times,* Nov. 8, 16, 1867; David Donald, *Charles Sumner and the Rights of Man* (New York, 1970), p. 339.

39. Chicago *Tribune,* Oct. 17, 24, Nov. 25, 1867; New York *Tribune,* Sept. 14, 1867; New York *Times,* Oct. 13, 21, Nov. 16, 1867; Philadelphia *Press,* Oct. 22, 26, Nov. 7, 11, 20, 1867; New York *Herald,* Nov. 13, 19, 22, 25, 1867; New York *World,* Nov. 20, 1867; Charleston *Courier,* Nov. 18, 1867; John Sherman, *Recollections of Forty Years* (2 vols., Chicago, 1895), I, 415–16; *Garfield–Hinsdale Letters,* Mary L. Hinsdale, ed. (Ann Arbor, Mich., 1949), p. 112; George T. Palmer, *A Conscientious Turncoat: the Story of John M. Palmer* (New Haven, Conn., 1941), p. 204; letters to E. Washburne, October, 1867, *passim,* E. Washburne Mss, LC; letters to J. M. Read, I, November, 1867, *passim,* Read Family Mss, Library Society of Philadelphia.

Five: Reconstruction and Impeachment: The Crisis

1. Thomas Ewing, Jr., to Hugh Ewing, Oct. 5, 1867, Ewing Family Mss, Library of Congress; Philadelphia *Press,* Nov. 18, 1867; New York *Tribune,* Nov. 21, 1867; *Cong. Globe,* 40th Cong. 1st Sess., p. 792; "Impeachment Investigation," *House Reports,* 40th Cong. 1st Sess., no. 7 (Cong. ser. #1314), p. 59.

2. Chicago *Times,* Nov. 28, 30, Dec. 1, 1867; New York *Herald,* Nov. 30, Dec. 4, 1867; Philadelphia *Press,* Dec. 4, 1867; W. Thorpe to Johnson, Dec. 5, 1867, Johnson Mss, LC; La Verne K. Bowersox, The Reconstruction of the Republican Party in the West, 1865–1870 (unpublished PhD dissertation, Ohio State University, 1931), pp. 83–85; *Cong. Globe,* 40th Cong. 2d Sess., p. 68; New York *Tribune,* Dec. 9, 1867; Chicago *Tribune,* Dec. 8, 1867.

3. Philadelphia *Press,* Nov. 16, 1867; New York *World,* Nov. 14, 1867; "Notes of Col. W. G. Moore," p. 113.

4. *Messages and Papers of the Presidents,* VI, 558–71.

5. *Cong. Globe,* 40th Cong. 2d Sess., pp. 99, 117, 209–10, 264–67, 453, 699–700.

6. *American Annual Cyclopaedia,* 1867, 1868, *passim* (North Carolina incorrectly given as Feb. 14, should be Jan. 14); Hume, Constitutional Conventions, pp. 672–73.

7. William A. Russ, Jr., "Disfranchisement in Virginia Under Radical Reconstruction," *Tyler's Quarterly Historical and Genealogical Magazine,* XVII (July, 1935), p. 32; Mobile *Advertiser and Register,* Nov. 27, Dec. 21, 1867; Charleston *Courier,* Dec. 7, 1867; New York *Tribune,* Nov. 16, 20, 1867; Chicago *Tribune,* Nov. 13, 1867; New York *Herald,* Dec. 14, 15, 1867; Ord to W. T. Sherman, Nov. 6, 1867, William T. Sherman Mss, Library of Congress; New York *Times,* Nov. 12, Dec. 26, 1867.

8. Charleston *Courier,* Nov. 8, 9, 1867; *American Annual Cyclopaedia,* 1867, pp. 309–10, 366, 763; Staples, *Arkansas,* pp. 149–51; Garner, *Mississippi,* p. 209; New York *Times,* Dec. 26, 1867, Jan. 16, 26, 1868; New Orleans *Picayune,* Jan. 12, 30, 1868; New York *World,* Jan. 16, 1868; Raleigh *Sentinel,* Nov. 30, 1867, Jan. 6, 1868; Nathans, *Georgia,* pp. 81–82.

9. See n. 8 above and Raleigh *Standard,* Dec. 11, 1867, Jan. 28, 1868; Mobile *Advertiser and Register,* Dec. 8, 1867; Charleston *Courier,* Jan. 20, 1868; New Orleans *Picayune,* Nov. 21, 1867.

10. "Report of the Secretary of War, 1868," *House Executive Documents,* 40th Cong. 3d Sess., no. 1 (Cong. ser. #1367), pp. 210–19, 221; "General Orders–Reconstruction," pp. 179, 180, 181, 184; *Cong. Globe,* 40th Cong. 2d Sess., p. 264; New York *World,* Dec. 17, 1867; Chicago *Times,* Dec. 7, 1867; Raleigh *Sentinel,* Dec. 20, 1867; New Orleans *Picayune,* Nov. 30, 1867.

11. Sefton, *US Army,* pp. 173–74; "Report of the Secretary of War, 1868," pp. 585–87; New York *Times,* Dec. 12, 1867, Jan. 5, 1868; Charleston *Courier,* Jan. 10, 1868.

12. Chicago *Times,* Dec. 30, 1867; New York *Times,* Jan. 15, 1868; "Report of the Secretary of War, 1868," pp. 82–93; "General Orders–Reconstruction," pp. 126–31.

13. Chicago *Times,* Mar. 12, 1867; Charleston *Courier,* Jan. 14, 1868; New York *Herald,* Dec. 31, 1867; Chicago *Tribune,* Jan. 4, 17, 1868; Philadelphia *Press,* Dec. 20, 1867; *Garfield–Hinsdale Letters,* p. 130; letters to E. Washburne from: J. C. Underwood, Dec. 9, 16, 1867, C. W. Buckley, Jan. 9, 1868, H. White, Jan. 16, 1868, W. H. Gibbs, Jan. 18, 1868, E. Washburne Mss, LC.

14. "Constitution of the State of Alabama," *Senate Miscellaneous Documents,* 40th Cong. 2d Sess., no. 32 (Cong. ser. #1319); *Official Journal of the Constitutional Convention of the State of Alabama; Held in the City*

of Montgomery, Commencing on Tuesday, November 5th, A. D., 1867 (Montgomery, Ala., 1868), pp. 87, 99, 186–87, 239–40, 267–68.

15. New York *Times,* Jan. 12, 17, 26, 1868; Mobile *Register,* Feb. 1, 4, 5, 1868; Charleston *Courier,* Dec. 12, 1867; Fleming, *Alabama,* pp. 516, 529–30; Philadelphia *Press,* Dec. 13, 1867; R. W. Patton to Meade, Jan. 8, 1868, George G. Meade Mss, Historical Society of Pennsylvania; "Report of the Secretary of War, 1868," pp. 84–85, 86, 88, 89, 91; "General Orders–Reconstruction," p. 129.

16. Stanley I. Kutler, *Judicial Power and Reconstruction Politics* (Chicago, 1968), pp. 101–2; Philadelphia *Press,* Jan. 10, 1868; Chicago *Tribune,* Jan. 12, 1868; *Cong. Globe,* 40th Cong. 2d Sess., p. 489.

17. *Ibid.,* pp. 476, 664; New York *World,* Jan. 17, 1868; Chicago *Tribune,* Jan. 24, 1868; Sherman, *Home Letters,* p. 367.

18. *Cong. Globe,* 40th Cong. 2d Sess., pp. 511, 663–64.

19. New York *Times,* Jan. 4, 1868; Philadelphia *Press,* Nov. 21, 27, Dec. 10, 19, 1867, Jan. 13, 17, 1868; New York *Herald,* Dec. 12, 13, 15, 1867; *American Annual Cyclopaedia,* 1868, pp. 202–3; New York *World,* Dec. 9, 1867, Jan. 8, 9, 1868.

20. New York *Herald,* Nov. 21, Dec. 14, 22, 1867; F. W. Kellog to Washburne, Dec. 16, 1867, J. B. Stockton to Washburne, Jan. 14, 1868, Daniel Richards to Washburne, Nov. 11, 13, 1867, E. Washburne Mss, LC; New York *Times,* Dec. 25, 26, 30, 1867; New York *World,* Jan. 22, 1868; Philadelphia *Press,* Nov. 13, 20, Dec. 24, 30, 1867; Chicago *Tribune,* Jan. 17, 1868; S. Bard to Yates, Nov. 25, 1867, Richard Yates Mss, Illinois State Historical Library; W. P. Kellogg to Chandler, Jan. 13, 1868, William E. Chandler Mss, Library of Congress; J. M. Read, I, to J. M. Read, II, Dec. 6, 1867, Read Family Mss, Lib. Co. of Phil.

21. S. S. Cox to Marble, Nov. 11, 1867, Manton Marble Mss, Library of Congress; C. H. McCormick to Barlow, Nov. 26, Dec. 20, 1867, W. D. Shipman to Barlow, Oct. 10, 15, 1867, Barlow Mss, Huntington Lib.; New York *World,* Jan. 2, 10, 1868; Welles, *Diary,* III, 244; E. Casserly to Sherman, Dec. 24, 1867, W. T. Sherman Mss, LC; Charleston *Courier,* Nov. 13, 16, Dec. 2, 11, 19, 1867, Jan. 9, 18, 1868; Chicago *Times,* Nov. 5, 12, 19, Dec. 9, 1867; S. Wells to Washburne, Jan. 2, 1868, E. Washburne Mss, LC; "Doolittle Correspondence," *Southern History Association Publications,* XI (January, 1907), 6–7; Cincinnati *Enquirer,* Dec. 19, 1867; T. Ewing, Jr., to T. Ewing, Sr., Oct. 12, 1867, Ewing Mss, LC.

22. New York *World,* Oct. 16, Nov. 14, 18, 1867; T. Ewing, Jr., to T. Ewing, Sr., Oct. 19, 1867, Ewing Mss, LC; draft of statement to cabinet,

Nov. 30, 1867, Johnson Mss, LC; "Notes of Col. W. G. Moore," p. 113; Grant to Sherman, Nov. 21, 1867, W. T. Sherman Mss, LC.

23. *Messages and Papers of the Presidents*, VI, 583–94; Chicago *Times*, Nov. 30, Dec. 14, 1867; New York *Herald*, Dec. 16, 18, 1867; Philadelphia *Press*, Nov. 18, Dec. 12, 1867; New York *World*, Dec. 14, 1867; Chicago *Tribune*, Dec. 18, 1867, Jan. 10, 1868.

24. New York *Herald*, Jan. 3, 1868; Philadelphia *Press*, Jan. 3, 1868; Charleston *Courier*, Jan. 8, 1868; New York *Times*, Jan. 16, 1868.

25. Badeau, *Grant in Peace*, pp. 77–83; "Notes of Col. W. G. Moore," p. 114; Grant to W. T. Sherman, Sept. 18, 1867, W. T. Sherman Mss, LC; John M. Schofield, "Controversies in the War Department," *Century*, LIV (August, 1897), 579.

26. Badeau, *Grant in Peace*, pp. 110–11; New York *World*, Jan. 15, 16, 1868; Sherman, *Home Letters*, p. 364; T. Ewing, Sr., to Johnson, "Sunday evening" [Jan. 12, 1868], Johnson Mss, LC (incorrectly filed at end of 1867 correspondence).

27. *Cong. Globe*, 40th Cong. 2d Sess., pp. 977–78, 1107–9, 1115; "Notes of Col. W. G. Moore," p. 115; New York *World*, Jan. 16, 1868; Badeau, *Grant in Peace*, p. 112; Sherman to Grant, Feb. 12, 1868, W. T. Sherman Mss, LC; Thomas and Hyman, *Stanton*, pp. 567–71; Hesseltine, *Grant*, pp. 103–11.

28. McPherson, *Reconstruction*, p. 262; Chicago *Tribune*, Jan. 15, 1868; Philadelphia *Press*, Jan. 14, 22, 1868; New York *World*, Jan. 14, 16, 1868; Thomas and Hyman, *Stanton*, pp. 569–70, 572–73; William T. Sherman, *Memoirs of General W. T. Sherman* (4th ed. rev., 2 vols., New York, 1891), II, 423–24.

29. *Cong. Globe*, 40th Cong. 2d sess., pp. 977–78, 1107–9, 1115; Julius M. Bloch, The Rise of the New York *World* During the Civil War Decade (2 vols., unpublished PhD dissertation, Harvard University, 1941), II, 389–92; Hesseltine, *Grant*, p. 111.

30. New York *Tribune*, Jan. 17, 1868; New York *World*, Jan. 16, 1868; New York *Herald*, Jan. 17, 1868; *American Annual Cyclopaedia*, 1868, pp. 648–49.

31. New York *World*, Jan. 15, 1868; Charleston *Courier*, Jan. 22, 25, 1868; McPherson, *Reconstruction*, p. 346; Sherman to Johnson, Jan. 27, 31, 1868, T. Ewing, Sr., to Sherman, Jan. 25, 1868, T. Ewing, Sr., to Johnson, Jan. 29, 1868, Johnson Mss, LC; Sherman, *Memoirs*, II, 432–33.

32. *Cong. Globe*, 40th Cong. 2d Sess., pp. 470, 788, 845–46, 1026,

1037, 1087, 1142, 1163–65; New York *Herald*, Feb. 13, 1868; Philadelphia *Press*, Feb. 14, 1868.

33. 6 Wallace 50 (1868); Philadelphia *Press*, Feb. 12, 18, 1868; "Alabama Election," *House Executive Documents*, 40th Cong. 2d Sess., no. 238 (Cong. ser. #1341), p. 2; *Cong. Globe*, 40th Cong. 2d Sess., pp. 1117, 1217, 1257; "Report of the Secretary of War, 1868," p. 97.

34. *Cong. Globe*, 40th Cong. 2d Sess., pp. 1336, 1400; David M. DeWitt, *The Impeachment and Trial of Andrew Johnson* (New York, 1903), pp. 345–73; Thomas and Hyman, *Stanton*, pp. 583–94; McPherson, *Reconstruction*, pp. 265–66; "Notes of Col. W. G. Moore," pp. 120–22.

35. Bowersox, Republican Party in the West, pp. 85–86; letters to Washburne, Feb. 24–26, 1868, *passim*, E. Washburne Mss, LC; E. Pierrepont to Dix, Feb. 25, 1868, John A. Dix Mss, Columbia University; New York *Tribune*, Feb. 24, 1868; New York *Times*, Feb. 24, 25, 28, 1868; Philadelphia *Press*, Feb. 25, 26, 28, 29, Mar. 18, 1868; Chicago *Tribune*, Feb. 23, 26, 28, 1868; McKitrick, *Reconstruction*, p. 505; letters to Johnson, Feb. 22–27, 1868, *passim*, Johnson Mss, LC; William A. Russ, "Was There Danger of a Second Civil War During Reconstruction?", *Mississippi Valley Historical Review* XXV (June, 1938), pp. 48–55.

Six: Reconstruction and Impeachment: The Settlement

1. *Cong. Globe*, 40th Cong. 2d Sess., pp. 1402, 1542–43, 1613–14, 1616–19, 1638–42; DeWitt, *Impeachment*, pp. 379–88. The other managers were John A. Bingham, George S. Boutwell, James F. Wilson, Benjamin F. Butler, Thomas Williams, and John A. Logan.

2. *Ibid.*, pp. 388–402; *Proceedings in the Trial of Andrew Johnson* (Washington, D. C., 1868), pp. 6–29.

3. *Cong. Globe*, 40th Cong. 2d Sess., p. 1385; letters to Johnson from: S. M. Johnson, Feb. 26, 1868, T. Ewing, Sr., Mar. 1, 1868, J. C. Kennedy, Mar. 4, 1868, Johnson Mss, LC; William N. Brigance, "Jeremiah Black and Andrew Johnson," *Mississippi Valley Historical Review*, XIX (September, 1932), 205–18; Thomas and Hyman, *Stanton*, pp. 598–99; Edward D. Townsend, *Anecdotes of the Civil War* (New York, 1884), pp. 130–31; Philadelphia *Press*, Feb. 27, 1868.

4. "Report of the Secretary of War, 1868," pp. 223–33; McPherson, *Reconstruction*, p. 346.

5. DeWitt, *Impeachment*, pp. 388–93, 397, 402; *American Annual Cyclopaedia*, 1868, p. 352; H. R. Linderman to H. McCulloch, Feb. 28,

Mar. 1, 1868, Johnson Mss, LC; New York *World,* Mar. 11, 25, 1868; Charleston *Courier,* Mar. 3, 5, 1868; New York *Herald,* Feb. 28, 1868; Cleveland *Plain Dealer,* Feb. 27, Mar. 2, 1868; New Orleans *Picayune,* Mar. 15, 1868.

6. *Cong. Globe,* 40th Cong. 2d Sess., pp. 1847, 1860, 1881–86, 2094, 2128, 2170; Cleveland *Plain Dealer,* Mar. 21, 1868; Chicago *Times,* Apr. 7, 1868; Kutler, *Judicial Power,* pp. 78–84.

7. *U. S. Statutes at Large,* XV, 41; *Cong. Globe,* 40th Cong. 2d Sess., pp. 1289, 1415, 1417, 1452, 1861.

8. Francis N. Thorpe, ed., *The Federal and State Constitutions* (7 vols.; Washington D.C., 1909), I, 306–32; II, 704–28, 822–42; III, 1449–69; V, 2800–22; VI, 3281–3305; Olsen, *Tourgée,* pp. 99–100, 105–6; Jack B. Scroggs, "Carpetbagger Constitutional Reform in the South Atlantic States, 1867–1868," *Journal of Southern History,* XXVII (November, 1961), 475–93, *passim;* Hume, Constitutional Conventions, pp. 92–96, 282–86, 339–41, 410–12, 488–93, 682–84.

9. "Report of the Secretary of War, 1868," pp. 77, 93–94; Davis, *Florida,* pp. 500–14.

10. New York *Times,* Mar. 9, 17, 20, Apr. 19, 1868; Simkins and Woody, *South Carolina,* pp. 107–9; Thompson, *Georgia,* pp 199–204.

11. H. E. Sterkx, "William C. Jordan and Reconstruction," *Alabama Review,* XV (January, 1962), 68; New York *Times,* May 7, 11, 1868; Charleston *Courier,* Apr. 6, 1868; Joel Williamson, *After Slavery: The Negro in South Carolina During Reconstruction* (Chapel Hill, N. C., 1965), pp. 351–52; Allen W. Trelease, *White Terror: The Ku Klux Klan Conspiracy and Southern Reconstruction* (New York, 1971), Parts I, II, *passim;* New York *World,* Apr. 7, 10, 11, 24, June 7, 1868; Mobile *Register,* Feb. 11, 18, Apr. 8, 15, 1868; Chicago *Times,* Apr. 13, 14, 1868; Raleigh *Sentinel,* Apr. 9, 14, 1868; New Orleans *Picayune,* Apr. 11, 18, 1868.

12. "Report of the Secretary of War, 1868," pp. 521–22, 533–36; "Votes Cast for New Constitutions," *House Executive Documents,* 40th Cong. 2d Sess., no. 284 (Cong. ser. #1343); "Election in Georgia, North and South Carolina," *House Executive Documents,* 40th Cong. 2d Sess. no. 300 (Cong. ser. #1345), pp. 2–3; "Elections in Southern States," *House Executive Documents,* 40th Cong. 2d Sess., no. 291 (Cong. ser. #1343), p. 15; *American Annual Cyclopaedia,* 1868, pp. 433, 434, 554, 698.

13. DeWitt, *Impeachment,* pp. 417–517; *Trial of Andrew Johnson,* pp. 251–406.

14. Charles Mason's journal, Apr. 26, 1868, Mason Mss, Iowa Dept. of Hist.; Cleveland *Plain Dealer,* Apr. 1, 1868; New Orleans *Picayune,*

May 7, 1868; *Trial of Andrew Johnson*, pp. 63, 157–60, 169–70, 231–33, 238.

15. Cincinnati *Enquirer*, May 2, 1868. The ten were Joseph Fowler (Tenn.), Peter G. Van Winkle (W. Va.), James W. Grimes (Iowa), William P. Fessenden (Maine), Lyman Trumbull (Ill.), Henry B. Anthony (R. I.), Edmund G. Ross (Kan.), John Sherman (Ohio), Waitman T. Willey (W. Va.), and William Sprague (R. I.).

16. Philadelphia *Press*, Apr. 20, 22, 1868; New York *Tribune*, Apr. 20, 1868; New York *Herald*, Apr. 28, 1868; Badeau, *Grant in Peace*, pp. 134–36.

17. *American Annual Cyclopaedia*, 1868; *passim;* New York *Herald*, Feb. 28, Mar. 10, Apr. 2, 1868; Charleston *Courier*, Mar. 12, 1868; New York *Times*, Mar. 13, 26, 1868; Philadelphia *Press*, Apr. 8, 9, 18, 21, 1868; Badeau, *Grant in Peace*, pp. 134–36; James L. McDonough and William T. Alderson, "Republican Politics and the Impeachment of Andrew Johnson," *Tennessee Historical Quarterly*, XXVI (Summer, 1967), 181; Chicago *Times*, Apr. 23, 1868; New York *Tribune*, Apr. 3, 1868; Trefousse, *Radical Republicans*, pp. 389–91.

18. DeWitt, *Impeachment*, pp. 516, 524, 546–47; S. P. Chase to H. B. Anthony, May 25, 1868, Andre de Coppet Collection, Princeton University, Robert B. Warden, *An Account of the Private Life and Public Services of Salmon Portland Chase* (Cincinnati, 1874), pp. 684–85; McDonough and Alderson, "Impeachment of Andrew Johnson," pp. 177–83; Thomas and Hyman, *Stanton*, p. 604.

19. New York *World*, Apr. 17, 1868; Hans L. Trefousse, "Ben Wade and the Failure of the Impeachment of Johnson," *Bulletin of the Historical and Philosophical Society of Ohio*, XVIII (October, 1960), 241–52; Horace White to Washburne, May 1, 1868, E. Washburne Mss, LC; George F. Edmunds, "Ex-Senator Edmunds on Reconstruction and Impeachment," *Century*, LXXXV (April, 1913), 864; Charleston *Courier*, Apr. 8, 9, 1868; Cincinnati *Enquirer*, Apr. 16, 1868.

20. New York *World*, May 12, 1868; DeWitt, *Impeachment*, pp. 522–49; New York *Times*, May 12, 13, 1868; Philadelphia *Press*, May 13, 14, 15, 16, 1868; B. F. Butler to Ward, May 12, 1868, Marcus L. Ward Mss, New Jersey Historical Society.

21. *Trial of Andrew Johnson*, p. 412; W. S. Hawley to Tilden, May 22, 1868, Tilden Mss, NYPL; Benjamin C. Truman, "Anecdotes of Andrew Johnson," *Century*, LXXXV o.s. (April, 1913), 438–40; Charles A. Jellison, *Fessenden of Maine* (Syracuse, 1962), pp. 244–45. The vote was 35–19 and the seven were Trumbull, Fessenden, Grimes, Fowler, Henderson, Ross, and Van Winkle.

22. New York *Herald*, May 13, 19, 1868; Philadelphia *Press*, May 14, 1868; Chicago *Times*, May 19, 1868; Ralph J. Roske, "Republican Newspaper Support for the Acquittal of President Johnson," *Tennessee Historical Quarterly*, XI (September, 1952), 263–73; New York *Times*, May 16, 17, 18, 1868; Chicago *Tribune*, May 19, 20, 21, 1868; New York *World*, May 15, 16, 29, 1868.

23. New York *World*, May 19, 29, 1868; Chicago *Times*, May 19, 1868; Philadelphia *Press*, May 21, 1868; McPherson, *Reconstruction*, pp. 364–65; New York *Times*, May 19, 20, 1868; Adam Sherman Hill, "The Chicago Convention," *North American Review*, CVII (June, 1868), 178–80.

24. *American Annual Cyclopaedia*, 1868, *passim*; New York *Times*, Feb. 6, 27, Mar. 19, 1868; Ira V. Brown, "Pennsylvania and the Rights of the Negro, 1865–1887," *Pennsylvania History*, XXVIII (January, 1961), 51–52; Gillette, *The Right To Vote*, p. 37.

25. Homer A. Stebbins, *A Political History of the State of New York, 1865–1869* (New York, 1913), pp. 310–11, Abbott, Wilson, p. 332, Hill, "The Chicago Convention," pp. 182–85; James G. Blaine, *Twenty Years of Congress* (2 vols., Norwich, Conn., 1884–86), II, 389.

26. *Trial of Andrew Johnson*, pp. 414–15; *Cong. Globe*, 40th Cong. 2d Sess., pp. 2505, 3786–87, 3792–93, 4473–74; Philadelphia *Press*, May 29, 1868; New York *World*, June 5, 1868; Chicago *Times*, May 29, June 6, 1868; Ralph J. Roske, "The Seven Martyrs?", *American Historical Review*, LXIV (January, 1959), 323–40; Jellison, *Fessenden*, pp. 250–51; Mark M. Krug, *Lyman Trumbull: Conservative Radical* (New York, 1965), pp. 268–70; Badeau, *Grant in Peace*, p. 137; Blaine, *Twenty Years*, II, 376; New York *Times*, June 5, 13, July 1, 1868; Bowersox, Republican Party in the West, p. 90.

27. McPherson, *Reconstruction*, p. 264; Townsend, *Anecdotes*, p. 135; Thomas and Hyman, *Stanton*, pp. 608–10; Schofield, "Controversies in the War Department," p. 582.

28. Mobile *Register*, June 2, 1868; New York *World*, May 29, June 2, 1868; Chicago *Times*, May 13, 1868; U. S. Statutes at Large, XV, 72–74; *Cong. Globe*, 40th Cong. 2d Sess., pp. 2399, 2463–64, 2701, 2965, 3331, 3363, 3466, 3484—85.

29. "Second Military District," *House Executive Documents*, 40th Cong. 2d Sess., no. 276 (Cong. ser. #1343), pp. 10–14; New Orleans *Picayune*, June 30, July 3, 1868; "Report of the Secretary of War, 1868," pp. 78–79, 108–10, 112–14; *American Annual Cyclopaedia*, 1868, pp. 18, 39, 272, 312, 434–35, 554, 697; *Cong. Globe*, 40th Cong. 2d Sess., p. 3441. Georgia was only partially represented as action there had lagged

behind the other states and her senators were not admitted before the end of the session.

30. Charles W. Ramsdell, *Reconstruction in Texas* (New York, 1910), pp. 200–1, 207–11, 229; "Constitution of Virginia," *Senate Executive Documents*, 40th Cong. 2d Sess., no. 54 (Cong. ser. #1317), New York *Times*, Apr. 18, 20, July 6, 8, 1868; John M. Schofield, *Forty-Six Years in the Army* (New York, 1897), pp. 400–3; *Cong. Globe*, 40th Cong. 2d Sess., p. 3887; Lowe, Virginia, pp. 306–7; 311–12, 324.

31. "Report of the Secretary of War, 1868," pp. 590–93; New York *Times*, July 7, 1868; W. H. Gibbs to Washburne, June 30, 1868, J. L. Alcorn to Washburne, June 29, 1868, E. Washburne Mss, LC; "Condition of Affairs in Mississippi," *House Miscellaneous Documents*, 40th Cong. 3d Sess., no. 53 (Cong. ser. #1385).

32. *U. S. Statutes at Large*, XV, 257, 706–11; *Cong. Globe*, 40th Cong. 2d Sess., pp. 3630, 3926, 3966, 3981, 4197, 4236, 4259, 4266, 4296, 4396, 4416–23.

Seven: Financial Questions

1. Arthur F. Burns and Wesley C. Mitchell, *Measuring Business Cycles* (New York, 1946), p. 78.

2. *Cong. Globe*, 40th Cong. 2d Sess., pp. 70, 537; Charleston *Courier*, Feb. 3, 1868; *U. S. Statutes at Large*, XV, 34; Sharkey, *Money, Class, and Party*, pp. 110–15.

3. "Report of the Secretary of the Treasury, 1867," *House Executive Documents*, 40th Cong. 2d Sess., no. 2 (Cong. ser. #1328), pp. v–vi; Irwin Unger, "Business Men and Specie Resumption," *Political Science Quarterly*, LXXIV (March, 1959), 46–70; *Cong. Globe*, 40th Cong. 2d Sess., pp. 95, 108, 123–28, 434, 1761, 1901–2, 2072.

4. *Ibid.*, 1060, 3887, 4216; *U. S. Statutes at Large*, XIV, 98–173, 471–85; XV, 34, 58–60, 125–68; Herbert R. Ferleger, *David A. Wells and the American Revenue System* (New York, 1942), pp. 62, 95–96, 102–5, 110–13; Edward Stanwood, *American Tariff Controversies in the Nineteenth Century* (2 vols., New York, 1903), II, 146–52, 154–58.

5. Herbert S. Schell, "Hugh McCulloch and the Treasury Department, 1865–1869," *Mississippi Valley Historical Review*, XVII (December, 1930), 405; "Report of the Committee on Fianance, Dec. 17, 1867," *Senate Reports*, 40th Cong. 2d Sess., no. 4 (Cong. ser. #1320), pp. 6–10; *Cong. Globe*, 40th Cong. 2d Sess., pp. 24, 64, appendix, pp. 182–84.

6. *Ibid.*, pp. 1177, 1464; "Report of the Secretary of the Treasury, 1867," pp. xxx–xxxi.

7. Chicago *Times*, Nov. 12, 16, 23, Dec. 1, 6, 7, 10, 13, 23, 31, 1867; Storey to Marble, Feb. 12, 1868, Marble Mss, LC.

8. *Ibid.*; *American Annual Cyclopaedia*, 1868, pp. 349–50, 377, 385, 494–95, 505–6, 603, 605–6; Cincinnati *Enquirer*, Nov. 28, 1867, June 8, 1868; Chicago *Times*, Dec. 31, 1867, June 25, July 2, 1868; Cleveland *Plain Dealer*, Mar. 11, 1868; *Cong. Globe*, 40th Cong. 2d Sess., p. 75.

9. *American Annual Cyclopaedia*, 1868, pp. 203, 448–49, 542–43, 619; New York, *Journal of the Assembly*, 91st Sess., 1868, pp. 63, 1425; Cincinnati *Enquirer*, May 13, 1868; Stebbins, *New York*, pp. 324–25; Irving Katz, *August Belmont: A Political Biography* (New York, 1968), pp. 164–66; New York *World*, Feb. 11, Mar. 12, Apr. 9, May 21, 1868.

10. *Ibid.*, Dec. 27, 1867, Feb. 18, Mar. 14, Apr. 9, June 3, 18, 20, 1868; New York *Herald*, Mar. 12, 14, June 26, 1868.

11. Cincinnati *Enquirer*, June 8, 10, 1868; Chicago *Times*, May 13, June 24, 29, 30, July 8, 1868; W. McLean to Marble, Mar. 22, 1868, Marble Mss, LC: McPherson, *Reconstruction*, pp. 367–68; New York *Tribune*, July 6, 7, 1868; George B. Woods, "The New York Convention," *North American Review*, CVII (October, 1868), 448–49.

12. S. Colfax to Sherman, Dec. 26, 1867, John Sherman Mss, Library of Congress; letters to Washburne from: C. W. Aylesworth, Nov. 12, 1867, B Close, Jan. 4, Feb. 1, 1868, J. Medill, Jan. 10, 1868, Brown, Feb. 2, 1868, C. H. Rosenthal, Feb. 26, 1868, E. Washburne Mss, LC; W. H. Painter to Cooke, Dec. 2, 1867, A. B. Nettleton to Cooke, Jan. 30, 1868, Jay Cooke Mss, Historical Society of Pennsylvania; Sharkey, *Money, Class, and Party*, pp. 92–97; Theodore Clarke Smith, *The Life and Letters of James Abram Garfield* (2 vols., New Haven, Conn., 1925), I, 415; *American Annual Cyclopaedia*, 1868, pp. 377–78, 603–4.

13. Chicago *Tribune*, Jan. 5, 9, 12, 14, Feb. 1, Mar. 10, 11, 15, 1868; *American Annual Cyclopaedia*, 1868, pp. 202–3, 350–51, 493–94, 619–20; New York *Times*, Feb. 6, Mar. 26, 1868; Woodward, *Political Parties in Oregon*, pp. 261–62; letters to Cooke from: L. S. Hubbard, Feb. 5, 1868, H. Cooke, Jan. 31, Feb. 6, 7, 8, 1868, W. E. Chandler, Jan. 31, Feb. 12, 1868, draft of letter, Jay Cooke to J. Sherman, Mar. 2, 1868, Cooke Mss, HSP; New York *Herald*, Mar. 23, 1868.

14. Hill, "Chicago Convention," pp. 173–78; *Cong. Globe*, 40th Cong. 2d Sess., pp. 2570–71.

15. *Ibid.*, pp. 3192, 3223, 3588–89, 3689; Philadelphia *Press*, July 2, 1868; New York *Times*, July 1, 1868; J. Medill to Washburne, May 1,

June 16, 25, 1868, H. Raster to Washburne, July 3, 1868, E. Washburne Mss. LC; H. Cooke to J. Cooke, July 3, 1868, Cooke Mss, HSP; Chicago *Tribune*, June 30, July 3, 1868.

16. *Cong. Globe*, 40th Cong. 2d Sess., pp. 3708, 4466, 4499; New York *Times*, July 14, 29, 30, 1868; New York *World*, July 30, 1868.

Eight: The Democratic Nomination

1. *American Annual Cyclopaedia*, 1868, pp. 203, 606; New York *World*, Mar. 12, Apr. 8, 9, June 4, 18, 20, 1868. The Democrats particularly relished the victory in Galena because Grant had once said that the only public office he desired was to be mayor of his home town.

2. *American Annual Cyclopaedia*, 1868, pp. 350, 377; New York *Times*, Jan 17, Feb. 28, Mar. 22, May 24, 29, 1868; Philadelphia *Press*, Mar. 30, 1868; Chicago *Times*, May 30, June 9, 1868; New York *Herald*, June 4, 1868; Cincinnati *Enquirer*, Oct. 22, 1867, Feb. 17, Mar. 5, May 8, 23, 1868; New York *World*, Jan 25, June 14, 1868; Pendelton to Marble, Nov. 13, Dec. 5, 1867, Mar. 3, 1868, W. McLean to Marble, Apr. 5, 1868, Marble Mss, LC; W. McLean to Seymour, Mar. 30, 1868, Horatio Seymour Mss, New York Historical Society; W. McLean to Barlow, Oct. 11, Dec. 28, 1867, Jan. 14, 1868, Barlow Mss, Huntington Lib.

3. James Buchanan to Bigler, Feb. 15, 1868, William Bigler Mss, Historical Society of Pennsylvania; S. S. Cox to Marble, Nov. 11, 1867, Marble Mss, LC; T. Ewing, Sr., to T. Ewing, Jr., June 14, 1868, Ewing Mss, LC; H. M. Humphrey to Tilden, Feb. 12, 1868, E. Casserly to Tilden, June 16, 1868, Tilden Mss, NYPL; New York *World*, Apr. 14, July 1, 1868; Roseboom, *Civil War Era*, pp. 408–9; E. L. Gould to Barlow, Mar. 21, 1868, R. Taylor to Barlow, Jan. 31, 1868, Barlow Mss, Huntington Lib.

4. New York *Herald*, Nov. 25, 28, 1867, Feb. 28, 1868; H. S. Orton to G. B. Smith, Jan. 17, 1868, G. B. Smith to W. H. Bowman, Feb. 28, 1868, George B. Smith Mss, State Historical Society of Wisconsin; *Letters and Literary Memorials of Samuel J. Tilden*, John Bigelow, ed. (2 vols.; New York, 1908), I, 223–24; George L. Miller to William Cassidy, Jan. 4, 1868, Horatio Seymour Mss, New York State Library; New York *Times*, Nov 29, 1867, Feb. 4, 1868; J. D. Van Buren to Marble, Nov. 26, 1867, Marble Mss, LC (incorrectly filed under June 26, 1867); New York *Tribune*, Mar. 10, 1868.

5. Chicago *Times*, Dec. 27, 30, 1867; Chicago *Tribune*, Jan. 11, 1868; Philadelphia *Press*, Feb. 25, 26, 1868; New York *World*, Dec. 3, 1867,

Feb. 26, 29, May 5, 1868; H. Smythe to W. G. Moore, Feb. 27, 1868, Johnson Mss, LC; J. B. Stillson to Barlow, Feb. 25, 28, 1868, Barlow Mss, Huntington Lib., S. L. M. Barlow to Chandler, Feb. 26, 28, 1868, W. Chandler Mss, LC; Philadelphia *Press*, Mar. 20, June 10, 1868; New York *Herald*, Mar. 20, May 8, 1868; Cleveland *Plain Dealer*, Apr. 18, 28, 1868; Chicago *Times*, May 26, 1868.

6. E. Casserly to W. T. Sherman, Dec. 24, 1867, W. T. Sherman Mss, LC; Raleigh *Sentinel*, Jan. 14, 22, Apr. 18, 1868; New Orleans *Picayune*, May 3, June 26, 1868; Mobile *Register*, Apr. 7, 1868; New York *Times*, Feb. 2, May 11, 17, 20, 1868; G. Halpine to Johnson, Dec. 24, 1867, Johnson Mss, LC; R. Taylor to Barlow, Jan. 16, 1868, Barlow Mss, Huntington Lib., M. M. Pomeroy to Marble, Jan. 3, 1868, Marble Mss, LC; Cincinnati *Enquirer*, May 13, 30, 1868; Cleveland *Plain Dealer*, Feb. 11, 1868; Charleston *Courier*, Mar. 18, Apr. 30, May 7, 8, 1868; Chicago *Times*, Dec. 8, 1867, Apr. 17, May 5, June 13, 1868; New York *Herald*, Feb. 28, Mar. 14, Apr. 22, June 4, 13, 1868; Tilden, *Letters*, I, 214—15; S. E. Church to Seymour, Dec. 27, 1867, Seymour Mss, N. Y. State Lib.

7. Letters to Tilden from: H. Seymour, Mar. 4, May 9, 1868, F. Blair, Jr., Apr. 21, May 20, June 2, 1868, M. Blair, June 5, 1868, W. S. Pierce, June 29, 1868, Tilden Mss, NYPL; Charleston *Courier*, Apr. 30, 1868; Warden, *Chase*, pp. 708—10; W. S. Pierce to Tilden, June 20, 1868, W. S. Pierce to Marble, June 15, 29, 1868, Marble Mss, LC; New York *Times*, Apr. 19, May 10, June 29, 1868; New York *Herald*, Mar. 14, 1868; New York *World*, June 9, 1868.

8. *Ibid.*, Mar. 26, 31, 1868; New York *Times*, Mar. 25, 1868; New York *Herald*, Mar. 13, 1868; Chicago *Tribune*, Mar. 22, 1868; David F. Hughes, Salmon P. Chase: Chief Justice (unpublished PhD dissertation, Princeton University, 1963), pp. 132—36; Cleveland *Plain Dealer*, Mar. 28, 1868; Chicago *Times*, Mar. 28, 1868.

9. Edward S. Perzel, "Alexander Long, Salmon P. Chase, and the Election of 1868," *Bulletin of the Cincinnati Historical Society*, XXIII (January, 1965), 6—7; New York *Herald*, May 6, 7, 8, 31, June 3, 9, 11, 12, 19, 1868; Charleston *Courier*, May 27, June 1, 8, 9, 1868; New York *World*, June 8, 15, 1868; W. B. Brown to Chase, May 27, 1868, W. C. Bryant to Chase, June 13, 1868, Salmon P. Chase Mss, Historical Society of Pennsylvania.

10. New York *Tribune*, June 11, 1868; Philadelphia *Press*, June 11, 1868.

11. Tilden, *Letters*, I, 228—29; J. Warren to Marble, May 23, 30, 1868, Marble Mss, LC; J. D. Van Buren to Chase, June 25, July 2, 1868,

Chase Mss, HSP; Katz, *Belmont*, pp. 167–70; New York *Times*, Oct. 5, 1867.

12. W. S. Pierce to Marble, June 15, 1868, W. Birch to Marble, June 12, 1868, Marble Mss, LC; T. Ewing, Jr., to T. Ewing, Sr., June 30, 1868, Ewing Mss, LC; Philadelphia *Press*, June 16, 1868; Chicago *Times*, June 7, 1868; August Belmont, *Letters, Speeches and Addresses of August Belmont* (n.p., 1890), pp. 114–17; New York *World*, June 10, 1868.

13. *Ibid.*, June 3, 8, 17, 1868; New York *Times*, June 29, 1868; Cincinnati *Enquirer*, June 13, 26, 27, 1868; Chicago *Times*, June 18, 20, 28, 1868.

14. *Ibid.*, June 17, 23, July 1, 1868; New York *World*, June 17, 23, 1868; Cleveland *Plain Dealer*, June 30, 1868; New York *Tribune*, June 29, 1868; Philadelphia *Press*, June 19, 29, 1868; C. A. Eldridge to Paul, June 12, 1868, George H. Paul Mss, State Historical Society of Wisconsin; New York *Herald*, June 24, 26, 1868; R. W. Newton to Johnson, June 24, 1868, Johnson Mss, LC. This is also the assessment of Gambill, *Northern Democrats*, pp. 289–91.

15. Chicago *Times*, June 6, 1868; New York *Herald*, May 2, 1868; New York *Times*, May 20, June 2, 4, 22, 1868; Raleigh *Sentinel*, May 15, June 3, 6, 1868; Cincinnati *Enquirer*, May 8, 1868; "The Correspondence of Robert Toombs, Alexander H. Stephens, and Howell Cobb," Ulrich B. Phillips, ed., *Annual Report, American Historical Association*, II (1911), 695–96; Mobile *Register*, Feb. 11, 27, Apr. 30, May 2, 1868; New York *Herald*, May 2, 21, June 10, 1868; New York *Times*, May 17, 1868; F. Smith to Johnson, June 27, 1868; Johnson Mss, LC.

16. Mobile *Register*, Apr. 7, June 13, 15, 16, 20, 23, 24, 1868; New York *Times*, June 16, 19, 29, 30, July 1, 1868; Raleigh *Sentinel*, June 13, 16, 19, 22, 24, 1868; "Howell Cobb Papers," Robert P. Brooks, ed., *Georgia Historical Quarterly*, VI (December, 1922), 391–92; Fayette Copeland, "The New Orleans Press and the Reconstruction," *Louisiana Historical Quarterly*, XXX (January, 1947), 200–1; Charleston *Courier*, Apr. 6, May 22, 25, June 10, 26, 30, 1868; New Orleans *Picayune*, June 21, 1868; J. A. Bayard to Barlow, May 29, 31, June 3, 10, 1868, J. B. Gordon to Barlow, June 5, 1868, W. M. Browne to Barlow, June 24, 1868, Barlow Mss, Huntington Lib.

17. New York *Tribune*, June 26, 29, July 2, 6, 1868; Philadelphia *Press*, July 2, 3, 1868; Detroit *Free Press*, July 3, 4, 1868; New York *Herald*, July 5, 1868. The vote in the New York caucus was Church-38, Chase-10, Hendricks-8, scattered-10.

18. *Ibid.*, July 4, 6, 1868; Hughes, *Chase*, pp. 141–42; Chicago

Times, July 4, 5, 6, 1868; New York *Tribune,* July 2, 1868; New York *Times,* July 1, 2, 3, 1868; Philadelphia *Press,* July 2, 3, 4, 1868; Cincinnati *Enquirer,* July 3, 1868; Charleston *Courier,* July 6, 1868; Perzel, "Long, Chase, and 1868," p. 10.

19. New York *Times,* June 30, July 3, 7, 1868; *U. S. Statutes at Large,* XV, 702–3; letters to Johnson, June 28–July 7, 1868, *passim,* Johnson Mss, LC.

20. McPherson, *Reconstruction,* pp. 367–68; Woods, "The New York Convention," pp. 449–50; Hampton M. Jarrell, *Wade Hampton and the Negro: The Road Not Taken* (Columbia, S. C., 1949), pp. 165–67; New York *World,* July 8, 1868; Coleman, *Election of 1868,* pp. 61, 203.

21. New Orleans *Picayune,* July 9, 1868; Woods, "The New York Convention," p. 455; "Howell Cobb Papers," pp. 391–92; *Official Proceedings of the National Democratic Convention Held at New York, July 4–9, 1868* (Boston, 1868), pp. 75–102.

22. *Ibid.,* pp. 104–37.

23. New York *Herald,* July 9, 1868.

24. J. D. Van Buren to Chase, July 24, 1868, Salmon P. Chase Mss, Library of Congress; New York *World,* July 9, 10, 1868.

25. New York *Herald,* July 10, 1868; S. Ward to Chase, July 10, 1868, Chase Mss, LC; J. D. Van Buren to Chase, Oct. 24, 1868, Chase Mss, HSP; James L. Vallandigham, *A Life of Clement L. Vallandigham* (Baltimore, 1872), pp. 423–24.

26. *Proceedings of the Democratic Convention,* pp. 141–61; Charleston *Courier,* July 15, 1868; Chicago *Times,* July 10, 1868; Coleman, *Election of 1868,* p. 240.

27. New York *Herald,* July 5, 1868.

28. J. Buchanan to Bigler, Mar. 13, 1868, S. J. Tilden to Bigler, Apr. 9, 1868, Bigler Mss, HSP; Charleston *Courier,* July 9, 1868; W. H. Bowman to G. B. Smith, Feb. 22, 1868, G. B. Smith Mss, Hist. Soc. of Wisc.; Tilden, *Letters,* I, 222–23; New York *Times,* June 17, 1868; Coleman, *Election of 1868,* p. 241; Stewart Mitchell, *Horatio Seymour of New York* (Cambridge, Mass., 1938), pp. 235–36.

29. *Proceedings of the Democratic Convention,* pp. 163–70.

Nine: The Election of 1868

1. Badeau, *Grant in Peace,* pp. 145–49; Richardson, *Chandler,* p. 94; Schofield, "Controversies in the War Department," p. 582; Grant to Wil-

liam W. Smith, Sept. 25, 1868, Grant Mss, LC; McPherson, *Reconstruction*, pp. 365–66.

2. This discussion is generally based on editorials and speeches in the New York *Times*, Chicago *Tribune*, New York *Tribune*, and Philadelphia *Press* during the campaign. Footnotes will be limited to those items that require further specific citation.

3. Statements by Wade Hampton and C. C. Langdon, in New York *Times*, July 28, Aug. 10, 1868; Mobile *Register*, Aug. 13, 1868; New York *World*, July 10, 1868.

4. For examples of veterans' activities see New York *Times*, July 10, 16, Aug. 8, 9, 17, 25, Sept. 5, Oct. 1, 2, 3, 1868. The Grand Army of the Republic took no part in the campaign, which was left to these independent veterans' groups.

5. Speeches by Henry Wise, Bedford Forrest, Howell Cobb, Robert Toombs, Raphael Semmes, and Zebulon Vance, in New York *Tribune*, July 17, 21, 28, 1868, and New York *Times*, July 16, Aug. 3, 17, 1868; New York *Herald*, July 29, Aug. 2, 3, 4, 1868.

6. New York *World*, July 18, Aug. 20, 1868; Cincinnati *Enquirer*, July 14, 16, 24, 1868. In general, treatment of the Democratic campaign is based on speeches in the New York *Times* and editorials and speeches in the New York *World*, Cleveland *Plain Dealer*, Washington *National Intelligencer*, Cincinnati *Enquirer*, Charleston *Courier*, New Orleans *Picayune*, and Mobile *Register*. Again specific items will be footnoted only if required.

7. New York *World*, July 14, Aug. 7, 14, 17, 21, 24, 25, 28, 31, Sept. 5, 1868. The New York correspondent of the Charleston *Courier*, Oct. 1, 1868, identified the author of the series as Gen. W. F. "Baldy" Smith.

8. New York *Times*, Aug. 25, Sept. 5, 1868.

9. New York *Times*, Aug. 6, 9, 17, 1868; Wood, *Black Scare*, pp. 126–28; New York *World*, July 13, 14, 1868; *Cong. Globe*, 40th Cong. 2d Sess., pp. 3911–12.

10. "Report of the Secretary of War, 1868," pp. 323, 525–26; New York *Times*, June 15, Oct. 13, 1868; Simkins and Woody, *South Carolina*, p. 110; Thompson, *Georgia*, pp. 209–14.

11. *Acts of the Sessions of July, September and November, 1868 of the General Assembly of Alabama, Held in the City of Montgomery* (Montgomery, 1868), p. 27; New Orleans *Picayune*, Aug. 15, Sept. 10, 1868; Charleston *Courier*, Aug. 4, Oct. 24, 1868; New York *Times*, Aug. 8, 12, 24, 1868; Mobile *Register*, July 23, Oct. 8, 1868; Davis, *Florida*, p. 540; Staples, *Arkansas*, pp. 284–86. In South Carolina the constitution disfranchised and disqualified for office anyone barred from voting or of-

ficeholding by the 14th Amendment. Democratic leaders argued, and election officials agreed, that as the 14th Amendment didn't bar anyone from voting the provision of the state constitution didn't either.

12. New York *Times*, Aug. 2, 10, 13, 31, 1868; Charleston *Courier*, Aug. 7, 26, Sept. 21, 29, 1868; Mobile *Register*, July 22, 31, Aug. 13, 1868; New Orleans *Picayune*, July 28, Aug. 13, 18, 1868; Herbert Shapiro "The Ku Klux Klan During Reconstruction: The South Carolina Episode," *Journal of Negro History*, XLIX (January, 1964), p. 37.

13. "Report of the Secretary of War, 1868," pp. xix–xxii, xxiv, 115, 120; New York *Times*, July 29, Aug. 2, 12, 20, Sept. 5, 1868; Otis A. Singletary, *Negro Milita and Reconstruction* (Austin, Tex., 1957), p. 36. On the subject of violence in the campaign in the South also see Trelease, *White Terror*, Part III.

14. New York *Times*, Aug. 12, 1868; *American Annual Cyclopaedia*, 1868, p. 42; *Messages and Papers of the Presidents*, VI, 653.

15. "Report of the Secretary of War, 1868," pp. xx–xxvi, xxx–xxxiii; Sefton, *US Army*, pp. 91–93.

16. "Report of the Secretary of War, 1868," pp. xxvi–xxxii, 125–28, 308–9; W. W. Holden to Gen. Miles, Oct. 7, 1868, R. Scott to Meade, Sept. 29, Oct. 3, 9, 1868, Meade Mss, HSP; Ralph L. Peek, "Aftermath of Military Reconstruction, 1868–1869," *Florida Historical Quarterly*, XLIII (October, 1964), 133; New York *Times*, Sept. 4, 5, 11, 1868; New York *World*, Oct. 23, 1868; Theodore B. FitzSimons, Jr., "The Camilla Riot," *Georgia Historical Quarterly*, XXXV (June, 1951), 116–25.

17. Kirkland, Troops in South, pp. 233–41; New York *Times*, Aug. 17, 18, 21, 27, Sept. 5, 8, 16, 1868; *Cong. Globe*, 40th Cong. 2d Sess., pp. 4520–22.

18. New York *World*, Aug. 21, 26, 31, Sept. 9, Oct. 2, 1868; New York *Times*, July 11, Sept. 4, 5, 1868. See eastern viewpoint in New York *World*, July 23, 24, Aug. 5, 11, Sept. 9, Oct. 13, 1868; New York *Times*, Aug. 12, Sept. 3, 1868. Western viewpoint in Cincinnati *Enquirer*, July 20, 25, Aug. 1, 4, 6, 7, 18, 1868; Cleveland *Plain Dealer*, Aug. 19, 1868; speeches by westerners reported in New York *World*, July 19, 27, 31, 1868; New York *Times*, Aug. 12, 1868.

19. New York *World*, July 19, 31, Aug. 8, 18, Sept. 28, 1868.

20. J. Cooke to H. Cooke, July 6, 1868, Cooke Mss, HSP; *Cong. Globe*, 40th Cong. 2d Sess.; p. 4178; Nugent, *Money and American Society*, pp. 108–9; New York *Times*, July 31, 1868.

21. See especially statement by Wells in New York *Tribune*, July 29, 1868; speeches by J. Sherman and E. Atkinson in New York *Times*, Aug. 23, Sept. 10, 25, 1868; Ferleger, *Wells*, pp. 211–19.

22. New York *Times*, July 14, 31, Aug. 11, 17, 20, 21, Sept. 6, 23, 29, Oct. 13, 1868; Philadelphia *Press*, July 11, 13, 1868.

23. Copeland, "The New Orleans Press," p. 201; William E. Smith, *The Francis Preston Blair Family in Politics* (2 vols., New York, 1933), II, 412; Mason's diary, July 10, 12, 1868, Mason Mss, Iowa Dept. of Hist.; R. W. Latham to Tilden, July 14, 1868, S. L. M. Barlow to Tilden, July 10, 1868, Tilden Mss, NYPL; D. S. Walker and C. G. Halpine to Chase, July 11, 1868, Chase Mss, HSP; New York *Times*, July 17, 28, Sept. 28, 1868; Chase to D. S. Walker and C. G. Halpine, July 13 [?] 1868, Chase to C. A. Dana, Oct. 1, 1868, Chase Mss, LC; S. Ward to Marble, Aug. 4, 1868, Ward to Barlow, Aug. 1, 1868, Marble Mss, LC; J. D. Van Buren to Seymour, July 20, 1868, J. D. Hoover to Tilden, July 15, 1868, Seymour Mss, N. Y. State Lib.; New York *World*, July 17, 1868; "Post-Bellum Days: Selections from the Correspondence of the Late Senator James R. Doolittle," *The Magazine of History*, XVII (August, 1913), 57–58; H. Seymour to Barlow, July 23, 1868, Barlow Mss, Huntington Lib.

24. Letters to and from Seymour, July 27–Sept. 5, 1868, *passim*, Seymour Mss, N. Y. State Lib.; J. Doolittle to Marble, Aug. 5, 1868, C. Vallandigham to Tilden, Sept. 2, 1868, Marble Mss LC; letters to Tilden from: H. Seymour, Aug. 7, 17, 1868, E. F. Pillsbury, Aug. 5, 1868, G. W. McCook, Aug. 24, 1868, J. Doolittle, Aug. 19, 1868, Tilden Mss, NYPL; Durkin, *Mallory*, p. 406; Perzel, "Long, Chase, and 1868," p. 13; New York *Herald*, Aug. 11, 12, 14, 1868; *Round Table* articles reprinted in Chicago *Tribune*, July 21, 1868, and Cleveland *Plain Dealer*, Aug. 31, 1868.

25. *Ibid.*, Sept. 4, 7, 12, 14, 1868; New York *World*, Sept. 2, 8, 9, 11, 14, 1868; N. E. Paine to Seymour, Sept. 8, 11, 1868, H. R. Shackleford to J. C. Spencer, Aug. 5, 1868, G. J. Tucker to Seymour, Aug. 31, 1868, M. Emery to Seymour, July 31, 1868, Seymour Mss, N. Y. State Lib.

26. New York *World*, Sept. 15, 16, 1868; Cleveland *Plain Dealer*, Sept. 15, 1868; Cincinnati *Enquirer*, Sept. 15, 16, 17, 1868; *Tribune Almanac*, 1869, p. 63; New York *Herald*, Sept. 5, 10, 1868.

27. Letters to Seymour from: E. E. Davis, Sept. 18, 1868, W. A. Wallace, Sept. 24, 1868, W. Cassidy, Sept. 25, 1868, J. B. Craig, Sept. 25, 1868, Seymour Mss, N. Y. State Lib.; W. Bigler to Tilden, Sept. 25, 1868, H. Seymour to Tilden, Oct. 1, 2, 1868, Tilden Mss, NYPL; New York *World*, Oct. 12, 13, 1868; Charleston *Courier*, Sept. 25, Oct. 8, 1868.

28. New York *World*, Oct. 16, 20, 21, 1868; E. Washburne to C. C. Washburn, Oct. 23, 1868, Cadwallader C. Washburn Mss, State Historical Society of Wisconsin; letters to E. Washburne from: H. White, Oct.

18, 1868, W. E. Chandler, Oct. 19, 1868, J. G. Blaine, Oct. 24, 1868, E. Washburne Mss, LC; Cleveland *Plain Dealer*, Oct. 14, 16, 1868; Cincinnati *Enquirer*, Oct. 15, 16, 19, 1868.

29. S. L. M. Barlow to Kernan, Oct. 14, 1868, Francis Kernan Mss, Cornell University; W. McLean to Barlow, Oct. 14, 15, 16 (3 items), 1868; Barlow Mss, Huntington Lib.; McJimsey, *Marble*, pp. 130–32; New York *World*, Oct. 15, 16, 18, 1868; Albany *Argus*, in New York *Times*, Oct. 18, 1868; Tilden to Marble, Oct. 17, 1868, W. Cassidy to Marble, Oct. 18, 1868, W. Cassidy to Tilden, Oct. 18, 1868, Marble Mss, LC; Gambill, *Northern Democrats*, pp. 302–4.

30. New York *World*, Oct. 19, 1868; New York *Times*, Oct. 16, 17, 1868: A. W. Randall to Tilden, Oct. 15, 1868, members of the Indiana Democratic Executive Committee to Belmont, Oct. 16, 1868, Tilden Mss, NYPL; Washington *National Intelligencer*. Oct. 16, 17, 20, 1868; New York *Tribune*, Oct. 16, 19, 20, 22, 1868; Cincinnati *Enquirer*, Oct. 17, 1868; Smith, *Blair Family*, II, 423.

31. New York *Times*, Oct. 17–19, 24–28, 1868; Cleveland *Plain Dealer*, Oct. 17, 19, 1868; Cincinnati *Enquirer*, Oct. 17, 1868; letters to Marble, Oct. 15–21, 1868, *passim*, Marble Mss, LC; Gambill, *Northern Democrats*, pp. 304–5; J. D. Van Buren to Chase, Oct. 17, 24, 1868, A. Long to Chase, Nov. 2, 1868, Chase Mss, HSP; Chase to A. Long, Oct. 27, 1868, Chase to J. D. Van Buren, Oct. 17, 1868 (2 items), Chase Mss, LC; Seymour to C. McCormick, Oct. 20, 1868, Cyrus H. McCormick Mss, State Historical Society of Wisconsin.

32. Text of speeches in New York *World*, Oct. 22–25, 27–31, Nov. 1–3, 1868.

33. New York *Times*, Oct. 17, 24, 28, 30, 1868; Charleston *Courier*, Oct. 19, 24, 1868; New Orleans *Picayune*, Oct. 15, 16, 22, 23, 1868; Katherine M. Chapman, "Some Benjamin Harvey Hill Letters," *Georgia Historical Quarterly*, XLVII (September, 1963), 312–13.

34. "Report of the Secretary of War, 1868," pp. xxxv–xxxviii, 303–8; "The Origin and Activities of the 'White League' in New Orleans," Walter Prichard, ed., *Louisiana Historical Quarterly*, XXIII (April, 1940), 525–43; Staples, *Arkansas*, p. 294; Shapiro. "Ku Klux Klan," pp. 37–38.

35. Alexander B. Callow, Jr., *The Tweed Ring* (New York, 1966), pp. 208–13; "Election Frauds in New York," *House Reports*, 40th Cong. 3d Sess., nos. 31, 41 (Cong. ser. #1389–90). For Southern material see n. 39 below.

36. Blaine, *Twenty Years*, II, 408. In the following discussion results for presidential elections are taken from Burnham, *Presidential Ballots*. All

other election results, as well as figures for congressional strength, are from *Tribune Almanac*, 1865, 1867, 1868, 1869.

37. Sharkey, *Money, Class, and Party*, pp. 82, 102–4, 182–83.

38. The elections of 1848, 1920, and 1946 show that the opposite has often been the case.

39. Shapiro, "Ku Klux Klan," pp. 35–39; Ficklen, *Louisiana*, p. 230; Thomas B. Alexander, *Political Reconstruction in Tennessee* (Nashville, 1950), pp. 193–94; Olive Hall Shadgett, *The Republican Party in Georgia from Reconstruction Through 1900* (Athens, Ga., 1964), pp. 14–15.

40. The vote would have been 160–157. As Charles Coleman points out, however, Grant's victory did not depend on the reconstructed states, as he would have won even if all eleven ex-Confederate states had voted for Seymour, *Election of 1868*, p. 363.

41. Alexander H. H. Stuart, *A Narrative* (Richmond, Va.; 1888), pp. 19–51; *American Annual Cyclopaedia*, 1869, pp. 455–61, 676–78, 709–10, 713.

BIBLIOGRAPHY

I. Manuscripts

Nathaniel Banks Mss, Illinois State Historical Library.
Samuel L. M. Barlow Mss, Henry E. Huntington Library.
William Bigler Mss, Historical Society of Pennsylvania.
Austin Blair Mss, Detroit Public Library.
John M. Broomall Mss, Historical Society of Pennsylvania.
William E. Chandler Mss, Library of Congress.
Salmon P. Chase Mss, Library of Congress.
Salmon P. Chase Mss, Historical Society of Pennsylvania.
James M. Comley Mss, Ohio Historical Society.
Cyrus B. Comstock Diaries, Library of Congress.
Jay Cooke Mss, Historical Society of Pennsylvania.
Henry L. Dawes Mss, Library of Congress.
Andre deCoppet Collection, Princeton University.
John A. Dix Mss, Columbia University.
Grenville M. Dodge Mss, Iowa State Department of History and Archives.
James R. Doolittle Mss, State Historical Society of Wisconsin.
Ewing Family Mss, Library of Congress.
Lucius Fairchild Mss, State Historical Society of Wisconsin.
Ulysses S. Grant Mss, Library of Congress.
Horace Greeley Mss, New York Public Library.
Timothy O. Howe Mss, State Historical Society of Wisconsin.
Andrew Johnson Mss, Library of Congress.
Francis Kernan Mss, Cornell University Library.
John Logan Mss, Library of Congress.
Cyrus H. McCormick Mss, State Historical Society of Wisconsin.
Hugh McCulloch Mss, Library of Congress.
Willett S. Main Diaries, State Historical Society of Wisconsin.
Manton Marble Mss, Library of Congress.
Charles Mason Mss, Iowa State Department of History and Archives.
George G. Meade Mss, Historical Society of Pennsylvania.
George H. Paul Mss, State Historical Society of Wisconsin.
Read Family Mss, Library Company of Philadelphia.
Horatio Seymour Mss, New York Historical Society.
Horatio Seymour Mss, New York State Library.
Philip Sheridan Mss, Library of Congress.
John Sherman Mss, Library of Congress.
William T. Sherman Mss, Library of Congress.

George B. Smith Mss, State Historical Society of Wisconsin.
William Henry Smith Mss, Ohio Historical Society.
Edwin M. Stanton Mss, Library of Congress.
Samuel J. Tilden Mss, New York Public Library.
Lyman Trumbull Mss, Illinois State Historical Library.
Marcus L. Ward Mss, New Jersey Historical Society.
Cadwallader C. Washburn Mss, State Historical Society of Wisconsin.
Elihu B. Washburne Mss, Library of Congress.
Waitman T. Willey Mss, West Virginia University Library.
Richard Yates Mss, Illinois State Historical Library.

II. Documents and Almanacs

"Alabama Election," *House Executive Documents*, 40th Cong. 2d Sess.,
no. 238 (Cong. ser. #1341).
American Annual Cyclopaedia, 1865–1869.
Appleton's Cyclopaedia of American Biography. 6 vols. New York,
1887–89.
Burnham, W. Dean, *Presidential Ballots, 1836–1892*. Baltimore, 1955.
A Compilation of the Messages and Papers of the Presidents, 1789–1897.
James D. Richardson, compiler. 10 vols. Washington, D.C., 1896–99.
"Condition of Affairs in Mississippi," *House Miscellaneous Documents*,
40th Cong. 3d Sess., no. 53 (Cong. ser. #1385).
"Condition of the South," *Senate Executive Documents*, 39th Cong. 1st
Sess., no. 2 (Cong. ser. #1237).
Congressional Globe, 39th and 40th Congresses, 1866–68.
"Constitution of the State of Alabama," *Senate Miscellaneous Documents*, 40th Cong. 2d Sess., no. 32 (Cong. ser. #1319).
"Constitution of Virginia," *Senate Executive Documents*, 40th Cong. 2d
Sess., no. 54 (Cong. ser. #1317).
"Correspondence Relative to Reconstruction," *Senate Executive Documents*, 40th Cong. 1st Sess., no. 14 (Cong. ser. #1308).
"Election Frauds in New York," *House Reports*, 40th Cong. 3d Sess.,
nos. 31, 41 (Cong. ser. #1389–90).
"Election in Georgia, North and South Carolina," *House Executive Documents*, 40th Cong. 2d Sess., no. 300 (Cong. ser. #1345).
"Elections in Southern States," *House Executive Documents*, 40th Cong.
2d Sess., no. 291 (Cong. ser. #1343).
"General Orders-Reconstruction," *House Executive Documents*, 40th
Cong. 2d Sess., no. 342 (Cong. ser. #1346).
"Impeachment Investigation," *House Reports*, 40th Cong. 1st Sess., no. 7
(Cong. ser. #1314).

"Interpretation of the Reconstruction Acts," *House Executive Documents,* 40th Cong. 1st Sess., no. 34 (Cong. ser. #1311).

McPherson, Edward. *The Political History of the United States of America during the Period of Reconstruction,* Washington, 1871.

Official Journal of the Constitutional Convention of the State of Alabama, Held in the City of Montgomery, Commencing on Tuesday, November 5th, A. D., 1867. Montgomery, 1868.

Official Proceedings of the National Democratic Convention, Held at New York, July 4–9, 1868. Boston, 1868.

Proceedings in the Trial of Andrew Johnson, Washington, 1868.

"Registered Voters in Rebel States," *Senate Executive Documents,* 40th Cong. 2d Sess., no. 53 (Cong. ser. #1317).

"Removal of Hon. E. M. Stanton and Others," *House Executive Documents,* 40th Cong. 2d Sess., no. 57 (Cong. ser. #1330).

"Report of the Committee on Finance, Dec. 17, 1867," *Senate Reports,* 40th Cong. 2d Sess., no. 4 (Cong. ser. #1320).

"Report of the Joint Committee on Reconstruction," *House Reports,* 39th Cong. 1st Sess., no. 30 (Cong. ser. #1273).

"Report of the Secretary of the Treasury, 1865", *House Executive Documents,* 39th Cong. 1st Sess., no. 3 (Cong. ser. #1254).

"Report of the Secretary of the Treasury, 1867," *House Executive Documents,* 40th Cong. 2d Sess., no. 2 (Cong. ser. #1328).

"Report of the Secretary of War, 1866," *House Executive Documents,* 39th Cong. 2d Sess., no. 1 (Cong. ser. #1285).

"Report of the Secretary of War, 1867," *House Executive Documents,* 40th Cong. 2d Sess., no. 1 (Cong. ser. #1324).

"Report of the Secretary of War, 1868," *House Executive Documents,* 40th Cong. 3d Sess., no. 1 (Cong. Ser. #1367).

"Second Military District," *House Executive Documents,* 40th Cong. 2d Sess., no. 276 (Cong. ser. #1343).

Thorpe, Francis N., editor. *The Federal and State Constitutions,* 7 vols. Washington, 1909.

Tribune Almanac, 1865, 1867–1869.

United States Bureau of the Census, *Ninth Census of the United States: 1870. Population.*

——*Tenth Census of the United States: 1880. Population.*

United States Statutes at Large, XIV, XV.

"Votes Cast for New Constitutions," *House Executive Documents,* 40th Cong. 2d Sess., no. 284 (Cong. ser. #1343).

III. Newspapers

Boston *Post*, 1866–67.
Charleston *Courier*, 1866–68.
Chicago *Times*, 1866–68.
Chicago *Tribune*, 1867–68.
Cincinnati *Enquirer*, 1867–68.
Cleveland *Plain Dealer*, 1866–68.
Mobile *Advertiser and Register*, 1867–68 (Mobile *Register* after January 30, 1868).
New Orleans *Picayune*, 1866–68.
New York *Herald*, 1867–68.
New York *Times*, 1866–68.
New York *Tribune*, 1867–68.
New York *World*, 1866–68.
Philadelphia *Press*, 1867–68.
Raleigh *Sentinel*, 1867–68.
Richmond *Whig*, 1867.
Washington *National Intelligencer*, 1866–68.

IV. Autobiographies, Diaries, Letters, Etc.

Belmont, August. *Letters, Speeches and Addresses of August Belmont*, N. p. 1890.
Bigelow, John. *Retrospections of an Active Life*. 5 vols. New York, 1909–13.
Blaine, James G. *Twenty Years of Congress*, 2 vols. Norwich, Conn., 1884–86.
Browning, Orville H. *The Diary of Orville Hickman Browning*, James G. Randall and Theodore C. Pease, editors. 2 vols. Springfield, Ill., 1925–33.
Chapman, Katherine M. "Some Benjamin Harvey Hill Letters," *Georgia Historical Quarterly*, XLVII (September, 1963), 305–19.
Cobb, Howell, "Howell Cobb Papers," Robert P. Brooks, editor, *Georgia Historical Quarterly*, VI (December, 1922), 355–94.
"Correspondence of Robert Toombs, Alexander H. Stephens, and Howell Cobb," Ulrich B. Phillips, editor, *Annual Report, American Historical Association*, II (1911).
Doolittle, James R. "Doolittle Correspondence," *Southern History Association Publications*, XI (January, 1907), 6–9.
——— "Post Bellum Days: Selections from the Correspondence of the

Late Senator, James R. Doolittle," *The Magazine of History* XVII (August, 1913), 49–64.

Edmunds, George F. "Ex-Senator Edmunds on Reconstruction and Impeachment," *Century*, LXXXV (April, 1913), 863–64.

Garfield-Hinsdale Letters, Mary L. Hinsdale, editor. Ann Arbor, Mich., 1949.

Grant, Jesse R. *In the Days of My Father: General Grant.* New York, 1925.

Grant, Ulysses S. *General Grant's Letters to a Friend*, James Grant Wilson, editor. New York, 1897.

Green, Wharton J. *Recollections and Reflections.* N. p., 106.

Hampton, Wade. *Family Letters of the Three Wade Hamptons, 1782–1901,* Charles E. Cauthen, editor. Columbia, S.C., 1953.

McClure, Alexander K. *Old Time Notes of Pennsylvania.* 2 vols. Philadelphia, 1905.

Moore, William G. "Notes of Colonel W. G. Moore, Private Secretary to President Johnson, 1866–68," St. George L. Siossat, editor. *American Historical Review*, XIX (October, 1913), 98–132.

"Origin and Activities of the 'White League' in New Orleans," Walter Prichard, editor. *Louisiana Historical Quarterly*, XXIII (April, 1940), 525–43.

Pomeroy, Marcus M. *Journey of Life.* New York, 1890.

Schofield, John M. *Forty-Six Years in the Army.* New York, 1897.

—— "Controversies in the War Department," *Century*, LIV (August, 1897), 577–83.

Schurz, Carl. *Intimate Letters of Carl Schurz, 1841–1869,* Joseph Schafer, editor, Madison, Wisc., 1928.

Sherman, John, *Recollections of Forty Years.* 2 vols. Chicago, 1895.

Sherman, William T. *Home Letters of General Sherman*, M. A. DeWolfe Howe, editor. New York, 1909.

—— *Memoirs of General W. T. Sherman*, 4th ed. rev., 2 vols. New York, 1891.

—— *The Sherman Letters.* Rachel Sherman Thorndike, editor. New York, 1894.

Stephens, Alexander H. *Recollections of Alexander H. Stephens*, Myrta L. Avery, editor. New York, 1910.

Strong, George Templeton. *The Diary of George Templeton Strong,* Allan Nevins and Milton H. Thomas, editors. 4 vols. New York, 1952.

Stuart, Alexander H. H. *A Narrative.* Richmond, Va., 1888.

Tilden, Samuel J. *Letters and Literary Memorials of Samuel J. Tilden,* John Bigelow, editor. 2 vols. New York, 1908.

Townsend, Edward D. *Anecdotes of the Civil War.* New York, 1884.

Welles, Gideon, *Diary of Gideon Welles*, Howard K. Beale, editor. 3 vols. New York, 1960.

Worth, Jonathan. *The Correspondence of Jonathan Worth*, J. G. de Roulhac Hamilton, editor. 2 vols., Raleigh, N. C., 1909.

V. Secondary Works

Abbott, Richard Henry. Cobbler in Congress: Life of Henry Wilson, 1812–1875. Unpublished PhD dissertation, University of Wisconsin, 1965.
Alderson, William T. The Influence of Military Rule and the Freedmen's Bureau on Reconstruction in Virginia. Unpublished PhD dissertation, Vanderbilt University, 1952.
Alexander, Thomas B. "Persistent Whiggery in Alabama and the Lower South, 1860–1867," *Alabama Review*, XII (January, 1959), 35–52.
—— "Persistent Whiggery in the Confederate South, 1860–1877," *Journal of Southern History*, CXXVII (August, 1961), 305–29.
—— *Political Reconstruction in Tennessee*, Nashville, 1950.
Badeau, Adam. *Grant in Peace*. Hartford, Conn., 1887.
Beale, Howard K. *The Critical Year: A Study of Andrew Johnson and Reconstruction*. New York, 1930.
Bentley, George R. *A History of the Freedmen's Bureau*, Philadelphia, 1955.
Blackburn, George M. "Radical Republican Motivation: A Case History," *Journal of Negro History*, LIV (April, 1969), 109–26.
Bloch, Julius M. The Rise of the New York *World* during the Civil War Decade. Unpublished PhD dissertation, Harvard University, 1941.
Bonadio, Felice A. *North of Reconstruction: Ohio Politics, 1865–1870*. New York, 1970.
Bowersox, LaVerne K. The Reconstruction of the Republican Party in the West, 1865–1870. Unpublished PhD dissertation, Ohio State University, 1931.
Bradley, Erwin S. *The Triumph of Militant Republicanism: A Study of Pennsylvania and Presidential Politics*. Philadelphia, 1964.
Brigance, William N. "Jeremiah Black and Andrew Johnson," *Mississippi Valley Historical Review*, XIX (September, 1932), 205–18.
Brock, W. R. *An American Crisis: Congress and Reconstruction, 1865–1867*. London, 1963.
Brown, Ira V. "Pennsylvania and the Rights of the Negro, 1865–1887," *Pennsylvania History*, XXVIII (January, 1961), 45–57.
Caldwell, Martha B. The Attitude of Kansas towards Reconstruction. Unpublished PhD dissertation, Kansas University, 1933.
Callow, Alexander B., Jr. *The Tweed Ring*. New York, 1966.
Carleton, William G. "Civil War Dissidence in the North: The Perspec-

tive of a Century," *South Atlantic Quarterly*, LXV (Summer, 1966), 390–402.

Carpenter, John A. *Sword and Olive Branch: Oliver Otis Howard*. Pittsburgh, 1964.

Caskey, Willie M. *Secession and Restoration of Louisiana*. University, Louisiana, 1938.

Clayton, Powell. *The Aftermath of the Civil War, in Arkansas*, New York, 1915.

Clemenceau, Georges. *American Reconstruction, 1865–1870*. New York, 1928.

Cole, Arthur C. *The Era of the Civil War, 1848–1870*. Vol. III of the *Centennial History of Illinois*, C. W. Alvord, editor. Springfield, Ill., 1919.

Coleman, Charles H. *The Election of 1868: The Democratic Effort To Regain Control*. New York, 1933.

Copeland, Fayette. "The New Orleans Press and the Reconstruction," *Louisiana Historical Quarterly*, XXX (January, 1947), 149–337.

Cox, LaWanda, and John Cox, "Negro Suffrage and Republican Politics: The Problem of Motivation in Reconstruction Historiography," *Journal of Southern History*, XXXIII (August, 1967), 303–30.

—— *Politics, Principle and Prejudice, 1865–1866*. New York, 1963.

Craven, Avery. *Reconstruction: The Ending of the Civil War*. New York, 1969.

Curry, Richard O., editor. *Radicalism, Racism, and Party Realignment: The Border States during Reconstruction*. Baltimore, 1969.

—— "The Union as It Was: A Critique of Recent Interpretations of the Copperheads," *Civil War History*, XIII (March, 1967), pp. 25–39.

Dante, Harris L. Reconstruction Politics in Illinois, 1860–1872, Unpublished PhD dissertation, University of Chicago, 1950.

Davis, William W. *The Civil War and Reconstruction in Florida*. New York, 1913.

Davis, Winfield J. *History of Political Conventions in California, 1849–1892*. Sacramento, Calif., 1893.

Dearing, Mary R. *Veterans in Politics: The Story of the GAR*. Baton Rouge, 1952.

Destler, Chester M. *American Radicalism, 1865–1901*. New London, Conn., 1946.

DeWitt, David M. *The Impeachment and Trial of Andrew Johnson*. New York, 1903.

Dilla, Harriette M. *The Politics of Michigan, 1865–1878*. New York, 1912.

Donald, David. *Charles Sumner and the Rights of Man*. New York, 1970.

Donald, David. "Devils Facing Zionwards," in *Grant, Lee, Lincoln and the Radicals: Essays on Civil War Leadership*, Grady McWhiney, editor. [Evanston, Ill.], 1964.

―――― *The Politics of Reconstruction, 1863–1867*. Baton Rouge, 1965.

Durkin, Joseph T. *Stephen R. Mallory*. Chapel Hill, N.C., 1954.

Eckenrode, Hamilton J. *The Political History of Virginia during the Reconstruction*. Baltimore, 1904.

Ellenburg, Martha Ann. Reconstruction in Arkansas, Unpublished PhD dissertation, University of Missouri, 1967.

Farnen, Russell F., Jr. Ulysses S. Grant: The Soldier as Politician (1861–1868). Unpublished PhD dissertation, Syracuse University, 1963.

Ferleger, Herbert R. *David A. Wells and the American Revenue System*. New York, 1942.

Ficklen, John R. *History of Reconstruction in Louisiana (through 1868)*. Baltimore, 1910.

Fishel, Leslie H., Jr. "Northern Prejudice and Negro Suffrage, 1865–1870," *Journal of Negro History*, XXXIX (January, 1954), 8–26.

―――― "Wisconsin and Negro Suffrage," *Wisconsin Magazine of History*, XLVI (Spring, 1963), 180–96.

Fitz Simons, Theodore B., Jr. "The Camilla Riot," *Georgia Historical Quarterly*, XXXV (June, 1951), 116–25.

Fleming, Walter L. *Civil War and Reconstruction in Alabama*. New York, 1905.

Foner, Eric. *Free Soil, Free Labor, Free Men: The Ideology of the Republican Party Before the Civil War*. New York, 1970.

Gallaway, B. P. "Economic Determinism in Reconstruction Historiography," *Southwestern Social Science Quarterly*, XLVI (December, 1965), 244–54.

Gambill, Edward L. Northern Democrats and Reconstruction, 1865–1868. Unpublished PhD dissertation, University of Iowa, 1969.

Garner, James W. *Reconstruction in Mississippi*, New York, 1901.

Gillette, William. *The Right to Vote: Politics and the Passage of the Fifteenth Amendment*. Baltimore, 1965.

Hamilton, J. G. de Roulhac. *Reconstruction in North Carolina*. New York, 1914.

Harris, William C. *Presidential Reconstruction in Mississippi*. Baton Rouge, 1967.

Hesseltine, William B. *Ulysses S. Grant: Politican*. New York, 1935.

Hill, Adam Sherman. "The Chicago Convention," *North American Review*, CVII (June, 1868), 167–86.

Hollis, John Porter. *The Early Period of Reconstruction in South Carolina*. Baltimore, 1905.

Hughes, David F. Salmon P. Chase: Chief Justice. Unpublished PhD dissertation, Princeton University, 1963.

Hume, Richard L. The "Black and Tan" Constitutional Conventions of 1867–1869 in Ten Former Confederate States: A Study of Their Membership. Unpublished PhD dissertation, University of Washington, 1969.

Hunt, Gaillard. Israel, Elihu, and Cadwallader Washburn. New York, 1925.

Hutchinson, William T. Cyrus Hall McCormick. 2 vols. New York, 1930–35.

James, Joseph B. The Framing of the Fourteenth Amendment. Urbana, Ill., 1965.

Jarrell Hampton M. Wade Hampton and the Negro: The Road Not Taken. Columbia, S.C., 1949.

Jellison, Charles A. Fessenden of Maine. Syracuse, 1962.

Jones, John William. Personal Reminiscences, Anecdotes and Letters of Gen. Robert E. Lee. New York, 1876.

Katz, Irving. August Belmont: A Political Biography. New York, 1968.

Kelley, Brooks Mather. A Machine is Born: Simon Cameron and Pennsylvania, 1862–1873. Unpublished PhD dissertation, University of Chicago, 1961.

Kendrick, Benjamin B. The Journal of the Joint Committee of Fifteen on Reconstruction. New York, 1914.

Kincaid, Larry. The Legislative Origins of the Military Reconstruction Acts, 1865–1867. Unpublished PhD dissertation, Johns Hopkins University, 1968.

—— "Victims of Circumstance: An Interpretation of Changing Attitudes Toward Republican Policy Makers and Reconstruction," Journal of American History, LVII (June, 1970), 48–66.

Kindahl, James K. "Economic Factors in Specie Resumption: The United States, 1865–79," Journal of Political Economy, LXIX (February, 1961), 30–48.

Kinsley, Philip. The Chicago Tribune: Its First Hundred Years. 3 vols. New York, 1943–46.

Kirkland, John Robert. Federal Troops in the South Atlantic States During Reconstruction, 1865–1877, Unpublished PhD dissertation, University of North Carolina, 1967.

Krug, Mark M. Lyman Trumbull: Conservative Radical. New York, 1965.

Kutler, Stanley I. Judicial Power and Reconstruction Politics. Chicago, 1968.

Larson, Henrietta M. Jay Cooke, Private Banker. Cambridge, Mass., 1936.

Linden, Glenn M. "A Note on Negro Suffrage and Republican Politics," *Journal of Southern History*, XXXVI (August, 1970), 411–21.

Lowe, Richard Grady. Republicans, Rebellion, and Reconstruction: The Republican Party in Virginia, 1856–1870. Unpublished PhD dissertation, University of Virginia, 1968.

McDonough, James L., and William T. Alderson. "Republican Politics and the Impeachment of Andrew Johnson." *Tennessee Historical Quarterly*, XXVI (Summer, 1967), 177–83.

McJimsey, George T. *Genteel Partisan: Manton Marble, 1834–1917.* Ames, Iowa, 1971.

McKitrick, Eric L. *Andrew Johnson and Reconstruction.* Chicago, 1960.

McLaughlin, Tom LeRoy. Popular Reaction to the Idea of Negro Equality in Twelve Nonslaveholding States, 1846–1869: A Quantitative Analysis. Unpublished PhD dissertation, Washington State University, 1969.

McPherson, James M. "A Brief for Equality: The Abolitionist Reply to the Racist Myth, 1860–1865," in *The Antislavery Vanguard: New Essays on the Abolitonists*, Martin Duberman, editor. Princeton, N.J., 1965.

Mantell, Martin E. New York and the Elections of 1866. Unpublished MA thesis, Columbia University, 1962.

Meade, George. *The Life and Letters of George Gordon Meade.* 2 vols. New York, 1913.

Meador, John Allen. Florida Political Parties, 1865–1877. Unpublished PhD dissertation, University of Florida, 1964.

Mitchell, Stewart. *Horatio Seymour of New York.* Cambridge, Mass. 1938.

Mitchell, Wesley C. *Gold, Prices and Wages Under the Greenback Standard.* Berkeley, Calif., 1908.

Morton, Richard Lee. *The Negro in Virginia Politics, 1865–1902.* Charlottesville, Virginia, 1919.

Myers, William S. *The Self-Reconstruction of Maryland, 1864–1867.* Baltimore, 1909.

Nathans, Elizabeth Studley. *Losing the Peace: Georgia Republicans and Reconstruction, 1865–1871.* Baton Rouge, 1968.

Nugent, Walter T. K. *Money and American Society, 1865–1880.* New York, 1968.

Oberholtzer, Ellis P. *Jay Cooke, Financier of the Civil War.* 2 vols. Philadelphia, 1907.

Olsen, Otto H. *Carpetbagger's Crusade: The Life of Albion Winegar Tourgée.* Baltimore, 1965.

Palmer, George T. *A Conscientious Turncoat: The Story of John M. Palmer.* New Haven, Conn., 1941.

Parker, William B. *The Life and Public Services of Justin Smith Morrill.* Boston, 1924.

Parrish, William E. *Missouri Under Radical Rule: 1865–1870.* Columbia, Missouri, 1965.

Patton, James W. *Unionism and Reconstruction in Tennessee, 1860–1869.* Chapel Hill, N.C., 1934.

Peek, Ralph L. "Aftermath of Military Reconstruction, 1868–1869," *Florida Historical Quarterly,* XLIII (October, 1964), 123–41.

—— "Military Reconstruction and the Growth of Anti-Negro Sentiment in Florida, 1867," *Florida Historical Quarterly,* XLVII (April, 1969), 380–400.

Pereyra, Lillian A. *James Lusk Alcorn, Persistent Whig.* [Baton Rouge], 1966.

Perzel, Edward S. "Alexander Long, Salmon P. Chase, and the Election of 1868," *Bulletin of the Cincinnati Historical Society,* XXIII (January, 1965), 3–18.

Pierce, Michael Dale. Andrew Johnson and the South, 1865–1867. Unpublished PhD dissertation, North Texas State University, 1970.

Porter, George H. *Ohio Politics during the Civil War Period,* New York, 1911.

Ramsdell, Charles W. *Reconstruction in Texas.* New York, 1910.

Randall, James G. *Constitutional Problems Under Lincoln.* Rev. ed. Urbana, Illinois, 1951.

Rawley, James A. *Edwin D. Morgan.* New York, 1955.

Reynolds, Donald E. "The New Orleans Riot of 1866, Reconsidered," *Louisiana History,* V (Winter, 1964), 5–27.

Richardson, Albert D. *A Personal History of Ulysses S. Grant.* Hartford, Conn., 1868.

Richardson, Joe M. *The Negro in the Reconstruction of Florida, 1865–1877.* Tallahassee, Fla., 1965.

Richardson, Leon B. *William E. Chandler: Republican.* New York, 1940.

Roseboom, Eugene H. *The Civil War Era, 1850–1873.* Vol. IV of *The History of the State of Ohio,* Carl Wittke, editor. Columbus, Ohio, 1944.

Roske, Ralph J. "Republican Newspaper Support for the Acquittal of President Johnson," *Tennessee Historical Quarterly,* XI (September, 1952), 263–73.

—— "The Seven Martyrs?" *American Historical Review,* LXIV (January, 1959), 323–40.

Russ, William A., Jr. "Disfranchisement in Virginia Under Radical Reconstruction," *Tyler's Quarterly Historical and Genealogical Magazine,* XVII (July, 1935), 25–41.

—— "Radical Disfranchisement in Georgia, 1867–71," *Georgia Historical Quarterly,* XIX (September, 1935), 175–209.

—— "Radical Disfranchisement in North Carolina, 1867–1868," *North Carolina Historical Review,* XI (October, 1934), 271–83.

Russ, William A., Jr. "Was There Danger of a Second Civil War during Reconstruction?" *Mississippi Valley Historical Review*, XXV (June, 1938), 39–58.

Schell, Herbert S. "Hugh McCulloch and the Treasury Department. 1865–1869," *Mississippi Valley Historical Review*, XVII (December, 1930), 404–21.

Schuckers, J. W. *The Life and Public Services of Salmon Portland Chase*. New York, 1874.

Scroggs, Jack B. "Carpetbagger Constitutional Reform in the South Atlantic States, 1867–1868," *Journal of Southern History*, XXVII (November, 1961), 475–93.

Sefton, James E. "The Impeachment of Andrew Johnson: A Century of Writing," *Civil War History*, XIV (June, 1968), 120–47.

—— *The United States Army and Reconstruction, 1865–1877*. Baton Rouge, 1967.

Shadgett, Olive Hall. *The Republican Party in Georgia from Reconstruction through 1900*. Athens, Georgia, 1964.

Shapiro, Herbert. "The Ku Klux Klan during Reconstruction: The South Carolina Episode," *Journal of Negro History*, XLIX (January, 1964), 34–55.

Sharkey, Robert P. *Money, Class, and Party: An Economic Study of Civil War and Reconstruction*. Baltimore, 1959.

Shipley, Max L. The Greenback Issue in the Old Northwest, 1865–1880. Unpublished PhD dissertation, University of Illinois, 1929.

Silvestro, Clement Mario. None But Patriots: The Union Leagues in Civil War and Reconstruction. Unpublished PhD dissertation, University of Wisconsin, 1959.

Simkins, Francis B., and Robert H. Woody, *South Carolina During Reconstruction*. Chapel Hill, N.C., 1932.

Singletary, Otis A. *Negro Militia and Reconstruction*. Austin, Texas, 1957.

Smith, James Douglas. Virginia During Reconstruction, 1865–1870. Unpublished PhD dissertation, University of Virginia, 1960.

Smith, Theodore Clarke, *The Life and Letters of James Abram Garfield*. 2 vols. New Haven, Conn., 1925.

Smith, Willard H. *Schuyler Colfax: The Changing Fortunes of a Political Idol*. Indianapolis, Ind., 1952.

Smith, William E. *The Francis Preston Blair Family in Politics*. 2 vols. New York, 1933.

Stampp, Kenneth. *The Era of Reconstruction, 1865–1877*. New York, 1965.

Stanwood, Edward. *American Tariff Controversies in the Nineteenth Century*. 2 vols. New York, 1903.

Staples, Thomas S. *Reconstruction in Arkansas, 1862–1874*. New York, 1923.

Staudenraus, P. J. "The Popular Origins of the Thirteenth Amendment," *Mid-America*, L (April, 1968), 108–15.

Stebbins, Homer A. *A Political History of the State of New York, 1865–1869*. New York, 1913.

Sterkx, H. E. "William C. Jordan and Reconstruction," *Alabama Review*, XV (January, 1962), 61–73.

Tatum, Georgia Lee. *Disloyalty in the Confederacy*. Chapel Hill, N.C., 1934.

Thomas, Benjamin P., and Harold M. Hyman. *Stanton: The Life and Times of Lincoln's Secretary of War*. New York, 1962.

Thompson, C. Mildred. *Reconstruction in Georgia*. New York, 1915.

Trefousse, Hans L. "The Acquittal of Andrew Johnson and the Decline of the Radicals," *Civil War History*, XIV (June, 1968), 148–61.

—— "Ben Wade and the Failure of the Impeachment of Johnson," *Bulletin of the Historical and Philosophical Society of Ohio*, XVIII (October, 1960), 241–52.

—— *The Radical Republicans: Lincoln's Vanguard for Racial Justice*. New York, 1969.

Trelease, Allen W. *White Terror: The Ku Klux Klan Conspiracy and Southern Reconstruction*. New York, 1971.

Truman, Benjamin C. "Anecdotes of Andrew Johnson," *Century*, LXXXV o. s. (April, 1913), 435–40.

Unger, Irwin. "Business Men and Specie Resumption," *Political Science Quarterly*, LXXIV (March, 1959), 46–70.

——. *The Greenback Era*. Princeton, N.J., 1964.

Vallandigham, James L. *A Life of Clement L. Vallandigham*. Baltimore, 1872.

Voegeli, V. Jacque. *Free But Not Equal: The Midwest and The Negro during the Civil War*. Chicago, 1967.

Warden, Robert B. *An Account of the Private Life and Public Services of Salmon Portland Chase*. Cincinnati, 1874.

Ware, Edith E. *Political Opinion in Massachusetts during Civil War and Reconstruction*. New York, 1916.

Warmoth, Henry Clay. *War, Politics and Reconstruction: Stormy Days in Louisiana*. New York, 1930.

Wharton, Vernon Lane. *The Negro in Mississippi, 1865–1890*. Chapel Hill, N.C., 1947.

Wiggins, Sarah Woolfolk. "Unionist Efforts To Control Alabama Reconstruction, 1865–1867," *Alabama Historical Quarterly*, XXX (Spring, 1968), 51–64.

Williamson, Joel. *After Slavery: The Negro in South Carolina during Reconstruction*. Chapel Hill, N.C., 1965.

Wilson, James H. *The Life of John A. Rawlins*. New York, 1916.

Winkler, Ernest W., editor, "Platforms of Political Parties in Texas," *Bulletin of the University of Texas,* September, 1916, no. 53.

Wood, Forrest G. *Black Scare: The Racist Response to Emancipation and Reconstruction,* Berkeley, 1968.

—— "On Revising Reconstruction History: Negro Suffrage, White Disfranchisement, and Common Sense," *Journal of Negro History,* LI (April, 1966), 98–113.

Woods, George B. "The New York Convention," *North American Review,* CVII (October, 1868), 445–65.

Woodward, C. Vann. *The Burden of Southern History.* Rev. ed. Baton Rouge, 1968.

—— "Seeds of Failure in Radical Race Policy," in *New Frontiers of the American Reconstruction,* Harold M. Hyman, editor, Urbana, Ill., 1966.

Woodward, Walter C. *The Rise and Early History of Political Parties in Oregon.* Portland, Ore., 1913.

Zubér, Richard L. *Jonathan Worth: A Biography of a Southern Unionist.* Chapel Hill, N.C., 1965.